I Never Promised Not to Tell

Revealing, Behind-The-Scene Stories
By A Veteran Writer Who Was Part of It

When Television and
A New Era of Politics
Came to a Southern City

By Grady Jefferys

ISBN: 1481210262
ISBN-13: 978-1481210263

Library of Congress Cataloging-in-Publication Data
Jefferys, Grady (Grady B.)

ISBN 1481210262
ISBN-13: 978-1481210263
First Edition

I never promised not to tell: revealing, behind-the-scene stories by a veteran
writer who was part of it. When a new era of television and politics came to a
southern city.

First Edition

DEDICATION

Dedicated to the memory of my only brother, Macon, who died before having an opportunity to read these stories, but contended that they should be told, and to my wife, Marie, who participated in many of the events from which these stories are drawn and who plays an indispensable role in all aspects of my life.

ACKNOWLEDGMENTS

Inasmuch as this book is based on my observations of and participation in events involving others as well as my interaction with others, it is appropriate that I acknowledge those who agreed for me to observe and participate and in many instances threw open doors of opportunity for me. The names of those who did so will be found throughout this book.

There are, however, others whom I must acknowledge and to whom I must express my appreciation: My friend and colleague from our newspaper days, Marshall Lancaster; my friend and colleague Charles Heatherly with whom I have partnered in the writing of other books; his wife, Evelyn; my son, Shayne, who has heard these stories and encouraged me to share them with others; my daughter, Linda Ferrell who provided some important reference material; my daughter, Alyse Shirley whose assistance in the preparation of this book was crucial, and my son, Brack, whose generosity made the production of this project much easier.

Thank you one and all. For any shortcomings in this book, I take full responsibility.

*Sooner Will Men Hold Fire In Their
Mouths Than Keep A Secret
Petronius*

Prologue

In today's world, television, advertising and political campaigns demand our attention and dominate much of our time However, only a relatively few people ever get to see and participate in the activities behind the TV cameras, in the offices of the ad makers and in the "smoke-filled rooms" where crucial political decisions are made. It was in those arenas that I spent more than 40 years.

In the media and political climate of the second decade of the 21st Century, when this book is being published, television, advertising and politics comprise a symbiotic three-legged entity that is deeply entrenched at local, state and national levels. Raleigh, North Carolina, in 2012, the nation's fifth fastest-growing city, is as good an example as one can find of the way this relationship originated and flourished over the years.

Many people who are aware of this relationship are deeply concerned about its impact on the quality of governance at all levels. Quite a few believe that the way television is used to influence elections -- the enormous amount of money that fuels what has become an engine of oversimplification, obfuscation, distortion and outright lies -- has polarized our political factions to a degree that places our democracy at risk.

In what is the most important aspect of our lives -- the selection of the people who exercise authority and power over our lives -- the public is bombarded with messages that largely do nothing but raise doubt about the character and qualifications of the candidates. For this, television stations that are granted access to the public's airwaves for the sole purpose of serving the public reap financial bonanzas with each election cycle.

In an industry whose sins far outnumber their virtues, the undermining of our most important democratic function is perhaps the most egregious. There are, however, many more wrongs for which television should be -- but isn't -- held accountable.

The current system did not emerge full blown in recent times. It is the result of the introduction of and constant growth of television to a position of dominance in the media world, the advent of specialized operatives known as political consultants and the combination of technology and media sophistication that enables the moods of voters to be measured and messages designed that address their hopes and desires as well as their darker prejudices.

Without television, the current system of choosing elected officials would be vastly different than it is now. Indeed, it once was quite different. That alone is reason for serious people to want to understand how and why it emerged as it did, but it is also important to understand what the medium has done for and against our society and its culture.

Toiling In Strange Fields

In 1956, at a young age, I left the family farm on which I grew up in Wake County, North Carolina and its fields of tobacco for a journey of more than a decade through the fields of television, journalism and advertising. After a dozen years of writing for the first two television stations in Raleigh, North Carolina, the second station in Charlotte, several newspapers and magazines and Raleigh's first advertising agency, I opened a business that over the next 40 years kept me immersed in politics and political consulting, public affairs, publishing and television, video and motion picture production.

Much of what I was involved in was occurring for the first time in Raleigh, and in some cases, for the first time in the country. With no hard and fast standards or rules in place, practices and procedures were made up along the way as powerful technological and cultural forces shaped the last half of the 20th and the first decades of the 21st Century. With some refinements, many of those early day practices and procedures endure.

I am not a historian, so this book is not a history of media in Raleigh and North Carolina. Rather, it is part memoir, part journalism, part critique and lament and part a sharing of secrets that some would like to keep secret.

Together these somewhat diverse components illuminate a time, a place and the people who were engaged in new and interesting endeavors.

Writing for a local television station in the 1950s and early 1960s provided little opportunity to make a significant contribution to society. What was required were mostly forgettable, often trivial, bits and pieces that enabled the broadcast day to flow without interruption in an orderly and coherent manner.

Snappy lines for on-camera performers were valued. However, over the decades, few local stations sought to achieve genuine excellence in their local productions. Most of them didn't even try for excellence. And some seemed unable to comprehend the concept of excellence. Most local stations filled their available time slots with cooking shows, programs aimed at 'babysitting' children, inane celebrity gossip programs and syndicated films of dubious quality.

For the television writer, however, merely meeting the daily demand provided a valuable opportunity to learn how to gather and synthesize information about a variety of topics and present it succinctly in sentences that flowed easily and were pleasing to the ear while conveying accuracy and clarity. Achieving competence in those areas set me on a career path that over more than four decades placed me near the centers of power and influence at national, state and local levels. It is from those centers of power and influence that I observed and often participated in events that enabled me to gather and store many stories and insights that as an inveterate storyteller, I never promised not to tell.

It is my hope that you will find in these pages much that will interest, amuse and, perhaps, amaze you and that any injury inflicted on others will be mitigated by the insight my recollections will provide into times past.

Becoming a Writer

Although I was a part of a large extended family, my nuclear family was quite small, consisting of my father and mother and my brother, Macon, two and a half years older than I. Our parents instilled in both of us an abiding belief in our own capabilities, a moral compass that demanded that we "do what's right" and the certitude that we must move the family status higher on the socio-economic ladder.

More significant to my own life, however, was my mother's insistence, unspoken and spoken, that my brother and I were endowed with intellectual abilities and character strengths that required us to excel at something. Through a dozen years of public school, a series of teachers reinforced what my mother had insisted on from the outset.

My father, Marshall Jefferys, a son of the soil, descendant of forebears who once owned large Virginia plantations and family farms just across the border in North Carolina, believed success and happiness lay in being one's own boss, responsible only to one's own ability to earn a living and manage his own affairs. For him, successful farming was the best way to achieve those goals, and he held hopes that either my brother or I or perhaps both would join him in operating and expanding the farming operation that had sustained our family in good times and bad. Both my brother and I grew up with fond memories of farm life, but with dreams more expansive than the fields that spread beyond our home.

As a young woman, our mother, Edna Mason Jefferys, had been a correspondent for her local newspaper. That early exposure to a world different than that of a farm wife might well have made her encourage— even push -- my brother and me toward the careers that we both pursued, sometimes obsessively.

From my earliest school years, teachers consistently noted that I had a "knack" for storytelling. My inherent interest in story telling was sharpened by dime western novels, books and stories by Jack London, Zane Grey, Ernest Hemingway, F. Scott Fitzgerald, Sinclair Louis, Frank Yerby and Thomas Wolfe, the writers who wrote for Argosy and True magazines, the powerful journalistic pieces in Life and Look magazines, the human interest stories in The Saturday Evening Post and as I grew older, the insightful work of Harry Golden, John

Updike, Phillip Roth, Tom Wolfe, Grace Matalius and the gritty novels of Norman Mailer, James Jones and the writers of dozens of other publications.

I loved the newsreels that were a part of at our weekly movie outings. They brought us the news of the world in a manner often more dramatic than the movies they followed. Later, as I struggled to learn how to convey information in words and pictures for television, I would recall the way the news stories were delivered in newsreels and seek to emulate that style. It worked.

When I learned of an opening for a writer at WNAO-TV, the first television station in Raleigh, I decided to seek the job. I did not know it at the time, but the small UHF station was struggling to survive. At the time I applied for the job, its days were probably already numbered. For me, however, a novice in the craft of writing and broadcasting and most everything else, as well as for a number of other people seeking new careers or simply a new chance in life, the station provided an exciting adventure that would have profound impact on our lives and leave indelible memories.

For several months after High School graduation, I had worked at several jobs and dithered with college, never able to decide what line of study or work to pursue. Years of regular movie going, my participation in High School dramatics and years of voracious reading of adventure stories had ignited a craving for something different than the routine or mundane.

Over the course of several years, however, I engaged in intensive study of those areas and issues that interested me – television and film production, journalism, government, politics, law and business – all of which were to loom large in the various paths that my career would take. In years that were to come, I gained knowledge and experience in all of those areas, winning national awards for motion picture and video writing and production, and for excellence in advertising and magazine publishing.

In January, 1956, however, I had none of the skills or abilities I would later acquire and develop and had achieved nothing. Perhaps it was my sheer audacity, perhaps it was luck, pluck, maybe a smattering of ability that I somehow was able to convey or merely an indication of the station's inability to attract better talent, but I won the position as the chief writer for the television station. I was 21 years old and had never been inside a broadcast station prior to applying for the job.

Table of Contents

A City and Its People Come of Age in The Best Years of Their Lives

For the men and women who were beginning to gain traction in their lives following World War II and for the younger residents of the cities and small towns and rural areas of the nation, then coming of age, the mid-1950s were the beginning of what many would come to consider the best years of their lives.

The city of Raleigh, State Capital of North Carolina, was a sleepy southern town of colleges, government workers, small businesses and tradesmen. Carved out of the worn out plantation fields of Joel Lane in 1792 to serve as the state's permanent seat of government, the city stood on the dividing line between the state's great coastal plain and the Piedmont plateau that rose in the west to become the foothills of the Blue Ridge and Great Smoky Mountains. To the east across the vast coastal plains were the Atlantic Ocean and a chain of barrier islands in which were embedded centuries of lore and legend,

As Raleigh grew, it clung to its original purpose and stubbornly resisted becoming either a tobacco market or a mill town.

The prosperous congregated in enclaves, relegating poor folks to separate neighborhoods, some quite grim. Black folks were shoved to the fringes of the city where they largely remained over the decades. Most of the prejudices and narrow-minded ideas that existed throughout the South and the nation could be found in Raleigh. The city was, however, a place of studied civility and good manners, where *country* folk could mingle with *Country Club* folk for the purpose of transacting business before going their separate ways.

Over the next half century, what many of us had known as Raleigh vanished, its identity sucked into a sprawling multi-county metropolitan area of some two million people, most of them from someplace else. The natives welcomed the newcomers' money, but resisted and resented their desire to do things "the way we did them up North." Over time, the newcomers out-numbered the natives, and altered forever not only the landscape but the politics as well as the morals and mores of the region. Although Raleigh became largely unrecognizable to those who grew up here in the 1940s and 1950s, it acquired a similarity to many other areas of urban sprawl that have metastasized around aging and somewhat seedy central cores that progressive minded folk have tried mightily to keep relevant.

I came of age in Raleigh in the 1950s, a decade in which I graduated from high school, obtained a driver's license, owned my first automobile, registered for the military draft, worked at several jobs, built a house, studied and became proficient in a craft that became a career, met and married a beautiful woman, with whom I have shared more than a half century of marriage and raised two sons and two daughters.

I was and remain an enthusiastic member of the group whom the editors at Time-Life publications said believed fervently that the "fabulous fifties" were "the best of times" – indeed, the best years of our lives. The decade was the cauldron in which many of the attitudes, much of the energy and technology as well as the mindset and mores that were to dominate the coming generations formed, percolated and finally erupted. It was, after all, the decade in which television, rock music and the civil rights movement reached out to the masses.

In the mid and late 1950s, North Carolina and especially the several counties and numerous smaller towns that spread out around the Capital City and would come to be known as the "Triangle Area" seemed to be on the cusp of something larger, more significant than the ordinary. Many of the men and women who had fought in foreign lands during World War II and later in Korea had returned, gone to college or into business and were moving what had been a sleepy farm-oriented economy in new directions.

At the end of the 1940s, the influential political scientist, V.O. Key described North Carolina as "the progressive Plutocracy ... the leader of what the South might become." Key based his belief on several factors: the state's press, more liberal than any in the South; the institutional strength of the University of North Carolina: a higher level of industrialization: and a history in which the plantation influence played a lesser role than it played in other states. Although Key's description of North Carolina was rather overstated, it served the state better than the state's earlier designation as "the Rip Van Winkle State."

In the following decades Raleigh, the State Capital, and the surrounding communities became one of the nation's major centers of medical and technological research.

In a state where the first state-supported university was established, the first airplane flew, the first Pepsi-Cola was formulated and sold, the first shopping center between Washington, D.C. and Atlanta was built, and which gave the world Camel and Lucky Strike cigarettes, glamorous movie stars such as Ava Gardner and pioneering and nationally-known journalists such as Edward R. Murrow, David Brinkley, Charles Kuralt and Vermont Royster, and literary icons such as Thomas Wolfe and O'Henry, it was easy to believe that the brass ring could be grasped by those who were willing to reach for it.

Television: The Medicine Show
Comes to Town
Anticipation and Disappointment

In the late afternoon of Sunday, July 12, 1953, officers and key staff members of the Sir Walter Television Corporation along with municipal, civic and religious leaders of Raleigh and Durham gathered in a small room at Asbury, North Carolina, at that time about six miles west of the city to participate in the first television broadcast in the area.

Among those present were John English, President of the Company, Frank Daniels, general manager of *The News and Observer* and vice-president of the television company, Charles Stone, general manager of the station, Hal Stanley, the station's news director and Byron Davis, program manager. Within months, the station manager, program manager and news director would be replaced, the early casualties of the struggling start-up.

President John English, an Erie, Pennsylvania businessman, would seek to guide the new operation from his home, several hundred miles away. Vice-President Daniels would maintain a studied indifference to the operation

The launch of the new station, so eagerly anticipated, was decidedly underwhelming. The maiden broadcast consisted of a locally produced short film showing familiar scenes of Raleigh, narrated by station announcer Mike Silver. Following the broadcast, the station would sign off to make adjustments aimed at improving reception. From July to October 1, 1953, the station would broadcast only films, with network programming to begin after suitable adjustments to the transmitter were made. The delay was the second major postponement by the station. It had earlier promised to be on the air in April, 1953, but problems with AT&T were blamed for the delay. That initial test, to determine the quality of reception produced mixed results. Some viewers said the picture quality was adequate. Most reported a great deal of "snow" in the pictures, a problem that would plague not only WNAO-TV, but other UHF stations then seeking to go on the air.

Although clumsy and crude, that first television broadcast from WNAO –TV was a harbinger of the future, a tentative unleashing of forces that in a relatively brief period would change the culture of regions as it changed the culture of our nation.

It can be argued that many of the changes are not in the best interest of the region or the country. To many critics, television's most egregious sin was to shift the cultural center of the country from middlebrow to lowbrow. Others believe that the medium that showed such promise for elevating understanding of government and politics has done the opposite, "dumbing down" complicated governmental policies into 15-second sound bites and political discourse to 30-second "attack ads."

Many viewers agreed with the comedian Fred Allen who noted that "television is a device that permits people who haven't anything to do watch people who can't do anything."

The critic Clive Barnes wrote that television is the first medium governed entirely by what people want...and..."the most terrifying thing is what people want."

Although the analogy offends TV folk, the comparison between the medium and the old medicine shows that came to town is accurate. Both TV and the medicine man provided entertainment chiefly to keep the audience around for the sales pitch.

Centuries before television, the print media, with its rich, multi-layered history and heritage, educated and entertained with explanations of civilization's experience and enduring records of much of its knowledge through text books that could be studied in schools of all kinds, through classic works of literature, a multitude of journals, offbeat periodicals and regular news publications that brought millions an understanding of country and community with a daily "rough draft of history."

Local television, with all the glitz and superficial glamour that it arrogates for itself has, in its first six decades, achieved little of genuine value. Moreover, at the local level, television has shown no inclination to strive for excellence and, therefore, local television is bereft of a definable, much less distinctive, heritage.

It is doubtful that Thomas Jefferson, who wrote in 1787 that if asked to choose, he would prefer newspapers without government over government without newspapers, would make a similar choice should he be asked to choose between government without television or television without government.

Nevertheless, we are intrigued by television. As the late television commentator Howard Cossell observed, "What is popular is not necessarily good and what is good is not necessarily popular." Most certainly, television is popular. Even as the internet commands the attention of more and more people, the television screen continues to dominate the free time of millions. Therefore, its origins are of interest to those who love the medium despite its flaws and shortcomings.

A Love Affair With Radio

For Raleigh residents as well as for the great majority of Americans, the first television station to come to town was a welcomed event, worthy of celebration. The promise of the medium – *radio with pictures* -- was for many people unbelievable. Even as transmitter towers and equipment were being assembled, many residents refused to believe that "moving pictures could be sent through the air."

For fans of the many traditional radio dramas, comedy shows, news programs, sporting events and variety shows, television would be like an endless reel of movies free for the viewing. Many wondered if the new medium called *television* could possibly be better than radio.

For more than 20 years, Raleigh residents, like those throughout the nation, had been engaged in a love affair with radio. In the mid-1950s, the city had three stations, WPTF, a 50,000 watt broadcasting behemoth with a signal that extended for hundreds of miles. Its only local competition were WRAL, a 250-watt stations with a signal that barely covered Wake County, and WNAO, a 10,000-watt station that signed on the air in 1949.

As network affiliates, the stations brought to Raleigh, drama, comedy, soap operas, and music from the entertainment capitals of the world and news and information from places where news was being made throughout the world.

At the local level, the stations provided venues for musicians, discussions of public affairs, community events and a daylong menu of programs that engaged and entertained listeners of all ages. Many of the local announcers such as WPTF's Jim Reid, Phil Ellis, Sam Beard, Jimmy Capps, Charlie Gaddy and Bill Hoke and WRAL's Fred Fletcher, Ray Reeve, Bill Armstrong, Bill Allspaugh and Jesse Helms developed large and loyal followings as program hosts, news and sports announcers and disc jockeys. Most of them made successful transitions to television while some chose to remain with radio.

For a number of years, WPTF announcer Jimmy Capps dominated late night listening with a program he called "Our Best To You." Often the program, which featured romantic ballads and poetry readings, captured 80 percent of the listening audience, an audience share much larger than the audience for early day television. Capps' fan base was huge and loyal, and he was voted one of the "10 most popular radio announcers in the nation."

On the N.C. State University campus during early fall and spring, when the windows of the dormitories were open, one could walk across the campus and never miss a moment of Capps' program. His program was on radios in virtually every dorm room, as it was in dorm rooms on campuses throughout much of North Carolina.

For countless couples parked on lovers' lanes, Capps's music and mellow tones and the glow of a car radio on a summer eve created the perfect ambiance for romance. When Capps died at age 47 of a rare and aggressive form of cancer, Bill Hoke, took over the program extending its longevity to almost 20 years.

WNAO radio attracted an audience, of course, but it failed to win the hearts of Raleigh and surrounding areas the way WPTF and WRAL had. However, WNAO radio personalities such as Mike Silver, Allen Browning, Lynn Sanner and Ted Powers brought a high degree of professionalism to their craft. All of them also doubled as television personalities when WNAO-TV signed on the air.

On WRAL, Ray Reeve's authoritative sports reports and amazing accuracy in announcing the play-by-play action of football and basketball games also became quite popular. The popularity of Reeve and Fred Fletcher who created a popular morning show called *Tempus Fugit (Latin for Time Flies)* along with the strong emphasis on local news reporting by Jesse Helms and Bill Armstrong enabled the small station to compete favorably with its much larger competitor, WPTF.

Reeve's growing popularity was a source of pride and revenue for WRAL, but his continuing "battle with the bottle" caused the station many problems. For much of his life and especially during his early career, Reeve was what is known now as an episodic alcoholic. He would remain sober and committed to his job for significant periods and without warning fall off the wagon, get drunk and do something outrageous that embarrassed the station and placed his future as a broadcaster in doubt. Often, he would simply disappear only to turn up later in bizarre places. Reeve's alcoholic escapades became well known throughout the area, and the stories about him became lurid and legendary.

Some of the more illuminating stories about Reeve were recalled by Bill Currie, a sportscaster and journalist who at various times was Reeve's superior at WRAL-Radio and other times a colleague in announcing play-by-play for football and basketball. Currie remembered when Reeve went missing for several days, causing concern among his family and colleagues. He eventually turned up in Roswell, New Mexico, walking barefoot down a city street with his pants legs rolled up to his knees, and his huge pot belly protruding from his unbuttoned shirt. "He was 'drunk as a skunk'" recalled Currie.

A.J. Fletcher, the owner of the station was a lifelong teetotaler, who, according to his associate, Scotty Stephenson, did not trust anyone who consumed alcohol. Reeve's growing popularity as a sports announcer and his outrageous behavior during his alcoholic binges left Fletcher in a quandary. People who knew of Fletcher's distaste for alcohol consumption were puzzled by his willingness to tolerate Reeve's antics.

Years later, I asked Fletcher about his predicament with Reeve.

"He was very good sports announcer," Fletcher told me. "He was very popular, and the station made money broadcasting sports. I tried every kind of persuasion, but nothing seemed to be effective in stopping his drinking.

"Following the episode in New Mexico, I called Reeve into my office and told him that for every episode involving drinking, I would dock his pay proportionate to the offense. I only had to do that one time, and I never had any other problems with him."

Reeve was not the only broadcasting personality who battled the bottle with occasional embarrassment for his employers. However, he was one of the most popular radio personalities in Raleigh and surrounding areas, and was the only broadcast personality who engaged in the kind of bizarre and egregious behavior that attracted widespread public notice and caused such painful embarrassment for himself, his family and the station that employed him.

How Heavy The Hand of Government

Amid the excitement surrounding the coming of the first television station, few in Raleigh knew enough about the new medium to consider the implications of the then inferior UHF technology that would restrict WNAO-TV's ability to serve the area. Few were aware of the way the heavy hand of government had been used to deprive the residents of a first class, high quality television broadcasting facility, and they had no way of knowing that future decisions by the Federal Communications Commission (FCC) to allow a VHF channel into the Raleigh market would place the UHF station, WNAO-TV, in an untenable competitive position.

There is no better example of the stubborn, wrong-headed, unfairness of a government bureaucracy ill serving the public than the FCC's decisions and actions regarding television in Raleigh, North Carolina as well as in more than a hundred other cities throughout the United States.

As Canadian businessman Lord Thomason observed in 1957, a VHF television station, unlike an early day UHF station, was a license to print money. "It goes on and on in perpetuity," he said, "unless the license is taken by the FCC, an occurrence so rare, as to be almost non-existent." From 1941 to 2010, in a nation of more than 300 million people, the Federal Communication Commission has given to only 1,784 individuals and corporations VHF television licenses "to print money." According to a 2011 report in *The Denver Post* "from the advent of commercial television in 1947 to 2011, the FCC has never pulled a television station's license."

Television had been deemed a practical technology in 1939 when Raleigh lawyer A.J. Fletcher and his son, Fred, first viewed a transmission at the World's Fair in New York and many had foreseen its eventual role in entertainment and information. However, the beginning of World War II in 1941 brought an abrupt halt to the development of the new medium. When the movement to establish television as a viable communications system resumed after the war in 1945, little, if any, thought was given to the enormous potential of the new medium for good – and bad. Decisions regarding the allocation of a priceless, but limited, asset belonging to all the people were made in the most cavalier manner imaginable, creating the unfair system that cheated the American public and continued to cheat it over the decades that were to follow.

In 1945, with the war over, the impetus for developing and expanding television emerged with great force. In response to the demand that year, the FCC allocated 19 VHF television channels, but channels 14 through 19 were reserved for military usage and two-way radio communications. The FCC was involved in the allocation of television channels because of its earlier role in allocating radio frequencies to states and communities.

Throughout its history, the FCC awarded television channel allocations for reasons known only to those making the decisions. Until 1997, when the U.S. Congress mandated that all future television channel allocations be awarded to the highest bidder in a nationwide auction, the FCC awarded television channels and licenses at no cost. The first auction, held two years later, garnered $58 million for 116 broadcast channels.

Why the FCC chose to give away valuable and limited publicly owned assets remains inexplicable to this day. Many critics of the FCC cannot understand why the commission's decisions were based on *subjective,* rather than hard *objective* factors. Many also wonder why the licenses were granted in perpetuity and why those who received them paid nothing for assets worth uncounted sums.

Suggestions that licenses be sold to the highest bidder and limited to a specific number of years, after which the licenses would have to be again offered to the highest bidder were routinely rejected by the FCC and the U.S. Congress until the landmark legislation enacted in 1997.

Under the old rules, when more than one applicant sought the same channel allocation, the FCC presumably attempted to determine which applicant might better serve the viewing public by requiring each applicant to file a comprehensive proposal setting forth its technical and programming plans and to submit to a tedious and exhaustive interrogation by FCC commissioners and their attorneys. Service to the public was and remains a vague concept with no hard and fast definition and virtually no enforcement by the FCC.

Unable to cope with the number of requests for television channel allocations, the FCC on September 20, 1948 imposed a freeze on television channel allocation that lasted until April 13, 1952. The freeze did not prevent those who had received channel allocations before the freeze from building and activating stations, and by the end of the freeze 107 VHF stations were already in existence. Ten of those channels were awarded to the two major radio networks, five to NBC and five to CBS, all of which were located in the major metropolitan areas of the nation.

When the freeze was lifted, the FCC decided to grandfather in all 107 stations that had been awarded in a helter-skelter fashion to applicants throughout the nation. Included in the grandfather clause were the 10 stations owned by NBC and CBS, which over the years would become major profit centers for the two networks and would guarantee the networks local outlets that reached a significant portion of the nation's television viewers for the networks' programs and, thus, enable both NBC and CBS to achieve dominance as television networks, dominance that would continue through the decades to follow.

By grandfathering the 107 stations the FCC could provide only enough additional VHF stations to provide two-channel service to roughly 90 percent of the nation's potential viewers, setting up fierce contests for what was being recognized as one of the most valuable franchises in communications history.

In 1952 the FCC adopted a channel allocation framework that awarded VHF channels to communities throughout the United States roughly "in proportion to market size." With only 19 VHF channels available and with six allocated to the military, only channels 2-13 were available for commercial use, the FCC chose to make channel allocations that mixed VHF channels 2-13 and UHF channels 20 – 60 in the same markets, oblivious to the competitive disadvantage that its decision would impose on the UHF stations.

The decision to allocate UHF channels to markets already being served by more powerful VHF channels or VHF channels to markets already being served by UHF stations doomed most of the UHF stations to failure. By the end of 1956, 395 VHF stations and 96 UHF stations were on the air. By 1960, 70 percent of the 575 channels allocated were UHF stations, but only 15 percent of them remained on the air. In 1980, in the nation's top 100 markets, 61 percent of the channel allocations had been UHF, but in those markets, only 14 UHF stations survived. All of the VHF stations allocated during those years not only survived, but flourished.

The development of cable service and the requirement that cable companies carry all channels leveled the competitive field somewhat for UHF stations and created a demand for additional networks, but for most of the early UHF stations cable distribution came too late to save them.

The decision by the FCC was more than a technical experiment or a philosophical concept. It resulted in enormous financial and personal pain as more than 150 UHF stations throughout the nation went dark. Many millions of dollars invested in the stations were lost and countless careers that were being nurtured in the early days of television were derailed.

More important to the nation, however, the FCC decision placed the enormous power and reach of the superior form of television in the hands of a few, creating a competitive advantage for the VHF stations that continued over many decades and in many areas constituted a monopoly.

Instead of mixing VHF and UHF stations in the same markets, the FCC could have decided that all stations would operate on the UHF band, thus enabling multiple stations to compete in markets throughout the nation and creating a need for multiple networks, many comprised of stations that could have pooled resources to produce programs of interest and importance.

Under such a system, dozens of networks would have been possible instead of the three that emerged principally to serve the VHF stations. A system in which any city or town could have several television stations, each associated with its own network, would have created generations earlier the kind of smorgasbord of content that cable and satellites brought to TV screens.

From the outset there would have been genuine competition, creating far more choices and more program diversity. More importantly, such a system would have expanded exponentially the market for television content, a market that would have been required by market forces to tap the creative energies of countless people in communities throughout the nation instead of relying almost entirely on the networks based in New York and later in Los Angeles.

The concentration of power in the three networks assured that the means of distribution would be controlled by network executives. Without assurance of distribution, the creative process was stifled, and an abundance of ideas were stillborn.

With dozens of regional, financially strong, networks serving stations equal in strength, the centers of television power and influence would have been dispersed across the country, reflecting a mix of entertainment, information and culture far more representative of the nation than that concentrated in New York and Hollywood.

The FCC has never provided a rationale for its decision to create an uneven and unfair competitive system. Today, that decision continues to be fiercely criticized by virtually everyone who understands its impact on the viewing public as well as on the men and women who lost money and careers in the wholesale failure of those early UHF television stations.

The Unfair Burden on UHF Stations

The new owners of the UHF Channel 28 might or might not have known how difficult it would be in the early 1950s to build a successful television station in a city the size of Raleigh. They could not have known how unfairly they would be treated by the government agency established solely to assure fairness in the governance of both radio and television broadcasting.

Owners of VHF television licenses in Raleigh as well as throughout the nation have been careful over the decades to conceal the rank unfairness by government that made it possible for them to prosper. The FCC's mandate that stations serve the public interest has been treated as a vague, non-specific notion that could be circumvented with ease. Every station devotes the lion's share of its time and effort to serving its own private interests and the interests of the network with which it is affiliated. Those interests rarely intersect with public interests at most stations. The time devoted to genuine public service by virtually every TV station is a puny effort aimed at making viewers *believe* the stations are serving the public interest and providing irrelevant data for FCC forms.

WNAO-TV might or might not have been committed to carrying out the FCC mandate to serve the public. Regardless of its intent, its ability to do so was seriously compromised by its technical shortcomings and its struggle to sustain itself. As a competitor to newspapers, existing radio stations and other media, the small station did not seem to be a harbinger of change that would eventually cause historians to look back to the mid-1950s and the spread of television to small cities such as Raleigh and hundreds of others as the beginning of a tipping point in which the visual medium of television would replace print media as the dominant form of mass communication in the U.S and the world.

Making the Best of a
Bad Situation

Almost from the moment WNAO-TV, Channel 28 signed on the air on July 12, 1953 it was plagued with problems. For the new station every day was a dispiriting, morale-draining struggle to keep a decent television signal on the air, sell enough advertising to pay its bills, keep embarrassing errors off the air and finally to persuade CBS to allow it to carry the network's daily schedule of daytime and prime time programs on a consistent basis that did not include inexplicable interruptions in daily and weekly series or even deletions of all or parts of the most popular programs on the network.

Almost as bad as the FCC decisions to mix VHF and UHF channels in the same markets were the affiliation contracts between the television networks in New York and the various local stations.

To understand the problems faced by local stations, one must understand what a television network is and why it exists. As Christopher Reed wrote in an excellent paper on the network-affiliate partnership, "The relationship between a national television network and its affiliates is perhaps one of the most unique and dynamic in all broadcasting."

In essence a television network, wrote Reed, "is merely an office building where executives package programs they do not own and obtain advertisers who pay the networks to have the programs transmitted over stations, most of which the networks don't own or control. The money paid by the advertiser is then divvied up among the stations carrying the programs and the networks that provided them.

"While it is clear that the network-affiliate model makes economic sense for the programmers, producers and advertisers, the suitability of this system to stations' ability to fulfill their duty to their communities has by and large gone unquestioned," wrote Reed.

"Though television schedules are peppered with local and regional programs, the bulk of the programming seen on most major market stations come from national sources, leaving many to wonder whether the traditional network-affiliate model leaves the local public interest underserved at best and completely ignored at worst."

Many of WNAO-TV's problems and its eventual demise resulted from its affiliation agreement with the Columbia Broadcasting System (CBS). Because WNAO-TV was a small UHF station in a small market, CBS had an overwhelming advantage at the negotiating table. In the mid-1950s, CBS' contracts could permit a local station to carry some of its programs for which it received payment, and prohibit the station from carrying others. In many cases, WNAO-TV was permitted by CBS to carry parts of a program, but not the entire program.

Imagine for a moment: You are watching your favorite dramatic show, and suddenly without any explanation, the dramatic conclusion is replaced by an old film short. Impossible to believe, but that was the problem confronting WNAO-TV and other UHF stations regularly in the early days of the medium.

According to their affiliation agreements, local stations were required to notify AT&T, the provider of coaxial services over which the programs were transmitted from the networks, to delete programs or program segments that they were not authorized to receive from the network.

Because of the scheduling chaos that resulted from the affiliation agreement and the outrage of viewers who were disappointed when favorite programs were not aired, WNAO-TV and possibly other stations in the same predicament opted to carry programs not specifically authorized by the network. If AT&T was not notified to delete a program or a segment of a program, the program or program segment was provided to the station.

The delivery of programs from networks to local stations is a much different process than it was in the 1950s and 1960s, but back then, failing to notify AT&T to delete non-authorized programs was a serious offense by the station and a violation of the network-station affiliation agreement. However, the alternative created such problems for WNAO-TV, it felt it had no choice. The term for this kind of action was known as "bootlegging the network."

At the direction of the Station Manager, John Bone, WNAO-TV began the practice of bootlegging CBS sometime prior to 1956, without mentioning it to the staff except for key members of the advertising sales department and to those responsible for preparing the daily program broadcast logs. When CBS discovered the practice, it would be cited in its decision to terminate its affiliation with WNAO-TV, leaving the station without a network or the means to create programming capable of competing with the two large VHF stations then operating in the market. However, if WNAO-TV had not been guilty of bootlegging the network, CBS most likely would have found other reasons to terminate its affiliation. The network seemed determined to become affiliated with one of the two larger VHF stations.

With its programming and technical problems, the launch of WNAO-TV that initially had generated considerable enthusiasm quickly became a frustrating disappointment for most of those who had eagerly looked forward to its sign on. Although WNAO Radio had been sold to investors from Erie, Pennsylvania who acquired a majority interest in WNAO-TV, the station's call letters, WNAO-TV, linked its lineage to *The News and Observer,* and this linkage was something of an embarrassment for the paper's owners and editors.

Compounding the problem for viewers who wanted to receive the Channel 28 signal was the requirement for either an outdoor UHF antenna or a special UHF indoor antenna/tuner. The outdoor antennas worked pretty well when there was a UHF signal to pick up, but to the great frustration of viewers, the Channel 28 signal often was not available as the station struggled to keep its equipment functioning properly. The indoor UHF antenna/tuner could be affected by many factors, including weather, radio interference or simply the configuration of the furniture in a room.

With few experienced in television in North Carolina, WNAO-TV employed programming, production, technical and sales people from across the Northeast and Midwest, areas in which local television stations had been operating for longer periods.

When I joined WNAO-TV in 1956, as Continuity Director or chief writer, the station had been on the air two and a half years, but was still struggling to find its way and gain traction in the market.

Many of the staff members who had been at bigger stations regarded WNAO-TV as a temporary stopover that they would leave as soon as a better opportunity presented itself. Those just starting out also looked toward bigger stations in larger markets and were using WNAO-TV as merely a learning experience.

Around the water cooler and in the break room, groups would cluster throughout the day, and the major topic of conversation was, "What station were you with?" or "How long you plan on being here?" Most of the staff members did not know the last names of their co-workers.

Although many WNAO-TV staffers were strangers to one another and were working in an unfamiliar geographical location, the esprit de corps was generally quite high. Despite the station's overriding problems, most staff members enjoyed the daily excitement that television broadcasting provided. Much of the time the mood at the station was more relaxed and easygoing than serious. Many staff members, even the most professional ones, willingly participated in practical jokes at the expense of on-the-air personnel. They especially enjoyed making life uncomfortable for the inexperienced who joined their ranks.

For many who were just beginning careers in television, a small start-up station in a relatively small Southern city provided a fairly easy entryway to the medium. For those who had, for various reasons, not been successful at larger stations in larger markets, WNAO-TV provided a second chance, an environment in which the demands would be fewer than in the more competitive markets and where mistakes and lack of professionalism might be more readily tolerated. The result was a disparate mixture of people, some with little real experience in television and some experienced people who carried personal and professional baggage resulting from difficulties at other stations that had resulted in their termination – either voluntarily or involuntarily.

A Glossy Façade, A Diverse Staff: Hopes and Dreams Hanging in the Balance

Initially, the TV station began operations from the offices of WNAO radio station, which were located next door to offices of *The News and Observer,* founder of the radio station and minority owner of the new television station.

The television operation soon required additional space, and both the radio and television stations moved to what had been Raleigh's most elegant night club, the Club Bon Aire, a handsome structure near the east entrance to Pullen Park, on Western Boulevard that combined a futuristic architectural appearance with what appeared to be a woodsy campus. (In 2012, a convenience store occupied the site.)

When WNAO-TV signed on the air as an affiliate of CBS and began broadcasting network programs it provided viewers with many of the better programs of the time such as *The Ed Sullivan Show, I Love Lucy, Playhouse 90,* and the early news and documentary programs by Edward R. Murrow, and other figures who came to dominate television news. To the casual observer, the station, with impressive offices and studios and a schedule of some of the more popular television shows, appeared to be substantial and on its way to success.

The station's executive staff was drawn from a wide area. John Bone, station manager, brought a wealth of experience and success he had achieved at Crosley Broadcasting of Cincinnati, Ohio, a pioneer in radio broadcasting that had also created a regional television network of Midwest stations.

Leo Ribitiski, operations manager, brought an unusual intellectual and somewhat mysterious background to the station. His resume was the stuff of legend. Although he rarely spoke of his past, it was generally known that he had led an underground Jewish resistance against Nazi Germany during World War II, and after the war made his way to the U.S. via South America where he found work at a Florida television station. He spoke nine languages and was said to *think in Latin.*

Joe Cutter, his assistant, was a talented announcer and writer who had both radio and television experience. After leaving the station, Cutter found success with the Andy Griffith Show and as a comedy skit writer for *The Jack Paar Show,* forerunner to the *Tonight Show With Johnny Carson.*

Earle Welde, the advertising sales manager, was one of the few members of the staff who had a degree in broadcasting. He had begun his career in radio, but his face, seriously scarred by what apparently had been a savage case of adolescent acne, and sparse hair that was becoming sparser by the day rendered him largely unsuitable for the visual medium. Welde was easy-going, hardworking and supportive of those who reported to him, but he always seemed disappointed that he was unable to have a career before the camera instead of behind it.

The job of Traffic Manager, a lower level position, was held by Daphene Molgilnicki, one of the few native North Carolinians employed by the station. Like me, she was able to obtain a job at the station although she had no experience in broadcasting and no academic preparation for her job. In short order, however, she made herself indispensable to the station, and was often the person CBS officials preferred to deal with on station-network matters.

The position of Continuity Director, the odd designation for the person who does virtually all of the writing for a station, also is a lower level management position largely unknown to the public. It was the job I was to acquire and thus at an early age to become engaged in many aspects of the station's operation, including regular appearances on a live afternoon show that in an informal setting provided programming information, public service material and community news.

On my first day at WNAO-TV, I had no idea how to write for television. What kept me from immediately getting booted out of the station was that no one else seemed to know how any better than I. My predecessor left the station with precious few instructions on how to carry on. My first assignments were to write more than a dozen promotional announcements and several public service notices. No instructions were given, and no one seemed the least bit interested in reviewing what I had written. I muddled through the day by trying to write copy that was similar to the copy I found in the files. No one complained. Oddly, there was no editorial oversight of television continuity writers. Local television writers sent their copy off to be broadcast without the input of a copy editor or anyone else. Sometimes advertisers or account executives might want to review a script for a commercial, but this was rare.

If an error went out over the air, it was written up along with others in "discrepancy" reports that eventually found their way to the FCC. No one wanted to be on the discrepancy report, so everyone sought to perform his job as error-free as possible.

I managed to keep my name off the discrepancy reports except for a few minor glitches, and in a few weeks, I became comfortable in my strange job. After three months I was given a merit raise for consistently completing my assignments before the end of each work day.

Because television requires the cooperation of several people, virtually everything except live interviews must be "scripted," and even live interviews are planned in advance so that the director is aware of the questions that will be asked, and the answers that will be given. This enables the director or master control operator to know in advance what is to be shown and what is to be said. Without scripts, there can be no coordination between those who are involved in the technical aspect of broadcasting and those actually speaking or performing on the air.

In the early days of television, providing on-screen credit to writers was not considered. Many, perhaps most, television viewers never gave a thought to the notion that what they were hearing was actually *written* by someone and that the visual sequences were determined by the writer as he or she wrote the script. As television evolved through the years, and although writers are crucial to its smooth operation, they rarely received on-screen credit. Today, television executives prefer to identify news writers and reporters as "producers." According to the Writers Guild of America, virtually all writers of non-fiction television material are credited on screen as producers – if they are credited at all.

The writers and reporters who do the actual leg work and produce the scripts for local stations as well as for news shows and programs such as *60 Minutes* on CBS are credited as producers, not writers. Much of what appears on television is undeserving of a credit for writing, however, disguising the writer as a producer is an oddity peculiar to television.

The nature of the television business seems to engender a kind of pervasive anxiety among many – especially those whose work product is placed before the public daily · to be either admired or criticized. Compounding the problem for persons working in television in the early days was the limited number of stations. Losing one's job meant relocation in another distant city. At WNAO-TV, anxiety, mitigated somewhat by a pervasive "gallows humor," was rampant. It was pretty well understood that the station was losing out in the competition with WTVD in Durham, and by early 1956, WRAL was beginning to construct its studios and administrative offices on Western Boulevard, just a few hundred feet from WNAO-TV.

Each day's progress toward sign on by WRAL-TV was a day closer to the end for WNAO-TV, and many of the station's employees were aware of the impending finality. Some, however, believed there would be a place for the smaller station, especially as fledgling ABC was beginning to offer a more comprehensive schedule of programming.

Scams and Gimmicks

In the early days, selling television time was a difficult task. Local businesses did not know how to use the medium and they distrusted the size of the audiences that stations claimed. The pressure on ad sales people was intense.

Television advertising sales people became especially adept at persuading advertisers to purchase advertising by convincing them that they would be effective in on-camera appearances in their advertising. Officials of aluminum siding companies, car dealerships, insurance agents and many other small businesses were particularly susceptible to the notion of appearing on television to pitch their own products or services. Oddly, many of those same types of advertisers continue to be susceptible to the lure of being "on television." Most of them do as much harm as good to their businesses. Quite a few appear ridiculous.

WNAO-TV's continuing difficulties in attracting advertisers made the station vulnerable to various advertising gimmicks that sometimes were nothing more than a scam. In the 1950s, the television networks were all caught up in a widespread scandal that involved rigging game shows and contests. The practice extended to local stations as well.

One of the more egregious scams in which WNAO-TV was involved was a rather convoluted contest that was offered to the station by an itinerant promoter who approached the station with a "guaranteed money maker." The promoter promised a 13-week series, with all commercials paid in advance. The station felt it could not turn down such a deal. The plan worked like this:

The promoter would sell advertisers a promotional plan in which customers who visited an advertiser's place of business would be given the opportunity to sign his or her name on a card and thus become eligible to win what was billed as a "free trip to Florida." Participating advertisers paid an advanced fee equivalent to the cost of approximately 13 20-second commercial announcements. A dozen advertisers were eligible to participate in each contest, so each week's contest yielded more than a dozen commercials for the station – all paid in advance.

Each week, during a film promoting the joys of a Florida vacation, a single name would be drawn from the cards turned in by the dozen advertisers. The winner would receive a free trip.

The promotion seemed to be working well for everyone. The commercials promoted the drawing, resulting in increased business for the participating advertisers, the station was enjoying an advertising windfall and a lucky person was winning a trip to Florida every week.

Very quickly, however, the winners discovered that that they would be required to pay for their travel to Florida and that the cost of a husband, wife or other companion would be extra and the extra exceeded the cost of what would be a normal cost. The complaints were loud and angry.

After setting up the program and signing all the advertisers, the promoter took his share of the profits and disappeared. WNAO-TV spent the advance money and was stuck with a 13-week contract that had several weeks to run. The station could have opted to cancel the program, return the money and move on. To eliminate the complaints, the station decided to award the trips to fictitious winners each week who, of course, would not complain. The scam went undetected by the advertisers or the viewers.

Decades later, television networks continue deception in their so-called "reality shows' that they promote as contests, but are carefully structured and edited for maximum dramatic effect.

Live From The Studio

Although WNAO-TV was technically ill-equipped and for most of its last two years operated with a skeleton staff, it made a valiant effort to carry two daily news shows and several locally produced live shows. Those early locally produced television programs on WNAO-TV, in addition to the news and sports, included daily episodes of *Romper Room, Good Afternoon,* a daily potpourri of conversation, program promotion and community public service news, and a clown show for children.

One of the station's most popular and enduring personalities was legendary country music entertainer Homer Drie, who had adopted the name Homer Briarhopper from an entertainment group known as the Briarhoppers that had appeared regularly on Charlotte radio station WBT as well as performing hundreds of live shows. Briarhopper worked as an early morning disc jockey on WNAO radio. His arrangement with the station required him to sell the advertising that appeared on his show and share the proceeds with the station.

By the time the station's regular employees arrived, Briarhopper had already put in a couple of hours of work. After his on-the-air shift, he immediately began working the phones selling advertising and booking live shows for him and the group of musicians who worked with him.

At 11 a.m. Briarhopper would return to the radio studios where he and his band would do a live music show. As soon as they completed their radio show, they would rush down to the television studio and do a half-hour show on live television. As soon as the cameras turned off, the entire band would gather their instruments and rush out the door to pile into Briarhopper's car.

Briarhopper and his band would accept any paying engagement that he could drive to from 12:30 p.m. and return in time to do his morning radio show. Briarhopper and his band met this daily schedule even though it appeared impossible, and he never seemed to be in a bad humor or out of sorts in any way.

Briarhopper often was the opening act for touring groups that came to Raleigh, and he usually brought some of the well-known stars to appear with him on his daily radio and television shows. Among them was a very young Elvis Pressley. Some staffers were amused by his performance on Briarhopper's TV show, but none realized that he would become the "King of Rock and Roll" and start a new musical genre that would sweep the nation.

The year 1956, was an election year, and in North Carolina, W.E. Debnam, a former newspaper reporter turned radio commentator, challenged the Democratic incumbent Harold Cooley for Cooley's Fourth District congressional seat. Debnam's family owned a weekly newspaper where he gained early journalistic experience. He later worked for radio stations and newspapers throughout the region, but gained his greatest popularity as a regular commentator on WPTF radio with a program entitled *Debnam Views the News* and with a book critical of Eleanor Roosevelt entitled *Weep No More, My Lady.*

Debnam was a political conservative and his commentaries were vigorous and sometimes eloquent presentations of the conservative perspective, a kind of forerunner to Jesse Helms who would achieve fame with conservative "Viewpoints" on WRAL-TV. As a part of his campaign to unseat Cooley, Debnam purchased a daily quarter hour of television time on WNAO-TV that ran Monday-through Friday for several weeks prior to the Democratic primary that was held in the spring. His political program aired before the daily television newscast at 6.p.m.

Debnam would arrive at the station less than 45 minutes before his broadcast was to go on the air. He usually wore a dark suit with a vest buttoned to the top and a dark hat, common to well-dressed gentlemen of the time. He had installed on an old manual typewriter a continuous roll of paper that eliminated the need for him to stop writing to insert new pages. Entering the office complex he would nod to those in the room, sit down at his desk and without removing his hat begin to type with two fingers at a dazzling speed.

For a half hour he would type non-stop, never pausing to gather new thoughts or consider what he had written. After some 30 minutes, he would stop writing and begin tearing the roll of typewritten copy into sheets, glancing at each momentarily. He would then rise, take his packet of freshly typed pages and go upstairs to the television studio. When the camera focused on him and he received the cue from the floor manager, he would deliver his material flawlessly. I could not understand how he could write so rapidly without pausing for thoughts and reviews and how his copy could flow so gracefully with no editing or rewriting at all. Debnam lost the primary election to Cooley, but it was not because of any deficiency in his writing ability.

Getting Better By Getting Smaller

As the months went by, the WNAO-TV staff seemed to shrink noticeably. By the Fall of 1956, the staff of 60 had been reduced by half, and shortly after the beginning of 1957, the staff of 30 was reduced further. I was glad to be among that dwindling group, but like all of the survivors of the draconian cuts, I saw the writing on the wall.

As the reductions in staff continued, Bone, Ribitiski and Welde called the remaining members together and urged us to "take up the slack."

With a smaller staff, working in much closer collaboration, however, the on-air errors virtually disappeared, resulting in improvement in the station's overall performance. The engineering department, under Lee Poole and Gene Reopelle, managed to find a way to keep the station on the air with few daily interruptions.

As the staff shrank, rumors of all kinds circulated throughout the station. Some of us even began to deliberately concoct bizarre rumors just to see how many people would actually believe them. Each day became a challenge to come up with some new fictitious plan that would either save or end the station.

Although uncertainty and anxiety permeated the station, the small staff carried on with a high degree of professionalism. Those of us who had survived the layoffs had reached the conclusion that we were essential, and this enabled us to carry out our responsibilities with a minimum of anxiety even though we never knew what the future would hold. We also had developed a high degree of camaraderie. As the much larger station grew closer to a reality, we dug in to demonstrate just how competent a small group could be under adverse conditions. Frankly, some of us had few other options in television, and virtually all of us had been bitten by the television bug. Although we worked hard, we enjoyed being a part of a generally exciting enterprise. Some of us even considered our jobs to be great fun.

Busted for Bootlegging: A Botched Cover Up

One afternoon in autumn of 1956, Station Manager John Bone summoned managers and staff to his office for a closed-door meeting. Bone told us that representatives from CBS wanted to examine program logs covering several months' operation, but that he had offered to submit random logs that did not include every day but would cover the period in question.

"Before we send in the logs, we need to review them and possibly make some corrections," said Bone. It quickly became clear what Bone was suggesting. He wanted the logs to be changed so as not to reveal the "bootlegging" that had been on-going for quite some time. He asked the group to report for work at 6 a.m. for the next several days until the "corrections" could be made.

The process of "correcting" the program logs went on for a week. It consisted of reviewing the teletype orders that the station had received from CBS, and where the orders did not correspond with log entries, making changes that disguised the station's "bootlegging" of programs it was not entitled to air.

About two dozen logs were changed during the "correcting" process. New logs were typed, back dated and copies packaged and sent to the CBS executives. As the succeeding days passed, the worried expressions on the faces of Bone, Ribitiski and Welde grew more pronounced.

After several weeks of waiting and worrying, Bone received a response from CBS. For serious infractions of the affiliate agreement between WNAO-TV and the Columbia Broadcasting System as well as for other reasons not enumerated, the contract between the network and the station would be terminated. Within the week, WNAO-TV was left without a fulltime network affiliation and a very difficult problem to explain to the viewers and advertisers.

CBS moved to WTVD in Durham. WRAL-TV had already announced its plans to be on the air before the end of the year, and everyone assumed that the station would carry the NBC lineup. Indeed, that is what occurred. WRAL-TV, Channel 5 signed on the air on December 15, 1956, ushering in a new era of television broadcasting in Raleigh and central North Carolina.

Station Manager Bone discussed the situation with managers and key staff, and it was decided that no in-depth explanation would be offered regarding the loss of its network affiliation, merely an announcement that the station would no longer carry the CBS network.

The brief statement did little to quell public dissatisfaction. Although CBS programs continued to be available, the popular NBC program lineup went into limbo, and viewers had no way of knowing when or whether the programs would be again available. Because of the difficulty of filling an 18-hour broadcast day, WNAO-TV reduced its broadcast day to only nine hours, eliminating all of the morning game shows and continuing soap operas that housewives tuned in to see.

Advertisers who had bought time next to network programs cancelled their contracts, although the station sought to keep them by reducing advertising rates. The combination of public anger and loss of advertising weighed heavily on Bone. The rest of us were too busy trying to make adjustments and keep things on an even keel to dwell on the real implications of the station's problems.

Bone could see the handwriting on the wall. He knew that without a network affiliation and with a big new VHF station soon to sign on the air, WNAO-TV's days were numbered. He also seemed to know that he would bear the responsibility for the failure and that at his stage in life, his options were limited.

The once genial and enthusiastic station manager began to look haggard and depressed. He rarely spoke to anyone, but each morning went immediately to his office where he secluded himself behind a closed door. Soon, however, he initiated a series of meetings in his office that became more and more bizarre. Every morning he would summon Program Director Ribitski, Sales Manager Welde, Traffic Manager Mogolniki, and me to his office. For several hours, he would relate tales of his success at the Crosley Broadcasting Company. The meetings and their stories which seemed pointless and irrelevant continued past the lunch hour, leaving less time for the work of preparing for the next day's broadcast.

Bone's haggard appearance became apparent to everyone, but the strange meetings grew a bit longer each day and a bit more pointless. His tales of successes at Crosley dominated the meetings and he would occasionally ask rhetorically why WNAO-TV could not use the Crosley experience as a way to achieve success.

After approximately eight weeks, the meetings ended. We soon learned the reason. The station owners from Erie, Pa. arrived at the station, went into a closed door meeting with Bone that lasted for several hours. In mid-afternoon, the owners and Bone left together. It was the last time we would see him.

He said no goodbyes, and no explanation was given for his leaving, although to those of us who interacted with him daily, the reason seemed clear enough. Those who had known Bone before the pressures of his job changed his personality and his behavior were saddened. We wondered what life held in store for the man who had once exhibited energy, vitality and good will toward those who reported to him and who seemed to lose it all as circumstances conspired to make life difficult for him.

The New Boss Takes Over

Bone was immediately replaced by Roger Bower, who had been hired as the manager of WNAO radio. Bower had an impressive broadcasting resume. However, his ego was larger than his resume. When he arrived at the station, he strutted through the offices and studios looking like he smelled something unpleasant.

In a rather long broadcasting career in New York during the days of big time radio network broadcasting, Bower had written, produced, and appeared in several successful national radio shows. As a sportscaster, he had announced the Army-Navy games, the annual Rose Bowl games and later announced the first Macy's Thanksgiving Day parade. Bower won numerous awards as a true broadcasting pioneer. Now, nearing retirement age, his best years were clearly behind him. Still most staff members were puzzled as to why he would be willing to accept the position of station manager of a not-too-successful radio operation in a small southern city.

One of the first things he did upon moving into his office was to hang pictures of himself with various celebrities on every square inch of wall space. With the walls totally covered, he would escort young female staff members into his office and in a manner far too physically intimate, patiently explain the circumstances under which each picture was taken. In the work environment of the 21 Century, Bower would likely be charged with sexual harassment for his behavior with subordinate females. In the 1950s, complaints about such behavior were virtually non-existent.

In a well-cultivated, well-trained baritone, with exquisite enunciation, Bower bored female and occasionally male visitors to his office with stories about his success as the moderator of a defunct radio show entitled *Can You Top This?*

Bone's bizarre preoccupation with past successes while the station for which he was currently responsible writhed in a downward spiral provided a sad spectacle. Bower's egomaniacal obsession with his past stardom was merely annoying.

Soon after assuming the position of Station Manager, Bower sought to energize the staff and attract advertisers with promises of better times for the station. He said the ABC network was going to increase its programming in the Raleigh-Durham market providing at least some network programs for the station and local viewers. The station would purchase a new package of newer movies that had not been seen in the area and that live programming would be increased. There would be no more layoffs and advertising sales would be coordinated between the radio station and the television station, offering a better advertising opportunity for local advertisers and promising to boost income for both stations.

Bower's promises were successful in building morale, but the reality of the situation soon became apparent to everyone as we all realized that Bower's promises were going to be difficult to keep. The rumor that the station would build a new 1,000-foot transmission tower and increase its power to a million watts spread through the station with a bit more credibility than most rumors. All of us took some satisfaction in watching WRAL-TV, which had signed on the air without first completing its studios, production and administrative facilities, struggle with its own technical and production problems, generally typical of a television start-up. We had finally figured out how to keep the small UHF station on the air virtually error-free, and we took delight in the errors that we observed on our big competitor.

The Rumor Mill Grinds On

As December, 1957, arrived, another rumor spread; the station had made a trade deal with an appliance distributor, and for our hard work in keeping the station on the air, each employee would receive, not a cash bonus, but a color television set. The excitement was palpable.

In early December, the staff was notified that the station's annual Christmas party would be held around the middle of the month at the station. Everyone considered the news regarding the party to be a good sign. We assumed that by having a Christmas party, the station was going to remain on the air. We took seriously the rumor regarding the gifts of color television sets for each staff member.

The night of the party, virtually all staff members attended, dressed in festive finery. The party was moving along at a good pace when Bowers, slightly tipsy, asked everyone to gather around. Everyone thought he was ready to pass out the color television sets. No one had actually seen any TV sets, but we thought perhaps they had been kept hidden to heighten the surprise.

As we waited with considerable anticipation, Bower stepped forward to announce that contrary to the rumors, which he, too, had heard, no color television sets would be given to anyone. That was the good news. The bad news? WNAO-TV would suspend operations at midnight, December 31, 1957. Everyone would be dismissed, however, engineers, announcers and a "few others" might be given jobs at WNAO radio. In the coming days, persons wishing to be considered for the radio jobs should be available to discuss their futures. The party quickly broke up, with some staff members weeping.

The Monday following the Christmas party with its devastating news as well as the remainder of the month was like an elongated funeral wake. Staff members whose work was not essential to keeping the station on the air said their goodbyes and began seeking new jobs.

By the end of December, only a handful of people remained. Those of us who had been engrossed in the day-to-day operation of the station, could not help but feel a bit of sadness as the past years in which a serious effort to operate a television station had been interspersed with actions and antics that vacillated between tragedy and farce were finally coming to a definite conclusion. It was now clear that the odd and troubling behavior of the top executives in this struggling organization had been a signal that the end was near for the first television station in Raleigh, North Carolina and that the final curtain soon would be lowered.

On New Year's Eve, 1957, Raleigh's first television station signed off, perhaps unnoticed by most holiday revelers. The station would remain "dark" until November 4, 1968, when WRDU-TV, licensed in Durham and unrelated to the earlier station, began operation. The station had studios on Highway 54 and its transmitter was located near Terrell's Mountain in Chatham County. It was owned by a company known as Triangle Telecasters. The station acquired part of the NBC network's program schedule, but shared some of it with WTVD in Durham.

Over the next decade, the UHF station struggled to compete successfully with the two well-established and dominate VHF stations, and in May, 1977, The Durham Life Insurance Company, owner of WPTF radio, purchased the station, thus achieving a goal of owning a television station it has first sought more than two decades earlier. The Channel 28 call letters were changed to WPTF-TV.

The Durham Life Insurance Broadcasting Company invested heavily in the station, even erecting a 1,300-foot transmitting tower. The investments failed to enable the UHF station to compete effectively with WRAL-TV and WTVD. It even failed to achieve better ratings than other UHF stations that were then in the Raleigh area.

In the summer of 1991, Durham Life sold all of its broadcasting assets. Its television station was sold to Paul Brissette who changed its call letters to WRDU.

Like his predecessors, Brissette failed to make the station profitable and in 1995, the station was again sold, eventually becoming a part of the Sinclair Broadcasting Company and an affiliate of MYNetwork TV.

As future events were to prove, the lowering of the curtain on the tragedy/farce that began as WNAO-TV would not be the last act in the Raleigh, N.C. television saga. Indeed, the station's struggles were the opening act, the dog and pony show that heralded the main events that were to follow.

In Anger Unkind Words
--And Defeat Is Snatched From The Jaws
of Victory

It was the third week of the Federal Communications Commission's hearing in the epic David versus Goliath struggle that pitted Capitol Broadcasting, operator of the 250-watt radio station, WRAL, against Durham Life Insurance Company, owner of the 50,000-watt station WPTF, for the allocation of the coveted VHF television Channel 5 for the Raleigh, North Carolina market. Tedium had settled over the hearings as they had droned on over the past weeks with statistics and data piled upon statistics and data and endless questions asked and answered.

Those in the room endured the tedium without complaint because they knew the outcome of these proceedings would have profound significance for the winning applicant as well as for Raleigh, North Carolina, a broad section of the central and eastern parts of the state and eventually the political future of the state and nation.

Among the small group that was enduring the tedium was Alfred Johnson Fletcher, known to his contemporaries as "Fletch," or "A.J." but almost universally to his employees and those younger as "Mr. A.J." Raised on a hardscrabble farm in the mountains of Northwestern North Carolina, the son of an iterant preacher, Fletcher, against great odds, had become a successful radio station owner, entrepreneur and lawyer. In the mid-1950s, nearing retirement age, Fletcher was still thin as a strip of store-bought bacon and tough as a boot strap with an intellect as keen as an old-fashioned straight razor. Competing against the most formidable contender that Raleigh could produce for one of broadcasting's most cherished prizes, he needed all the toughness and intellect he could muster.

Also in the room was Fletcher's trusted associate, Mrs. Scotty Stephenson and Fletcher's second son, Frank, a former Washington, D.C. FCC lawyer, who understood the application procedure perhaps better than any of the participants. As Capitol Broadcasting Company's legal counsel, Frank Fletcher's detailed knowledge of FCC regulations and requirement was a secret weapon that leveled the playing field significantly in the ongoing contest.

The hearing was one of the last hurdles confronting the two contenders for the television allocation, a gift from the government that many considered a "license to print money." The stakes were enormous, and the battle had been going on for over five years, a battle Fletcher remembered as the "hardest, most nerve-wracking of his entire life." It had raged from the late 1940s to the mid-1950s. As the hearings continued with the outcome very much in doubt, Fletcher was beginning to wonder if the prize would be worth the long fight he had waged.

Durham Life, the owner of the 50,000-watt radio broad-casting behemoth, WPTF, had for years been considered the logical recipient of the television channel allocation. As a broadcast entity, its reputation and history were stellar. Since the 1920s, the station had proven to be a highly regarded, well-run operation that had entertained and informed the residents of Raleigh, Central North Carolina and thousands of others who could receive its signal as far away as Washington, D.C. and Atlanta, Georgia. The station had been profitable for years and was backed by the financial strength of the Durham Life Insurance Company, a major business institution in North Carolina and the South.

At the outset Durham Life Broadcasting considered Capitol Broadcasting's application for the television license to be a minor nuisance. The company was so confident of its ability to win the channel allocation, it had already begun building a television studio, and it had proceeded at a rather slow pace. However, the contest between Durham Life Broadcasting and Capitol Broadcasting had intensified with each passing year, and Capitol's position had strengthened with each passing month. What once appeared to be a certain win for the bigger, more established company became uncertain.

"At first," recalled Fletcher, "public sentiment was almost decidedly against us. No one thought, apparently, that Capitol Broadcasting could possibly be successful in obtaining a grant or in building a worthwhile station if we got it."

The gradual and now accelerating change in public sentiment resulted from the exceptional efforts of WRAL Radio staff members, such as George Hall, Scotty Stephenson, the Station's news staff and others who worked tirelessly for the channel allocation. By the time the hearings had begun, no one could predict the outcome.

As Capitol's position strengthened, WPTF decided it needed legal talent not then available in Raleigh. It retained Attorney Kenneth Royall, a retired Army General who was associated with a large, well-connected New York firm. Although retired from the Army, Royall stilled liked to be referred to as General Royall. At six feet, six inches tall and over 225 pounds, the former General presented an imposing figure.

Realizing the tedium that had settled over the proceedings, the hearing commissioner, (a Mr. French, as Fletcher recalled), offered a suggestion designed to reduce the tiresome details and expedite the process. Royall became irate at the suggestion. Rising to his full height, towering over the much smaller commissioner, he bellowed, "Your honor, I am not going to let you tell me how to try my case!" The commissioner allowed Royall's outburst to go unchallenged.

The angry words the Durham Life lawyer leveled at the man who would ultimately make the decision as well as his overbearing demeanor, gave A.J. Fletcher a surge of confidence in the outcome. The hard chair on which he was sitting somehow seemed softer.

Fletcher's son, Frank, turned to his father with a look that spoke volumes. Fletcher cast a glance at his associate, Mrs. Stephenson, and gave her a wink and a tiny smile.

"Watching the reaction of the hearing commissioner to the General's outburst, I just knew things were going to turn out in our favor," said Fletcher. "Frankly, I thought Royall had played hell and my confidence in winning went up." Fletcher's confidence was well placed. After some three more weeks of hearings, the FCC ruled that WRAL would receive the Channel Five television allocation, and the decision was upheld through the appeals process initiated by WPTF.

Recalling the incident nearly two decades later still produced a chuckle from Fletcher. Even in private quarters, the General would not consider the commissioner's suggestions, recalled Fletcher. He went so far as to declare that he would not agree to anything that he, himself, did not first suggest, recalled Fletcher. "The old boy still thought he was in the Army where everybody had to jump when he gave an order."

The FCC said its decision to give Capitol Broadcasting the prized VHF television channel allocation was based on Capitol's promise that the station owners would manage all phases of the station's operation in a "hands-on" manner.

With the allocation of VHF television Channel Five in Raleigh, with its coverage reach many times greater than the existing UHF channel 28, the Federal Government unfairly, profoundly and permanently titled the competitive field against the smaller UHF station as well as those that would come later. The pattern was repeated across the country. In Raleigh, the FCC decision enabled A.J. Fletcher and his family to achieve financial success and political influence that otherwise would not have been so readily available.

For over a half century, Channel Five would dominate the television market in Raleigh and central and eastern North Carolina. For much of that time, the only other commercial VHF station permitted in the market – WTVD, Channel 11 in nearby Durham – was owned in part and managed by Fletcher's son, Floyd.

There is no evidence that the Fletchers, in winning such a favored advantage, did anything illegal. They played the game by the rules. They just played it better than their competitors. The fault lay not with the players, but with the game and the rules under which the game was played.

WRAL-TV, The Early Hectic Years

Soon after winning the Channel Five television allocation, A.J. Fletcher and several of his employees stood under a funeral home tent on a rainy morning and broke ground on Western Boulevard in Raleigh for what he proclaimed would be a complex of offices, studios and production facilities on beautifully landscaped grounds.

Fletcher fully expected to begin broadcasting from the facility he envisioned from the moment the new station signed on the air. It was not to be.

The construction process bogged down as numerous problems delayed construction. Impatient to get on the air, the Fletchers decided to begin operations on December 13, 1956 -- in temporary quarters.

Into the old Grass Roots Opera House at the corner of Morgan and Hillsborough streets in Raleigh were jammed dozens of people – the men and women responsible for most of the station's operation – programming, promotion, advertising sales, news, an art department, a film development facility as well as the traffic and continuity departments.

Only the station's two top executives, A.J. Fletcher and his son, Fred, had private offices.

The station had offered me a job shortly before the last days of WNAO-TV, and in early January, 1958, I joined the crowded staff in the old opera house.

The engineering and production personnel operated from the station's transmitter site at Auburn, about 10 miles away, but were constantly in and out of the offices, meeting with the operations director, sales and continuity people. People wandered through the building continually, adding to what seemed to be a state of complete chaos.

Although WRAL-TV had promised to be superior to the struggling WNAO-TV, the promise was not kept in the early days. Many of the station's early problems resulted from the logistical dilemma caused by the separation of the production and programming departments. A major part of the logistics problem stemmed from the requirement that all of the material for programs and commercials for a full day's broadcast be prepared and organized in a set of copy books for delivery to the transmitter site at least a day in advance.

At WRAL-TV, multiple writers – from the promotion department, the advertising department and the programming department – prepared copy which was then organized in the copy books by a clerical worker. The written material for an 18-hour broadcast day was delivered to the transmitter/production site without being reviewed by anyone who understood the way a broadcast operation functions. Announcers, master control operators and directors at the Auburn transmitter/production site, complained daily in lengthy discrepancy reports about errors in the material, missing graphics and often scripts that were not available when needed. The errors made WRAL-TV appear to viewers to be more incompetent than WNAO-TV, which had been virtually error-free for most of its last 16 months. The errors were a source of continuing embarrassment and frustration for WRAL-TV.

Although many of the WRAL-TV staff members had broadcast experience, much of their experience was in radio, which, although somewhat similar to television, requires an entirely different skill set.

Despite the crowded conditions and confusion in the temporary offices at the Grass Roots Opera House, a sense of optimism and an atmosphere of creative energy flowed throughout the station. A disparate and ambitious group had come together from throughout North Carolina and the nation, and creativity and innovation were encouraged by Program Director George Hall who, himself, was a fountain of ideas. Television directors Earle Ashe, George Brenholtz, Hank Cheney and Ross Shaheen were brimming with ideas they wanted to see developed and broadcast.

A remarkable amount of responsibility was given to people who were quite young. Operations/Program Director Hall, who passed away in early June, 2011, was at the time 28 years old, five years older than I. All of the television directors were about the same age as I. Indeed, few staff members were older than 30.

Over the course of a few weeks and months, many of the former WNAO-TV staffers -- Daphene Mogolniki, Lee Poole and Gene Reopelle, Paul Montgomery, Bill Johnson, L.A. Lentz, Ted Powers, O.B. Garris, Edrie Davis and others – made the move to WRAL-TV. The station welcomed them into the WRAL-TV organization graciously and enthusiastically, adding vitality and energy to the station that contributed to the overall optimistic atmosphere. It was clear that WRAL-TV was a station on the way to bigger and better things, unlike WNAO-TV, that for its last two years had mounted a failed holding action against a shutdown.

New Studios – At Last

To everyone's relief, after a series of disappointing and costly errors in the design and construction of the WRAL-TV production building on Western Boulevard, progress was visible. The Fletchers, inexperienced in the television industry, had hired as operations manager, Ted Cramer, who represented himself as an experienced television manager. Based on his resume, Cramer was given the responsibility of overseeing the design and construction of the production, administrative and executive offices for the station. The Fletchers had hoped to have at least the production building completed prior to signing on the air in December, 1956, but a year later, the building was still not complete and costs were soaring.

A.J. Fletcher fired Cramer and sought to prosecute him on various charges. Fletcher was so incensed by Cramer's failures as well as what he believed to be his dishonesty, he had posted on the property a notice that anyone sighting Cramer on the premises should call the police and have him arrested. The signs remained on the property for several months after the production building was completed and occupied.

Sound and Fury Signifying--*Nothing*

From the outset, WRAL-TV management seemed determined to demonstrate its commitment to local service and local programming. Hall, who had great interest in live theatre, was especially interested in live television production. In addition to the NBC network's schedule of daytime and primetime programs, the station embarked on an ambitious schedule of locally produced programs. With a full staff of television directors, new ideas for live programming were encouraged, and each day's schedule included several live interview and information programs.

The popular *Romper Room* program was picked up with Margaret Brickell as the "teacher." A noon news and interview program was added to the schedule and several other interview shows were begun. However, except for the *Cap'n Five Show,* featuring announcer Herb Marks and Paul Montgomery, most of the locally produced programs failed to attract audiences large enough to attract advertisers. One by one they were stricken from the program schedule.

Despite the failures of local programs, soon after the production and administrative offices were completed, Fred Fletcher, president of Capitol Broadcasting, decided to resurrect his successful radio program *Tempus Fugit* as an hour-long television program five days a week.

Although Fred Fletcher's radio show had been successful, there were serious doubts among many at WRAL-TV as to whether Fletcher could be successful on television. At the time, he was middle-aged, somewhat overweight and completely bald. He looked very much like what he was – a cigar-smoking business executive. Members of the station's senior staff thought it unseemly for a top executive of the station to appear on television every day, often participating in frivolous and sometimes silly behavior. Fred's desire to perform apparently was a family trait. After all, his father, A.J. Fletcher began appearing in numerous operas when he was nearing 60 years of age.

Fletcher's appearance was deceptive. He was an engaging person of genuine goodwill to virtually everyone. He was the executive who was approachable, who was willing to listen to younger subordinates and who generally would provide the approval one might be seeking for a new project. Although most people doubted that he would be a hit on television, virtually everyone wished him well.

As Fred Fletcher's daily *Tempus Fugit* settled into the noon time period, the need for material grew more urgent. Performers from the Grass Roots Opera Company were always available if they were in town. Another favorite was Shelton Lewis, who worked as my assistant for several months.

Lewis was a Frank Sinatra look-alike with a singing style very much like the famous crooner. A native of Wendell, son of a funeral home owner, Lewis had spent a number of years in New York seeking a career on Broadway. After many disappointments, he had given up on New York and returned to Raleigh.

After several years as a performer with the Grass Roots Opera and in other venues around the country, Alec Dantre joined the WRAL-TV staff working in the film department where he edited movies, inserted commercials in syndicated film shows and performed many other tasks. With a powerful, well-trained voice, Dantre was often called on to appear on *Tempus Fugit* where he invariably wowed the viewing audience.

My involvement in the show was to prepare "humorous material" as requested. The request would often come from Fred Fletcher who would stop by my office and say, "How about whipping up something funny for the show?" Often he would make the request as he was on his way to the studio for the rehearsal.

Whether the material I prepared was funny or not depended on one's taste. The most that can be said about it is that it was offbeat and whacky, much of it similar to the offbeat material that Steve Allen had done on *The Tonight Show* and which David Letterman would do decades later on his late night show.

Being a part of the production of live television shows was almost always interesting and often exciting. However, those locally produced programs during WRAL-TV's early years were of little significance, and none was deemed worthy of preserving on videotape. None was controversial or political in nature. Most were designed to carry out the station's commitment to public service, attract and maintain audiences and thus create opportunities to sell local advertising. As the years passed, virtually all local program production was devoted to news and weather and sports.

The Beginning of The Jesse Helms' Era

George Hall was clearly upset when he came into my office. "Mr. A.J. is going to put Jesse Helms on every Sunday," he said.

"This is going to cause trouble for the station," said Hall. He then said that we needed to be very careful in developing the format for the show with an opening that noted that the show did not necessarily reflect the views of the station, that they were the personal views of Helms and any guests that he might have.

Hall and I kicked around the format, with Hall dictating commentary to open and close the show, then deciding against it. He finally set down a number of statements that needed to be made at the beginning and ending of the show, and asked me to write it up so it flowed. He then reviewed the scripts, made a few changes, and thus was launched, the first in what would become one of the most popular and certainly the most controversial television programs in North Carolina.

The first show was called *Facts of the Matter*. Eventually, the name of the program was changed to *Viewpoint*, and was scheduled not just once a week but daily on a statewide network of approximately 100 radio stations as well as on television.

The viewpoint program became the launching pad for Helms successful election to the U.S. Senate, and a 30-year tenure that made him the nation's most recognizable member of Congress and the living symbol of old fashioned political conservatism.

In 1960, after several months of weekly programs, A.J. Fletcher and Jesse Helms began discussions that would lead to Helms joining the station as Executive Vice President of News Operations. In effect, Helms became operations manager of the station, eclipsing the role of Fred Fletcher and other managers.

The Helms commentary was controversial from the start. The week after its initial airing, WRAL-TV had to grant time for an opposing view, a pattern that would be repeated over the weeks and months to come.

When A.J. Fletcher offered Helms the position of Executive Vice President in charge of News Operations, Helms was slow to accept the position. He insisted that in addition to his executive role, he be given the opportunity to broadcast a daily *Viewpoint* editorial on any subject that he deemed important, regardless of how controversial it might be.

Many management people at the station were concerned. They feared a daily broadside often critical of the actions and activities of the federal government could be dangerous for the station. They feared it could result in a loss of the station's prized license.

A.J. Fletcher was not unaware of the risks. However, years later, he told me what he told the station executives who were not in favor of the Helms' daily editorial.

"I had been concerned for a long time that the only editorial voice in this part of the state was that of *The News and Observer*," he said. "One of the reasons I worked so hard to get the television channel was to be able to offer another opinion on the issues of the time."

A.J. Fletcher's reaction to the warning that the station might lose its license chilled the hearts of those whose future was tied to its continued operation. "By God, if we lose it, we lose it," he said, and for the next decade or so, Helms voiced a daily editorial that pulled few punches and skirted few issues, no matter how controversial they might be.

By the time Helms joined WRAL-TV on a full time basis, I had left the station, and I came to know him under circumstance that left me with conflicted feelings. Although we never agreed on political issues or candidates, we always had a friendly relationship, and he was unfailingly supportive of many projects that I initiated over the years and in the U.S. Senate always available to offer any assistance he or his office could provide.

Helm's enthusiastic endorsement of a book I wrote in 2003 about the tobacco buyout program, a program he had initiated in the U.S. Senate, was most certainly a factor in the book's success throughout tobacco producing states.

TV News Without The Glitz

Except for Helms' Sunday afternoon programs, politics was not an issue in the programming or news departments during the early days of WRAL-TV. News Director Bill Armstrong, a hard-working, no-nonsense journalist with prior newspaper experience and a small staff of about four people concentrated on a daily early evening news show devoted to hard news. Photographers Owen Balance, O.B. Garris, occasionally announcer Russell Capps and news secretary Dorothy Buffaloe made up the "hard news" staff. The daily *Stateline* edition was the principal news offering. Ray Reeve's sports segment and a weather segment known as *The Atlantic Weather Man,* with announcer Bob Knapp dressed as a service station attendant, rounded out the early evening news.

Despite the pressures of researching, writing and appearing on a daily news show, Armstrong was one of the most even-tempered persons one could meet. Deadline pressure never rattled him, but if someone intercepted the early afternoon edition of the *Raleigh Times,* the newspaper where he had earlier worked as a reporter and editor, Armstrong's placid disposition erupted into frustrated anger. The reason was quite clear. With a limited staff and a daily news show to fill, Armstrong, as did many broadcast journalists, then and now, relied on the daily newspaper as a source of news – without credit, of course.

Videotape: Television's Game Changer

From the outset, the inability to record live television programs or programs transmitted by the TV networks created great frustration. A live commercial that ran multiple times, required an announcer and a crew to be available for each broadcast, increasing operating costs for the station and limiting advertising sales. Any locally produced program vanished after a single showing because production costs did not cover repeating the production over and over.

For weeks the rumors had circulated that WRAL-TV was going to acquire a videotape machine, and when the memo requesting staff's presence in the station's main studio was received, it was assumed that the rumor was true. When all were assembled at the designated hour, A.J. Fletcher himself stepped forward to make an announcement.

"The station has just purchased a videotape machine," he said. And he said he was advised that the machine would perform wonderful things and would be a great asset to the station.

"I'll leave it to those who know more about its capabilities to explain them," he said. "I want you all to know that this new videotape machine cost slightly more than $75,000. It is one of the most expensive pieces of equipment in the station, and I want you to treat it as such."

The purchase of the videotape machine, said Fletcher, "indicates the station's commitment to building and operating the best broadcast facility that money can buy."

That early videotape machine was the size of a U-haul trailer. It recorded images in black and white on videotape that was two inches wide. At the time WRAL-TV purchased it, there was no technology for editing content recorded on the tape. In the following weeks, production and engineering people spent long hours trying to figure out ways of editing recorded content.

The need for editing was obvious. Errors that occurred during a recording session appeared on the tape. There was no way to delete them, so if a serious error was made during recording the entire commercial or program had to be re-recorded. Engineers attempted to cut the tape with a razor blade and splice it back together, much like film was spliced. Cutting and splicing didn't work. The splice appeared as a blob-like image that ruined a commercial and distracted from a program.

While the engineers fiddled, largely in vain, the production people envisioned a new and expanded horizon using videotape. No longer did commercials have to be produced over and over again in news programs and other live events. They could be recorded and inserted, freeing production people to concentrate on the program content and improving overall production values. Programs could be produced and recorded during the week for weekend showing without the need to bring in extra staff. The possibilities seemed infinite. If only a way could be found to edit the tape.

The solution to the editing dilemma proved to be simple, but costly. A second videotape machine was required. With two machines, corrections could be made on the second machine and with the press of a button could be switched to the other machine, replacing content with errors with error-free material. Confronted with the problem and its solution, the station bit the bullet and acquired the second videotape machine.

The ability to record live television programs and to edit them if necessary, enabled WRAL-TV to expand its offering of locally produced programs. Within a short period, virtually all of the station's previously live programs except news were recorded on videotape.

The station began airing programs such as professional wrestling, country music productions such as *The Happy Show,* featuring Gerald Young and Hayden Ivey, two   former members of *The Jim Thornton Show* that had been a major late Saturday night staple of WTVD in Durham for a number of years. The station, however, did not consider any of its locally produced programs to be worth the cost of the tape that would be needed to preserve them. As quickly as the programs were broadcast, the tapes were wiped clean or used for other material.

For many of the production people, the videotape machines were, despite A.J. Fletcher's admonition, treated like a delightful toy, enabling the program and production staff to experiment with new ideas and to try new programs. The only content deemed worthy of preserving, however, was commercials. As soon as they became out of date or no longer usable, the tape on which they were recorded was wiped clean. With the touch of a button, all of the early history of local television vanished, all of it regarded as not worth the cost of the tape that would have preserved it.

Cue Cards and
Miscommunication

Regular viewers of late night network shows with David Letterman and Jay Leno are familiar with the use of cue cards. Despite the development of sophisticated electronic teleprompters, the two comedians continue to use a system that was standard in the early days of television. Cards with big handwritten print were preferred for short pieces that were delivered on camera, and scrolls were used for longer form material that was delivered on camera. In television jargon, those printed scripts were referred to by virtually everyone in the station as "idiot sheets." That term was coined by studio stage hands who resented having to hold a few sentences of copy in front of announcers who were unwilling or unable to memorize lines.

Soon after WRAL-TV production people became comfortable with the videotape system, the station agreed to promote the current United Fund (now known as the United Way) by programming a popular movie and providing the time that normally would be used by commercials for United Way promotional messages. Public Relations consultant Ben Park was handling the campaign, and he had persuaded Mrs. Luther Hodges, the wife of the then Governor Luther Hodges, to serve as the hostess for the Sunday afternoon special movie showing.

The production people were asked to be on their best behavior for the taping session in which the state's First Lady would appear in a well-designed set and deliver messages encouraging people to contribute to the campaign.

In a production involving taping or live performances, the floor manager coordinates all the activity and assures that all the bits and pieces are at the right place at the right time. In the taping session with Mrs. Hodges, the floor manager was L. A. Lentz, who later became a successful cinematographer and independent film and video producer. In the session with Mrs. Hodges, one of Lentz's major tasks was to be sure that the right script was held in front of the camera so that Mrs. Hodges could read it with ease.

Lentz, enthusiastic and eager to do a good job, was solicitous of Mrs. Hodges, continually asking her as cameras were moved in and out of position if she could see the "idiot sheet." Each time Lentz used the phrase, Mrs. Hodges would get a puzzled look on her face. Finally, she exclaimed, "Young man, why do you keep talking to me about an idiot sheet. Do you think I'm an idiot?"

Lentz was embarrassed, of course, but despite his best effort, he could not explain to the wife of North Carolina's governor why she must read something called an "idiot sheet." Despite that incident and efforts to rename the cards and scrolls, the name hung on through the years.

In WRAL-TV's early days, a relaxed work environment existed at the station. Creative and production people were given considerable latitude in suggesting, developing and implementing ideas. Both A.J. and Fred Fletcher, the two top executives were not strict taskmasters. The break room often doubled as a kind of public forum in which employees could discuss everything from the poetry of e.e. cummings to the state of the television industry. Mid-morning and mid-afternoon breaks often lasted much longer than the 15 minutes that were officially allotted for them.

The relaxed work environment continued under the management of Jesse Helms. As an executive, Helms enjoyed enormous respect and affection among WRAL-TV staffers. He loved a good argument and was amenable to changing his mind if he thought a staff member had a better idea than he.

When Helms entered politics, a number of WRAL-TV staffers joined his Senate staff and later his campaign organizations. With the departure of Helms, Jim Goodman brought in a management team that, according to a number of employees, changed the environment rather significantly.

"When Goodmon brought in his management team, the atmosphere changed immediately, recalled Earle Ashe, one of the station's earliest production directors. "I could argue with Jesse about anything and often get my way," said Ashe. "You couldn't do that with Goodmon's management team."

Years later, I discussed the relaxed environment that existed at WRAL-TV in the early days with then President Jim Goodmon. I told Goodmon that my impression as an employee was that "it was like the television station was a huge, expensive toy that those of us who worked there were being permitted to play with and have fun with every day."

"I know how it was," said Goodmon, "it was one of the things I wanted to change as soon as I was placed in charge of the station." Goodmon said he found it odd that his grandfather and his uncle would allow the kind of unstructured atmosphere to persist at the station. Some of the long-time WRAL-TV employees who had watched Goodmon grow from a small lad to top executive at the station had difficulty accepting him in the new role. Those who resisted his authority either found employment elsewhere or were eased out of the company.

Unexpected Generosity

A.J. Fletcher, often regarded as tight with a buck, could be quite generous, and my wife and I are the grateful recipients of his generosity. Our oldest son, who was born during my first year at the station, was a premature baby who had a number of health issues associated with his premature birth.

During his first year, he spent several months in and out of Rex Hospital in Raleigh and his condition was worsening to a grave status. My wife and I made the decision to transfer him to Duke Hospital where some of the world's preeminent pediatricians practiced state-of-the-art medicine. Upon arrival at Duke, our son's care was given over to a team of specialists none of whom we knew. We were told they were the best in the business. Our son remained in Duke Hospital for two weeks. His condition was finally diagnosed correctly and a treatment routine prescribed that restored him to health. Because his condition had begun at birth, our medical insurance did not cover his care. We owed thousands of dollars to Rex Hospital, and an unknown amount to Duke.

When my wife called to tell me he was eligible for discharge, I made arrangements to leave work early, pick up our son, and then come back to work to complete pending assignments. On the way out, I encountered Scotty Stephenson and told her I was going to check our son out of the hospital.

Jokingly, I said, "I'm trying to figure out how to get him out without paying the bill which I have no way of doing. I guess I'm going to have to kidnap him." Mrs. Stephenson smiled and went her way.

At Duke Hospital, I went to my son's room where my wife was waiting and told her I was going to the checkout office and plead my case. "I guess they will let us work out a payment plan over time as Rex is doing," I said.

At the checkout office, I nervously asked how much the bill was. The lady looked at the paperwork and said with a smile. "Mr. Jefferys, this bill has been paid."

My heart skipped several beats. "It's been paid?" I said. "By whom?"

She again looked at the paperwork. "By a Mr. A.J. Fletcher," she said.

I was flabbergasted. I have never learned how much the bill was. Certainly, considering the number of specialists and the procedures that were performed, a bill of several thousand dollars would have been in order.

I tried to express my gratitude to the Fletchers, but my effort was quickly dismissed. It was never mentioned while I was there.

After more than five years as a television continuity writer, I began to consider the long-term implications of the job. There were moments of satisfaction from meeting the needs of television, and certainly the job was often fun and placed me in the company of congenial and interesting people.

Looking ahead, though, I could not envision myself doing the same kind of work as I grew older. Moreover, I could not identify any job in local television at which I would really want to spend many years.

I had begun writing for television at age 21 and, at 26, I had written countless bits and pieces and a few programs that were more than that. In reflecting on my work over the years, however, I could not identify any work that was of genuine significance. With some reluctance, I decided to resign from WRAL-TV and join the J.T. Howard Advertising Agency as a copywriter.

My resignation did not end my relationship with WRAL-TV or the Fletcher family. Indeed, for many years after my resignation, my relationship with WRAL-TV and the Fletcher Family seemed to strengthen, and I found ways to remain in television that enabled me to make more significant and lasting contributions.

A.J. Fletcher: A Study in Contradictions
Rock Hard Principles,
Family Discord

There is no larger legendary figure in broadcasting in North Carolina and the Southeast than Alfred Johnston Fletcher, and probably no person of stronger principles and more contradictions.

Fletcher was an avowed political conservative who remained a registered Democrat for his entire life and was irritated when his favorite grandson and heir registered as a Republican; a family friend of Melville Broughton, but an admirer of Bob Scott, Broughton's opponent in the 1968 Governor's race, a friend and benefactor of individuals and institutions with more liberal leanings than he and a former contributor to *The News and Observer,* with whose editorial policies he strongly disagreed.

I was employed by WRAL-TV for not quite three years, from January, 1958 through part of 1960. My employment, however, resulted in a long-lasting relationship with A.J. and Fred Fletcher, as well as his grandson and principal heir, Jim Goodmon, and one of A.J. Fletcher's granddaughters, Barbara Fletcher. Our relationship ebbed and flowed over more than two decades.

Several years after I left the station, years in which I worked as a copywriter at the Howard Advertising Agency and also wrote for newspapers and magazines, I decided to write a magazine profile of A.J. Fletcher. He was receptive to the idea and gave me ample time to discuss his life and times. Following its initial publication in a local magazine, the article was published in a couple of national magazines as well as several newspapers in various parts of the country, including New Hampshire and Florida.

A few years later, for another magazine, I wrote a profile of Jim Goodmon. Those articles led to a plan for me to write a biography of Fletcher that resulted in my spending many hours asking questions and listening to Fletcher discuss his life and times. For a number of reasons the book project did not come to fruition. The first draft of the book was circulated to a number of people who had spent many years working with Fletcher. Each of them had their own impressions of him that often were contradicted by the impressions of others with equal credibility. Moreover, after absorbing the comments of the various people who were reviewing the manuscript, I feared that it would be impossible to write a book that would achieve a consensus among those who would have some editorial authority over the final product, an authority I had failed to obtain in the contract. The difficulty was the subject of the book, a man of enormous and profound contradictions.

In my discussions about various approaches to the book, Goodmon, who had been one of the stronger advocates for the book, seemed to have lost interest in the project and without a strong advocate among the Fletcher organization, I strongly suspected that we would be in an endless struggle to achieve agreement and that with so many differing views, it would be impossible for me to write the kind of book I felt the public would find interesting and readable.

About the same time, the agency that I had established was retained by several large clients who required much of my time. I let the A.J. Fletcher book project languish, and it soon appeared that the Fletcher organization had lost interest. As the project languished, Fletcher's health began to fail and, at age 93, he passed away. With his death, interest in the book project sank even lower. Sometime later, I was asked to make the first draft available to Howard Covington for inclusion in a book he was writing on the national opera company. After his retirement, Fred Fletcher asked me for a copy of the manuscript for possible use in a book of his memoirs.

The hours I spent with A. J. Fletcher asking questions and listening to his recollection of his life and times solidified an unusual friendship that began earlier between the aging owner of the television station and a young writer still trying to make his way in the world of broadcasting.

For reasons unknown to me, Fletcher and I hit it off from our first meeting. Before meeting him, I had heard many stories about his business acumen, his toughness in deals, and his ability as an insurance surety lawyer. The stories depicted him as a foreboding, intimidating individual one would be wise to steer clear of.

My introduction to Fletcher occurred in a parking area shortly after I began my job at WRAL-TV. Parking for the employees was on a first come first served basis in the small area behind the opera house that served as the station's administrative offices.

Occasionally, I would find space to wedge the small sports car I had recently purchased into the space next to a very expensive Cadillac. Staff members with normal sized cars seemed reluctant to park next to what I came to learn was "the boss's space."

One day after work, Fletcher and I were leaving at the same time. I had seen him around the station, but had never actually had a conversation with him. I nodded at him in recognition, a bit hesitant to initiate a conversation, and he responded by asking me if I were "Jefferys, the new continuity writer" and if I owned the small sports car next to his.

I told him I was the new continuity writer and that I did, indeed, own the car next to his.

With a kind of wistful look, Fletcher said, "I've always wanted a small car like that. I suspect it's fun to drive."

I told him I had traded a large Buick for it, and he smiled.

"I drive this Cadillac," he said, "not because I like Cadillacs, but because the station has an arrangement with the Cadillac dealer. The dealership buys a lot of advertising on the radio and TV stations, and I buy Cadillacs because they are such good advertisers. But I would really prefer a small car like you drive."

Laughing a bit, he said, "Maybe you should get a bumper sticker that says 'Stamp out Cadillacs.'"

We both chuckled and went our separate ways. As he drove away, I couldn't help but think, "He's nothing like I thought he would be." In the following weeks and months, we would occasionally be leaving at the same time and Fletcher continued to show an interest in my car. At 65, regarded as a hard driving, hard-nosed conservative as tough as an old boot, A.J. Fletcher had a yen for a sports car rather than the luxurious sedan he owned--just one of the many contradictions I would learn about him.

Months later, after the Channel Five studios and executive offices were completed on Western Boulevard, I occupied an office next to what was then a lovely glass fronted reception area. Employees and visitors to the administrative building had to pass my office both entering and leaving.

Fletcher had his own private entrance to his palatial office overlooking the WRAL gardens at the rear of the administrative building. However, he frequently passed my office on his way to other parts of the building. He invariably would stop and generally share a brief, humorous story with me. As an employee and later as a writer with unusual access, my impressions of A.J. Fletcher were quite different from those of many other people.

Born in the nineteenth century, decades before radio and television broadcasting were envisioned, A. J. Fletcher was the seventh of 14 children, the son of an itinerant preacher who supported his family with small donations from church members and subsistence farming in the rough hills of Ashe County.

When Fletcher was a child, the family moved to Oak Hill, Virginia, where his father was pastor of a church. Virtually all of Fletcher's formal education, less than five years, he recalls, occurred at the nearby Oak Hill Academy.

With such a meager educational foundation, Fletcher, before establishing WRAL-TV, was able to attend Wake Forest University long enough to learn enough law to pass the North Carolina Bar exam and become a nationally recognized expert in insurance surety law, establish an insurance company that he was able to see flourish, begin Raleigh's second radio station and a statewide radio network, and other businesses, including a cemetery that became something of a landmark with its landscaping and pink cherry trees.

His early years were marked by numerous attempts to earn money. He started and operated newspapers in Mooresville, Fuquay-Springs and Apex. In Apex, he met and, against the wishes of her family, courted and wed Margaret Utley. The family's opposition to the marriage was so strong, Fletcher packed a pistol at the wedding and on his honeymoon. Utley family members eventually came to approve of Fletcher, and the couple enjoyed a long marriage that produced three sons and a daughter.

As a 12-year-old boy living with his sister and her husband and working odd jobs in North Wilkesboro, N.C., Fletcher heard an aria from the opera *Foust*. The music ignited an improbable love affair with opera that Fletcher pursued with a passion many thought odd, "It is true that from the date I heard the Siebel Aria from Foust, I had been partial to music of that style," he said.

"My interest in the theatre was not confined to opera, however," said Fletcher. At various points in his life, he had performed in a production of *You Can't Take It With You* as well as the title role in Shakespeare's *Macbeth*.

Over many years, Fletcher sang in church choirs, organized various music shows in the small towns in which he lived, and as he was able to do so, took voice lessons to train his natural baritone. What Fletcher called "the bridging between church music and opera" occurred rather by accident.

Fletcher recalled that he was standing on the corner of Harget and Salisbury streets in Raleigh one day, waiting for the light to change when John Cole, an accountant with Carolina Power and Light Company and a good musician on piano or organ, came up and asked if he would fill in as Devilshoof in the production of *The Bohemian Girl,* then in rehearsal at the Raleigh Little Theater. The production was scheduled to present its first performance in two weeks.

Cole explained that the singer who had been rehearsing the part had been called out of the city. Fletcher hardly hesitated before agreeing to accept the role.

Fletcher said that performing that role in *The Bohemian Girl* convinced him that opera--especially opera in English--could play an important role in the cultural life of Raleigh and the State and that a local opera company could provide opportunity for aspiring artists who wanted to develop their talents.

From that beginning, Fletcher hired directors, bought trucks, stage props and costumes and went about the state meeting with local music clubs seeking to promote his concept of opera in English. Not only was Fletcher the chief sponsor, organizer and promoter, he also appeared in lead roles in various productions.

Fletcher was 58 years old when he formed the Grass Roots Opera Company and began performing in various productions in the small towns and cities throughout North Carolina in the company of sometimes young and attractive women from around the state and around the country.

"My family and a lot of my friends thought I had lost my mind," recalled Fletcher. "Some members of my family as well as neighbors accused me of neglecting my wife. They said I left her at home with no money and often no food in the house to run off with a bunch of young women in harebrained foolishness." Fletcher denied the accusations of neglect, but to quell the criticism he persuaded his wife to take a role in contacting and setting up meetings with music clubs, groups Fletcher came to hold in disdain for what he perceived to be their lack of genuine commitment to the promotion of good music and the development of singers.

Fletcher's involvement with his opera company gave rise to numerous rumors in Raleigh regarding his womanizing – rumors of which he was unaware or with which he was unconcerned. Some were quite ugly and some so comical as to be unbelievable.

In 1985, while publishing and editing a North Carolina insurance trade journal, I interviewed Earl Johnson, founding partner in the firm of Johnson and Moore. In 1985, Johnson, at 88, was believed to be the oldest insurance agent in North Carolina still working. During the course of our conversation, I asked Johnson if he knew A. J. Fletcher.

"Fletch? Sure, I knew Fletch," said Johnson.

He then began to chuckle. "Let me tell you about Fletch," said Johnson. "Everybody knew he favored the ladies, but Fletch didn't know that people knew that about him. We had offices in the same building as Fletch, what used to be the First Citizens Bank Building on Martin Street. The building was L-shaped. From offices on our side of the building, we could look across the way right into Fletcher's law library.

"Well every afternoon, around 4 O'clock, a lady would visit Fletch. He would escort her into the law library and people in the offices on our side of the building could look right into Fletcher's library and watch a quite steamy encounter," said Johnson.

I found the story incredible. However, it was confirmed by others of Johnson's and Fletcher's generation, many of whom delighted in relating risqué tales as well as other stories that contradicted the public impression of Fletcher.

"Fletch was not nearly as straight laced as some people thought he was," recalled Johnson. "He loved a good story as much as anyone – and he did like the ladies."

Certainly, Fletcher could be oblivious to ordinary needs that others may have considered to be of critical importance. One day, I was meeting with him in his office at the rear of the administrative building at WRAL-TV's studio when his secretary, Mrs. Bryan, quietly entered the office and whispered, "Mr. Fletcher, there is a police officer here who says he needs to see you."

Without dismissing me, he asked Mrs. Bryan to show the officer into his office. The young Raleigh policeman entered and with some hesitation presented Fletcher with a condemnation notice from the city for Fletcher's rather large brick home in one of the city's best neighborhoods.

Fletcher was nonplussed. He accepted the notice, thanked the officer and explained to me that after his second marriage, he and his new wife found no need to use all of the large home and had established a comfortable apartment in the upper story of the home.

"I just haven't been paying much attention to the rest of the house since then," he said. "I guess the neighbors figured I was going to let it fall down, but my house is not the only one that needs attention. The house next door to mine really does look like it's going to fall down. One of the walls actually leans right much."

One day, I received a phone call from Fletcher's secretary, asking if I would be able to meet with Fletcher and Benjamin Swalin, the long-time director of the North Carolina Symphony. Swalin wanted to publish a book about his life and times with the symphony, and he wanted the Fletcher Foundation to fund the publishing and distribution of the book.

Fletcher wanted my views on the project before he agreed and he wanted me to sit in on his meeting with Swalin.

The meeting began in a cordial and congenial manner with Fletcher interested in and supportive of Swalin's proposed project. After a half hour or so, Swalin's tone and demeanor seemed to grow angry as he recounted numerous slights he had endured from many sources as well as his great disappointments with his career and life and the many resentments he harbored against numerous individuals.

Fletcher listened with growing amazement. "Do you have a title for your book that expresses a theme?" he asked.

"Yes," said Swalin. I plan to call my book *The Mean Streets of Music.*

Fletcher was somewhat aghast at Swalin's ranting. He quickly signaled that the meeting needed to be concluded and as tactfully as possible sent Swalin on his way.

After Swalin left, Fletcher turned to me and said, "What a big old blowhard he turned out to be!" We chuckled a bit, and Fletcher asked me to give him an estimate of what I thought it would cost to publish and distribute a book about Swalin and the North Carolina Symphony. He thanked me and said he did not wish to pursue the project.

A Wrenching Decision

By 1977, A. J. Fletcher had already determined that the ownership of Capitol Broadcasting would pass directly to the two sons of his late daughter, Betty Lou, whose death at an early age of an illness not fully understood, had devastated Fletcher. His only daughter was clearly the apple of his eye, and his involvement in the lives of his daughter's two sons was far more intense than his involvement in the lives of his other grandchildren.

In recalling the death of his daughter, Fletcher sank into a dark mood, a mood I had never before encountered in the hours we had spent together.

"I just never could get a good answer as to what was wrong with her," Fletcher said. "The doctors just didn't seem to know, and Betty Lou just lay there and got sicker and sicker until she died."

Betty Lou Goodmon's death wracked the Fletcher family with grief – and anger. Fingers of blame were pointed, and, Fletcher recalled, with a sense of embarrassment and humiliation that the family was so distraught "a ruckus erupted during the wake at Brown-Wynne Funeral Home that caused damage to the casket.

"I'll never get over it," said Fletcher with a sad sense of resignation.

Fletcher's grandson, Jim Goodmon, replaced Fletcher's daughter as the "apple of his eye." It might have been guilt over the questions surrounding the death of his daughter, or just simply a matter of a grandfather having a favorite grandson, but early on, Fletcher began grooming Goodmon to take over the broadcasting empire he had established.

Fletcher said he saw in Goodmon, the combination of attitude and aptitude that he wanted in his successor. In a move that wrenched the hearts of

I Never Promised Not To Tell

close family members and perhaps severed blood ties forever, Fletcher made his choice by accepting his son Fred's resignation at age 65, and moving Goodmon to the presidency of Capitol Broadcasting.

Before Fletcher's decision was announced publicly, I received a call from Fred Fletcher, asking if he could stop by my office for a visit. I immediately said yes, and he came to my office shortly after the phone call. I was baffled. Fred Fletcher and I had enjoyed a very cordial relationship while I worked at WRAL-TV and later as I worked elsewhere. We did not, however, have a relationship in which we casually dropped by each other's offices. It was something of an event for the President of Capitol Broadcasting to want to stop in for a chat, and I waited for his visit with great curiosity.

When he arrived at my office, Fred Fletcher was despondent. He quickly got to the point. "Pop has asked me to resign," he said. "He's leaving everything to Jim and Ray Goodmon, and I'm out. He said I was too old to run the station, but he didn't even get the damn station on the air until he was 65.

"He always knew I wanted the opportunity to run WRAL for five years without being in his shadow. I know you've spent a lot of time with Pop. Do you have any idea why he's cutting out me and my family – and do you have any idea what I can do to change his mind?"

"Have you told your dad that you wanted the opportunity to run the station without his influence?" I asked.

I was shocked by Fred Fletcher's response.

"I haven't spoken to Pop, and he hasn't spoken to me in five years," said Fred Fletcher.

"You can't be serious," I said "You and he sit in offices next to each other. You must have had some conversation."

"None at all," said Fred Fletcher. "I don't think Pop cares about me or has any respect for me. You've talked to him for hours. What do you think?"

Considering Fred Fletcher's despondent state, I felt obliged to share with him what his father had told me.

A.J. Fletcher said he loved all of his children equally. He said he felt he had been generous with all of them over the years. He said his son Frank, a lawyer, and "the one more like his daddy, went in another direction, and did not need to inherit the station." He said he had given his son Floyd some three hundred thousand dollars' worth of Capitol Broadcasting stock and had redeemed it at par value when Floyd was advised by his lawyer that he should not own shares in two television stations. He said he had given his son Fred more stock than he had given to anyone else, and that it paid an annual dividend that was quite significant. Although A. J. Fletcher admired Fred's public relations skills, he doubted that Fred was tough enough to deal with the financiers, the technical and regulatory problems and the relationship with the network.

"I don't think he would do well in that role," said A. J. Fletcher.

A.J. Fletcher said that he felt he had done right by Fred over the years. "He has earned a generous salary with more than generous bonuses, and I never refused him any financial help that he requested," said A.J. Fletcher. "I estimate that while he worked at Capitol Broadcasting Company, I have given Fred more than $1 million in excess of his annual salary and bonuses. Just recently I provided the funds for the additions that he made to his house -- many thousands of dollars that I don't expect to be repaid."

When I finished telling Fred what he father had told me, he sat quietly for a few moments. "I guess everything has been decided," he said.

"Maybe things would change even now if you started talking to your dad," I said. "I don't think you should wait for him to initiate the conversation. If you are uncomfortable, write him a letter. Anything that would get the two of you to talking again."

Fred thanked me for my time and asked if he could stop in again. I assured him he would always be welcome.

A.J. Fletcher's decision regarding the transfer of ownership and authority was final. Over the decades that were to follow, WRAL-TV prospered. It became a pioneer in technological advancements and expanded the Capitol Broadcasting Company's holding throughout the state and the region. However, the station made virtually no progress in improving the content of television.

Over the years, it appears that some of the hard feelings that resulted from A.J. Fletcher's decision regarding the future ownership of the station had dissipated. In 1992, I interviewed Fred Fletcher for a bicentennial commemorative video on the city of Raleigh. He seemed at ease with his life and his career and no longer seemed to harbor disappointment or hard feelings toward anyone at the station.

Is There A Future For Local TV?

Although an avalanche of video floods the United States every minute of every day with what seems to be a never ending buffet of special interest programming, it has not swept away the persistent nostalgia of what we fondly remember as the "golden age of television." Whether such a "golden age" really existed or whether it is a wistful yearning viewed through a distorted prism of time remains a matter for discussion and debate.

Although the audience for mainstream network television has been in a free-fall for more than a decade, in 2013, there was no doubt that the three networks that dominated television for decades had been successful in holding the attention of large numbers of viewers and that among the many hours devoted to the trivial and banal, there have been a few programs of significance and lasting value.

In times of tragedy and sadness, network television has often bound the nation together, providing understanding of and context for our suffering and providing an outlet for our collective mourning and healing.

Satellites and fiber optic cable have rendered local television stations irrelevant for the great majority of television providers and viewers of today. Hundreds of cable stations now transmit programs without the need for local stations. It is only the traditional television networks that continue to send their programs to local stations that in turn broadcast them to specific areas and/or transmit them to local audiences via cable or satellite.

Although hundreds of local television stations exist throughout the United States, their principle mission is -- as it has always been -- to serve as conduits for the broadcast networks with which they are affiliated and to sell advertising. In the media world of the early

21st Century, counting the number of people watching a particular program is dicey. The networks continue to believe that the best way to determine the size and the demographics of various audiences is through local television stations. To accomplish this on a national scale requires large numbers of stations on which to distribute their programs. Although the broadcast networks have grown resentful over the standard practice of paying stations to carry programs, they are fearful of change. Local stations are fearful of losing the steady stream of revenue from the networks, and they continue to require the involvement of networks to fill their schedules – a responsibility that local stations have proven to be either unable or unwilling to discharge without network support.

Regular viewers of *network broadcast* television of a certain age can remember and reflect on programs and personalities that over the years have made lasting impressions -- programs such as *Captain Kangaroo, The Hallmark Hall of Fame, I Love Lucy, The Ed Sullivan Show, Playhouse 90, All In The Family, Meet The Press, The Andy Griffith Show, Perry Mason, Gunsmoke, 60 Minutes, Seinfeld, and Cheers,* and personalities such as Bob Hope, Jack Benny, Arthur Godfrey, Johnny Carson, Walter Cronkite, David Brinkley, Charles Kuralt, Dan Rather, Tom Brokaw, Bob Newhart, Carol Burnette, Mary Tyler Moore, Alfred Hitchcock, Joan Rivers and perhaps a dozen more not on this list.

No such memories exist for the programs of local television stations. From the mid-1950s to the second decade of the 21st Century, there is not a single program or series of programs produced by local stations that can be cited as genuinely "significant" in the life and times of the people of the area. Older, regular viewers might recall nostalgically programs they viewed as children or teenagers. Female viewers might have memories of programs aimed at stay-at-home homemakers. Were any of those programs of genuine significance? The answer most assuredly is no.

Moreover, for the most part, the personalities that have appeared on local television are easily forgotten as they move from station to station seeking larger markets, more airtime for themselves and bigger paychecks.

To those of us who were present at the beginning, television, except for its remarkable technical improvements, does not appear to have changed very much. Local stations continue chiefly to serve as conduits for their networks, and despite the technical advances, do not originate any programs of significance. Local television's connection to show business continues to give the medium a certain superficial glamour when viewed from afar.

In the earliest days, there was no practical way to preserve the programs that were produced by local stations. However, as noted earlier, when videotape became readily available, most local stations did not consider their local productions *worthy* of preserving. Therefore, there is no basis for comparing the work of early times with current efforts, no record on which to look back for review and reflection, only the memories of those who were there and those who watched.

Production was limited to what could be accomplished in a studio with two very large cameras, very small budgets and very little access to talent pools. Technical limitations challenged the creativity of those who wanted to expand the horizons of the medium -- and usually won. If a program consisted of people sitting or standing in pre-arranged spots in a studio before two cameras, local television was up to the task. Programs that required more were rarely considered, much less produced.

Few who were in early day television regarded themselves as pioneers. However, we felt in our bones that there was something magical about the medium, even as it frustrated us in our efforts to make it worthy or significant at the local level. For ambitious, creative and talented people, local television was so limiting and so frustrating they moved on to other fields or found other ways of remaining a part of the medium. Many look back on the failures to make the medium more significant with regret.

At the beginning of the second decade of the 21st Century, after more than 60 years as the dominant force in entertainment and mass communications, television, like most other mass media, finds itself on the slippery slope of old age. The halcyon days of its youth evaporated quickly, as did its so-called "golden age;" The medium that settled into a comfortable middle age, secure in the belief that the bond that existed between it and its mass audience would endure, all too quickly, has become old media, no longer relevant to the young viewers whose affections it has so earnestly craved and courted.

As Phil Zachary, president of Curtis Media, the largest owner of radio stations in North Carolina said in 2010, "We are trying to find a way to survive with a hundred-year-old technology, largely unchanged in a century, in a media climate that may undergo a revolution the next time a kid in a garage comes up with the next new thing."

Television is a 70-year-old technology seeking to hold on in the age of satellites, computers and the rapidly expanding capability and acceptance of the internet as a source of entertainment as well as information. There is real concern, indeed, fear among the men and women who have devoted most of their most productive years to an industry that now seems vulnerable to sweeping changes from virtually every direction.

In a society in which demographics and the market climate are undergoing constant change, local television station continue to obediently carry the programs provided by the networks with which they are affiliated and for which they are paid to carry. Original, locally produced programs remain so rare as to be unnoticed.

This traditional role of local television stations to serve principally as conduits for the originators of content is not just challenged and compromised by the internet, it is rendered obsolete, and it is only a matter of time before networks decide to end the shopworn "affiliation" arrangements that have limited television competition over the decades.

To evaluate or critique local television, one must consider local television news, inasmuch as few stations produce any other type of local programming. As a way of satisfying the FCC requirement that they serve the public interest, local TV stations have concentrated on news shows. However, to show that their news programs were actually serving the public interest, the stations needed proof that the shows being aired *were being watched.* To support their contention, the stations needed ratings.

To boost ratings for news shows, many of which were not necessarily entertaining, stations began hiring a new type of professional – "news doctors" or as they preferred to be called, "news consultants." The task of these "consultants" was to determine what the public liked, not what it needed, and to deliver what was wanted. The consultants sold the news the same way marketing consultants sold packaged goods or automobiles.

Early on stations employed former newspaper editors to run their news departments. Those early day TV news directors resented mightily the intrusion of the news "consultants," usually younger people who had little experience in the news business, but were savvy in marketing. As the consultants dominated TV newsrooms the ratings for local news went up as the value of the news content went down. But the news shows with dual anchors, funny sportscasters and engaging weathermen proved to be popular. Stations began to make money on news and as they made more money, they devoted more hours to local news programming.

Sadly, the increased hours have provided only an increased number of truncated accounts of murders, car chases, car crashes, fires, missing persons, other acts of violence and mayhem, consumer tips and much more attention to the weather. Dan Rather, the veteran and sometimes controversial CBS anchor, was correct when he noted that television news had been "tarted up and dumbed down."

To many serious journalists, one of the major mistakes of local television is their insistence that "pictures drive the story." Those journalists who argued that pictures are useful, but not always essential to good journalism lost the argument long ago. Those who prevailed in arguing that pictures are more important than the words have never demonstrated competence in using pictures to tell stories.

Soon after sign on, WRAL-TV, as did other stations, invested in film processing equipment. I often wondered why. Film was rarely used for program or advertising purposes. It was possible to record sound on a special kind of film that contained a magnetic strip for the sound portion. The sound and the picture on this "single system" film capability could not be synced so that the picture and the sound would start and end at the same point. The result was usually a herky-jerky effect that appeared to the viewer to be an error. Moreover, the black and white 16 millimeter film had to be photographed and at the station by 3 p.m. in order for it to be processed and edited in time for the early evening program three hours later. Such a tight deadline provided very little time for coordinating visual and narrative material.

The result was often simply a mishmash of images that appeared on the screen while the newscaster read stories for which the pictures had little, if any, relevance. Still, there seemed to be an obsession with acquiring and using news film. Garris and Balance, the station's two news photographers were in a constant state of movement, racing here and there and back to the station.

Balance, a middle-aged man with a perpetually florid face, always seemed to be on the verge of some kind of seizure as he rushed about to gather what often were irrelevant images of news events. I learned after I left the station that as he was rushing from the newsroom with camera in hand, he suffered a fatal attack.

Sometime later, Armstrong and his successor, Sam Beard, discussed with me the use of news film, which too many journalists and viewers often seemed to be of no real purpose.

Armstrong said the reason was that "people liked to see themselves on television. News film provided the opportunity for viewers who were involved in a news event to see themselves on television. The film made people watch, and it also made television appear to be much more engaged in news gathering than it really was."

Beard said, "I personally don't give a damn about news film. It is mostly an aggravation to acquire, process, and use on the air. I'm not opposed to using pictures in the news, but frankly, the way news film is used in television is ridiculous.

"Photographers are rarely able to photograph news as it occurs. They arrive after a news event has occurred, so there is usually little if anything to photograph except perhaps the burned structure where a fire occurred or the damaged car or covered victims of wrecks or other violence.

"If a photographer is on the scene as a news event is occurring, he has little factual information to convey, so the pictures don't really tell much. We use news film mainly so that we don't have to put all our news stories on cue cards. We can read the copy while the film is being shown."

More than a half century later, with breath-taking advances in video and mobile broadcasting, the same problem exists. Today, as was the case more than 50 years ago, the great majority of news video provides little, if any, understanding of a news event. Many studies have indicated that the pictorial material in most television news stories impedes understanding and is largely a distraction. Nevertheless, the notion that moving pictures are the most important part of a television news story remains an intransigent article of faith in most television newsrooms, including WRAL-TV.

The fact is local television news, equipped with helicopters, news teams and big vans of equipment, is a largely irrelevant enterprise directed to a segment of the population that does not understand the difference between being entertained and being informed.

Many people often watch local television news, but the serious men and women who truly want to be informed -- the very viewers who have the greatest impact on the local, state and national agenda -- go elsewhere for genuine news. Local television news executives seem to be unaware that genuine news is information that enables men and women to be well informed citizens, knowledgeable about the affairs of national, state and local governments, able to understand when government is acting in the interest of citizens and when it is not. In short, genuine news is the information that enables citizens to govern themselves. It is not always exciting or even interesting and does not always provide good pictures, but it is always important.

Instead of real news, local television – and to a lesser degree network television – provides a *semblance* of the news. The goal is to give the impression that the stations are delivering news when they are not. It is in a station's economic interest to attract large number of young, often immature and undeveloped viewers who will respond to the 30-second advertising messages that support the news.

Television news executives and reporters contend that television is entitled to the constitutional guarantees expressed in the first amendment. Truth is, however, local television, dependent for its existence on a government-issued license and the support of advertisers, cannot be independent, "honest brokers of information" and, therefore, have no claim on the rights granted to a truly free press. As Rather observes in his book, *Rather Outspoken,* the large, diversified corporations that own the main television networks are too invested in securing the goodwill of members of the legislative and executive branches of government to allow the kind of unfettered freedom envisioned by the constitutional amendment.

Advertisers do not like to be associated with program content that is controversial or even unpleasant. Moreover, they understand that television advertising is mostly effective among young, impressionable viewers whose tastes are unformed. Therefore, TV stations have little interest in attracting older, more experienced, more sophisticated and more discriminating viewers who rarely respond to most television advertising.

The helicopters, the vans, the large amounts of equipment and the prominent signage that adorns equipment are not necessary to cover the kinds of stories usually broadcast by television. They are merely props in an elaborate, on-going deception engaged in by most local television stations.

Rushing to the scene of a traffic accident, an act of violence or a destructive fire in a large, intrusive vehicle, whipping out lights and cameras and setting up what looks like a movie set as the "news team" goes into action is not conducive to news gathering. It is first and last "news theatre" aimed at exciting the emotions of viewers and giving them the impression of personal engagement and involvement.

The creation and production of worthwhile television content is tedious, frustrating, often enervating, and time consuming. The most important news story of the day might very well provide no opportunity for interesting pictures. If it doesn't, there is an excellent chance the story won't be broadcast. Can ignoring important news events because they are not visually interesting ever be serving the public interest?

In an unforgettable address to the National Association of Broadcasters on May 9, 1961, Newton Minnow, then Chairman of the Federal Communication Commission, said, "Broadcasting possesses the most powerful voice in America. It has an inescapable duty to make that voice ring with intelligence and with leadership."

How well did television meet its responsibilities some 50 years ago? In laying out the case against television, Minnow challenged television station owners to sit down before their own TV sets and watch the programming on their stations from sign-on to sign-off.

"I can assure you," he said, "that you will observe a 'vast wasteland.'

"You will see a procession of game shows, violence, audience participation shows, formula comedies about totally unbelievable families, blood and thunder, mayhem, violence, sadism, murder, private eyes, gangsters, more violence and carnage. And, endless commercials - many screaming, cajoling and offending - and, most of all boredom."

Will it ever be thus? Perhaps. Perhaps not.

Part II

Advertising and Politics: A Symbiotic Relationship of Big Egos And Sharp Elbows

In one form or another, advertising has been with us for a very long time, such a long time, it is known as the world's "second oldest profession," but like the world's oldest profession, its history is not something in which its practitioners can take pride. Instead, the history of advertising is largely an ignoble record of hawking and huckstering that employed exaggeration, overstatement, deceit, dissembling and outright lies.

Given advertising's history, I often wondered if President Franklin D. Roosevelt really meant it when he said that had he not gone into politics, he would have gone into advertising. There is no denying the similarity between politics and advertising or the symbiotic relationship that over time has become entrenched as each feeds off the other.

In the early part of the 21st Century, there is much gnashing of teeth and rending of garments by those who bemoan the awful state of politics: the polarization, the nasty campaign tactics, the huge amounts of money that are raised and spent sometimes only to assure election to minor offices.

Participating in the North Carolina "political process" has never been an activity for the faint of heart. For those who labor under the misconception that politics should be conducted according to the rules of the Marquis of Queensbury, please take note: North Carolina's political campaigns – especially those for the office of Governor, and in recent times for the U.S. Congress and Senate – are conducted mostly according to the rules that govern "professional wrestling" on TV.

North Carolina has not achieved the reputation of Chicago or New Orleans, but campaigns such as the

Frank Porter Graham vs. Willis Smith for the Senate, the various "slash and burn" campaigns of the North Carolina based "National Congressional Club in behalf of the late Jesse Helms and other hand-picked candidates have given the State a reputation as a place where politics is a bare knuckle enterprise of sharp elbows and oversized egos. Moreover, North Carolina's history of denying minorities the right to vote is as grimy, sordid and shameful as any other southern state's and perhaps worse than some.

In the period of "reconstruction" following the Civil War, the Republican Party, the party of Abraham Lincoln, with the overwhelming support of black people, consolidated its political power in North Carolina to the growing resentment of many white people who were bitterly opposed to black people holding positions of authority in government.

The political campaign of 1898 provides a troubling example of how vicious politics could be in the genteel Tar Heel State. In that campaign, Furnifold Simmons, chairman of the Democratic Party, developed a three-pronged campaign to wrest political control of North Carolina from the Republicans whose leader was Governor Daniel L. Russell.

Simmons recruited the Raleigh *News and Observer, Charlotte Observer, Wilmington Messenger and* the Wilmington *Morning Star* to publish articles designed to inflame public opinion against the Republican Party and its support by newly enfranchised black voters. Effective public speakers such as future Governor Charles B. Aycock, Robert Glenn and Wilmington native Alfred Moore Waddell took to the stump across the state to reinforce the inflammatory articles in the newspapers,

The third element of the campaign were night riders on horseback such as the Red Shirts who sought to intimidate blacks and press white people to vote for Democratic Party candidates.

In the port city of Wilmington, where black people had taken control of the city's municipal government, the

Red Shirts and other white groups paraded through black sections brandishing guns, and the newspapers sought to inflame whites with stories of black violence. A group of white citizens plotted to take control of the municipal government regardless of the outcome of the election and was successful in doing so.

The Democrats were successful in winning control of State government and with the election of Governor Aycock, began decades of dominance in North Carolina.

For over a century, North Carolinians honored Aycock. Josephus Daniels, publisher and owner of *The News and Observer,* held high office under President Woodrow Wilson and Franklin D. Roosevelt, and Daniels' *News and Observer* became in later years a champion of civil rights. However, their political excesses left both Aycock and Daniels with legacies that are forever stained.

In 2012, the numerous efforts to require photo identification of voters, regarded by many as an effort at voter suppression, were rooted in the blatant in-your-face intimidation that was commonplace before the advent of radio and television broadcasting. The nasty political attack ads that dominate television, nuanced just enough to avoid widespread public backlash, can be traced to the ugly handbills of an earlier time. The desire to influence the outcome of elections by whatever works, is an old habit in North Carolina and the nation.

Money has always been crucial to politics. It is the fuel that keeps political engines running. While much of it is spent in highly visible ways, much is spent in ways that are beyond the view of the media or the public. In election after election, bags of cash have been gathered to purchase the votes of the unsophisticated or the uncaring. The late Matilda Johnson of Harnett County recalled that in the 1930s and '40s, candidates for the State Legislature in her community of Coats, N.C., would gather residents by the carload, give each of them a couple of dollars and drive them to the polls to vote for a predetermined slate of candidates.

For years, transporting thousands of dollars to political manipulators to guarantee a certain electoral outcome has been standard procedure in hotly contested counties. In the mid and late 1960s, the general consensus was that $25,000 in small bills (not an insignificant amount in those days) was required to assure the "right outcome" in counties west of Asheville.

In predominately black sections of the state's larger cities, it was common knowledge that a certain amount of "walking around money" had to be provided to assure an appropriate "turnout" and outcome.

Tabloid and mainstream newspaper headlines of the early 21st century provide ample proof that money continues to loom large in North Carolina politics, whether to win a coveted appointment or to assure that an illicit love affair will remain secret.

For decades, politicians and political parties chafed at the power of the press to influence political campaigns through the promotion of favored candidate and/or parties and their willingness to deny comparable press treatment to candidates and parties they opposed. In many areas of North Carolina the outcome of elections could be predicted by the coverage in the major newspaper.

The advent of television and its power virtually to take a candidate into the homes of voters, the availability of large amounts of money and the growing reluctance of people of prominence to be personally involved in the rough and tumble of politics gave birth to a new profession and a new kind of professional – the political consultant.

First and foremost, the political consultant understood television and polling and the interaction between the two. Many become consultants after considerable experience in media. Today, political consultants bring their broad-based understanding of media and how to use it to candidates who generally know little about the nuances of publishing and broadcasting. They play dominant roles in the creation and production of messages for electronic media as well as in the content of those messages, which ultimately shapes the governance of local, state and national entities.

For the political consultant, a new campaign presents an opportunity to script a new saga that might have genuine significance to a state or the nation. Political consultants often are required to remake candidates, teach them how to speak, how to answer questions and deflect those they are unable or unwilling to answer. Sometimes, it is necessary for the consultant to provide advice and guidance on such personal matters as a shiny bald head, discolored teeth, body odor or bad breath. In short, the consultant often has to rewrite the entire narrative of a campaign although the ending is rarely certain at the beginning.

In an enterprise of volatile emotionality, the consultant must always "keep his cool" and base his decisions and actions on clear reason and logic. In matters of the campaign, the consultant is the "smartest one in any room" – or at least must pretend to be.

More than any other factor in the modern history of politics, television diminished the role of political parties in selecting candidates and of newspaper editors and publishers in setting political agendas and influencing the outcome of elections. With television, politicians no longer had to kiss the rings or any part of the anatomy of newspaper editors. However, they had to deal with their consultants, political gunslingers who made their reputations by winning elections.

Managing media campaigns for political candidates does not make one kinder and gentler toward fellow citizens. Political campaigns take a toll on the human psyche. In a political campaign, especially a campaign for an important office, the stress level starts out high and increases each day until the votes are counted. Tempers grow short. Character and personality flaws rise to the surface for all to see.

By and large, political candidates are endowed with oversized egos, some so large as to be pathological. They often expect the subordination of the personalities of volunteers and staff to their own egos. Professional consultants are not motivated by affection for the candidate or devotion to his ideology. They must make hard decisions and carry out difficult tasks, and their careers depend on winning. Few are able or willing to subordinate their personalities to the personality and ego of the candidate. The tension can get intense.

Much of what is wrong with the nation's political campaign processes today is the willingness of candidates to place themselves completely in the hands of people whose role is not good government, but whose only goal is to win the election. This willingness stems from a sense of terror that strikes many candidates when they truly realize the enormous challenge that a successful campaign poses, the huge expenditures, the demeaning compromises, the exhausting schedules and the ever-present fear that despite everything they do, they might experience failure, a rejection by fellow citizens of their community, their hometown – alas their entire state.

Controversy over money between candidates and consultants is always a flashpoint in political campaigns. Candidates tend to overstate the amount they will have to spend and when they will have it. How much money is available, how much to spend, when to spend it, who will be paid and when – these issues can cause nasty conflict.

At the outset of every election cycle, virtually every candidate who seeks an elective office believes he or she can win. Even the long shots, those pathetic figures with no funds, no organization and no hope, often feel that just maybe they can "catch lightening in a bottle." Nobody runs for political office in the hope or expectation of losing.

As the first full-time political media consultant in North Carolina, one of the first in the nation, who has been in the trenches for 45 campaigns over a 40-year span, I should have greater insight into and understanding of the factors that cause people to seek public office. Alas, I know not much more now about what motivates candidates than when I first started in 1968.

I have learned, however, that essentially there are two principal kinds of candidates – those who want to *do something* and those who want to *be something*. Both kinds of candidates can achieve success, sometimes even greatness. Both kinds, however, can pose great danger to the common weal.

Why people, accomplished, successful and seemingly sane, choose to put themselves into the meat grinder of a campaign escapes me. The same question could be asked of those who manage political candidates, political campaigns or the crucial media campaigns that drive them.

There is the money, of course, significant sums often earned in a relatively brief period. But there is more: For a writer, a wordsmith who often labors anonymously without fame or fortune at thankless writing tasks, there is no place where words are more important or more valued than the political arena. Simple, but powerful, phrases have mobilized our nation for wars and ended them, changed the way people interact with different races, generated money for worthwhile causes and focused the attention of the world on various issues of importance.

A competitive political campaign has many of the elements of thoroughbred horse racing, of contact sports, of world-class chess or high-stakes poker. Coexisting with the pervasive stress is almost constant excitement. There is nothing quite like the "thrill of victory" for a successful political campaign can change the course of history. And there is nothing quite as excruciating as the "agony of defeat" that one experiences when a long, hard-fought campaign comes up short.

My path to political consulting ran from pioneering television writer to award-winning ad writer to newspaper and magazine journalist – all of which served to sharpen the wits and steel the nerves as a participant and an observer. Certainly, that path would have never been opened to me had I not joined the J.T. Howard Advertising Agency in 1960 – just in time to experience the thrill of victory in a Lt. Governor's campaign, and the agony of defeat when our congressional candidate lost his campaign to unseat a legendary figures in the 10th congressional district.

By 1960, advertising had gained a bit of respectability and was poised to move even further in that direction by heralding what became known as advertising's "creative revolution."

The revolution originated in New York and was largely confined to the "Big Apple's" Madison Avenue shops until The J.T. Howard Advertising Agency, quite a small operation in Raleigh, N.C., began to win top honors in national advertising competitions. The success of the Howard Agency in demonstrating that talent and ability resided throughout the land was a catalyst in advertising's creative revolution spreading to the hinterlands.

In 1964, the Howard Agency's unprecedented creative approach in the use of television and print media in a successful gubernatorial campaign for a largely unknown mountain lawyer and judge demonstrated the power of advertising in the electoral process. The success of the campaign and the national publicity that accompanied it awakened other ad makers to the power of media when used in new and creative ways and thus was set in motion the political advertising trends that continue to the present.

For those who create it, advertising is an anxiety-ridden endeavor that often impoverishes the spirit of those who create it while enriching those for whom it is created. In advertising agencies, bitter struggles routinely occur among art directors, copywriters, account executives and their clients over matters both large and small -- the overall direction of a campaign, the concept of an ad, the size of pictures, the length of copy and even the typography that is used.

Many of the more heated disagreements result from a question of "who gets the credit" for work that often is undeserving of notice, much less credit.

Can This Marriage Be Saved?

The two men confronted each other across the table in the small conference room. Both were in their late 30s, one a dark haired New York Jew, a combination of Walter Matthau and Sammy Glick; the other a compact, muscular product of one of North Carolina's poorer mountain regions. Violence seemed imminent.

On this tense day in 1968, they had worked together for about a decade, each playing his respective role in building a successful advertising agency that had achieved notice and regard for its creativity among the media elite in New York, Chicago and other media centers of the nation.

Clutching a rolled up magazine, with which he pounded the table that separated them, Charles C. (Chick) McKinney bellowed, "Listen, you son-of-a-bitch, if your name ever appears in another article – any article -- about this agency, I will kill you! I am not just saying it! I will kill you! You got that?"

The color drained from the face of Mike Silver. It was clear that he believed McKinney and that he was scared. This was not the first time McKinney had exposed a violent side. On several occasions, he had caused consternation in the agency by wrecking his office in fits of anger and frustration over proposals that were not accepted or ads that were rejected. Until now, however, his anger had not been directed at any individual in such an overt manner.

"I didn't initiate the article," said Silver. "I didn't even know the damn magazine was going to publish an article on the agency." The confrontation occurred at the end of the day, shortly after most staff members had left. It was precipitated by an article in a small, somewhat esoteric magazine read chiefly by advertising professionals. The article had credited Silver with creating the advertisements that had won top honors in a recent show.

It was not the first time that Silver had reaped the credit for work done by others at the J.T. Howard Advertising Agency. *The News and Observer* had honored him for his advertising achievements as The Tarheel of The Week, a designation carefully and secretively determined by the editors of North Carolina's most influential publication. When local and regional publications wanted a comment about media, Silver was often the person they called.

Certainly Silver had a winning way with people and an engaging manner with words. His quotes were always on-target, often humorous and usually quite graceful.

That he had virtually nothing to do with the creation of advertising at the agency was irrelevant in his mind, and in his interactions with media, as he did with clients, he used his skills to promote the agency.

McKinney's anger had been building for quite a long time. A serious, driven commercial artist with underdeveloped interpersonal and verbal skills, he had been a major catalyst in moving the small Raleigh, North Carolina agency from the ordinary to the extraordinary in media circles. He was incensed when reporters and editors gave or implied credit to Silver for work he had done.

Silver was the Howard Agency's principal account executive, a job at which he excelled. He had joined Jack Howard in the mid-1950s after a stint as an on-air personality on WNAO radio and WNAO-TV. Initially, he had been responsible for many chores at the agency -- copywriting, account work, soliciting free-lance commercial artists and photographers to produce magazine and newspaper advertisements that were the agency's stock in trade.

Silver had moved to Raleigh to attend engineering school at N.C. State University. After a few semesters, he decided to transfer to UNC-Chapel Hill and acquire a degree in radio, television and motion picture production. Following graduation he had landed the job with WNAO radio and television.

Silver loved North Carolina and the southern culture. He married a non-Jewish woman with whom he had a son, and later they adopted a daughter. He settled in to make Raleigh and North Carolina his permanent home.

As the Howard Agency grew, Silver became the full time account executive, giving up his copywriting and ad-making chores to others. At the time of the confrontation with McKinney, it had been nearly a decade since he had actually written an ad.

McKinney grew up near Spruce Pine, North Carolina, a scenic area that even in the best of times was one of the poorer regions of a not-too-prosperous state.

As a child of the depression era 1930s, McKinney was embarrassed by his family's financial status and determined to improve his lot in life. After high school, he began college in Tennessee, but completed his studies by acquiring a degree in industrial management from UNC-Chapel Hill. He had no formal training in art, but was gifted in ad design and layout and was a good sketch artist, although he denigrated his ability in that area.

For McKinney, the most recent article crediting Silver with work that he and I and copywriters Jim Johnston and Jan Karon had done was almost the last straw. For months, he had talked with me about his desire to leave the Howard Agency and establish a boutique agency that specialized in creative work.

For McKinney, the certainty in his life was that he did not want to spend any more time with Mike Silver.

But as often happens, perversity sneaks in and changes everything. Less than six months after the violent exchange at the J.T. Howard Agency, Chick McKinney and Mike Silver put aside their differences and launched the advertising agency known initially as McKinney & Silver and later as McKinney. In the coming years, the new agency would become the major advertising agency in North Carolina and one of a handful of agencies outside the major media centers with national and international acclaim and a roster of blue chip national clients.

McKinney and Silver remained partners in one form or another until Silver's death, and even though McKinney delivered a warm eulogy at his memorial services, those of us who knew them well knew that theirs' was a union of convenience, a loveless marriage that assured that even at the moments of their greatest achievements, neither could rid themselves entirely of the taste of ashes.

Flashback: Eight Years Earlier

In 1960 the J.T. Howard Advertising Agency occupied a suite of six rooms in a non-descript building on Morgan Street in Raleigh, slightly less than a block west of the State Capitol. The staff included Jack Howard, who had founded the agency in `1945, his wife, and staffers Mike Silver, Chick McKinney, accountant James Mills, and secretaries, Minnie Lee Wellman and Fleming Sawyer.

In the coming years, the agency would play key roles in shaping the governance of North Carolina as well as in defining the state for dozens of industries and millions of vacationers. The work of its creative staff would be recognized nationally for its excellence, and the agency would serve as an incubator for several men and women who would achieve state and national recognition. However, in 1960 there was nothing remarkable about the small business. Its chief distinction was that when it was established, it was the only full-service advertising agency in Raleigh, then a small city of about 50,000 people. Only a few similar businesses existed in North Carolina, a state not known for being on the cutting edge of the communications industry. Howard, a New York native, had established the agency when he was 30 years old, after a number of years selling newspaper ads for New York publications and later for *The Raleigh Times* and *The News and Observer* in Raleigh.

Early on Howard had attempted to keep his job with the newspaper and operate his agency on the side. Former *N&O* publisher Frank Daniels Jr., recalls that when the paper learned of his moonlighting, it gave him a choice: keep the newspaper job and give up the agency or give up the newspaper job and keep the agency. Howard opted to keep the agency.

"Looking back on it," said Daniels, "Jack probably made the right decision."

The first years were difficult, but Howard had brought the agency to a profitable state and was reasonably comfortable with his business and the life it provided for him and his family. Adding Silver to the staff in the mid-1950s made life easier for him.

Howard and Silver got along well with each other. Howard allowed Silver to become a part owner of the agency, a practice he would extend to other employees who expressed an interest in owning a share of the business.

After a number of years of employing freelance artists, the agency brought McKinney into the firm, and allowed him to become one of three owners, with Howard retaining a majority ownership position. From the outset, McKinney introduced a kind of low-level tension to the agency. Although he could be quite personable, he had an edge about him, an attitude that implied that he had superior judgment in all matters pertaining to the advertising business.

By 1960, advertising as a business, craft or profession, had overcome some, but not all of, an unsavory history. In his remarkable book, *The Mirror Makers,* author Stephen Fox wrote that before the onset of the 20th Century, business and society considered advertising as a part of the publishing business "an embarrassment -- the retarded child, the wastrel relative, the unruly servant kept backstairs and never permitted into the parlor.

"A firm," wrote Fox, "risked its credit rating by advertising. Banks might take it as a confession of financial weakness. Everybody deplored advertising. Nobody, advertiser, agent or medium, took responsibility for it."

The advertising business was unregulated by any governmental entity and was, according to Fox, "conducted in the half light of bunkum and veiled appearances" where publishers routinely lied to agents,

agents lied to publishers as well as to their clients, and everybody involved lied to the public.

Nearly a hundred years later, in the late 1950s, the stigma had not entirely disappeared. People went into advertising, not to improve society or to find satisfaction through self-expression. They went into advertising for the money. Advertising jobs -- especially those at flourishing agencies -- paid significantly higher salaries than most media jobs. In the days when a dollar was far more valuable than it is now, an advertising man who could generate customers and "move merchandise" for a business was handsomely paid.

In the 1880s, the New York Department Store, Wanamakers, hired John F. Powers to write ads for the store. Powers was from an upstate New York farm, with not much education or experience. However, at Wanamakers, his ads increased annual store sales from $4 million to $8 million annually, and Powers became known as the first "great copywriter" and the most influential adman of his time. Later as a freelance copywriter, Powers earned the then unheard-of-fee of $100 a day.

Stories abound of admen (and they were mostly men) – principally copywriters – who earned enormous incomes from clients who profited from their "way with words." The stories also indicated those high-earning writers enjoyed total autonomy and brooked no interference from their clients – exaggerations, to be sure – but a harbinger of a trend that decades later would develop and evolve among those who in advertising's short-lived "creative revolution" became "stars" of the ad business.

Many writers and others who left jobs at newspapers and magazine and later at radio and television stations to go into advertising were regarded by those who didn't as "sellouts." Sadly, many of those who left other media jobs for advertising regarded themselves the same way.

Memorable Characters: Chick McKinney, Driven To Succeed

Soon after I joined the J.T. Howard Agency, in the early spring of 1960, Chick McKinney and I began working as a team. We quickly became friends, and over the next eight years, I might well have been McKinney's *best* friend and closest confidant. A number of artists who joined the Howard Agency and were supervised by McKinney left in anger and bitterness, sometimes hurling obscenities at him as they slammed the door on their way out.

John Gilbert, a talented graphics specialist, recalls McKinney as a man with a volatile temperament who could be overbearing in his relations with other. "He was the only art director I ever saw drop kick a Polaroid camera through a door in a fit of frustration," said Gilbert.

Harry Zepp, an experienced artist who had spent many years with the Young and Rubican Ageny in New York, joined the Howard Agency only to be assigned the most mundane technical chores.

As time passed, the animosity between McKinney and Silver grew. However, McKinney and I worked together -- often side by side -- for nearly a decade without anger or conflict.

We wrestled with ads, frequently disagreeing over many aspects, but without anger. We commiserated when clients muddled up our ads, demanding copy changes and making what we considered stupid suggestions regarding visuals and layouts. We also shared many stories about our experiences as children and teenagers, McKinney growing up in the mountains, I growing up on a Wake County tobacco farm, within the shadow of the State Capitol.

For years, McKinney remained resentful that his father never constructed a swinging bridge over the mountain stream that separated the McKinney house from the road. To catch the school bus each morning, McKinney had to cross the stream on a 'foot log.' If it were a cold morning, the foot log would be icy and almost impossible to cross without getting wet. A foot log is simply a large tree trunk that was laid across a stream. Its top side sometimes was flattened with an adz or an axe to make it easier to walk on. Only the poorer families had to cross the stream on foot logs." McKinney saw the foot log as a symbol of his family's low economic status.

Unlike McKinney, I grew up with fond memories of my childhood and adolescence and none of the resentments that troubled him. To me, some of the experiences that McKinney resented seemed like experiences I would have enjoyed. I could never persuade him that he should try to look on his past with a more positive perspective.

McKinney aspired to the "good life" surrounded by things of beauty and comfort, and he was willing to put forth whatever effort was required to achieve them. He often said he had an intense dislike of advertising, but was convinced that it held the key to the life he wanted to achieve, and that if he worked hard enough that life was within his reach. His goal, he said was to "get rich enough to get out of advertising," a goal he accomplished a number of years before his death at age 75.

At the Howard Agency, the central operating philosophy for every project or assignment was "give it your best shot."

For McKinney, his "best shot" meant that within the constraints of time and budget, he was required to put forth his very best effort. Difficult and contentious and even intimating to some people, McKinney never asked any colleague or subordinate to work harder or longer than he was willing to work. The problem for many people was that few were willing to work as long or a hard as McKinney, and although they respected him for his work ethic and professionalism, they did not always agree that every project warranted the effort that he was willing to put forth.

For many years, McKinney struggled with verbal communication. Although he was extremely intelligent, he was not a student of literature or history, had done poorly in English studies and had read very little other than technical material pertaining to art and the textbooks he was required to read in high school and college. His college major in industrial management was not the best preparation for the intuitive field of advertising. He knew nothing of the use of metaphor and simile. His attempts to write -- a letter or an ad -- often left him frustrated.

McKinney was a devoted fan of George Lois, the New York advertising and communications man who, according to *Business Week,* was a "supernova," the original 'Mr. Big Idea'" who, since the 1950s, had exerted "a titanic influence on world culture." Lois is principally an artist, who also writes, and he insisted that "in all great ideas, the words come first." Despite McKinney's limitations, he was determined to become, like Lois, a competent writer, and he believed that his determination to do so would compensate for any inherent shortcomings he might have. Often, he would spend hours on a paragraph, writing and re-writing it until it seemed he was torturing himself. No respecter of hours, he often was the last person to leave the office.

In the advertising business, McKinney was celebrated for his creativity; however, those of us who knew him well admired his drive and tenacity in producing advertising, but to us it seemed that his creativity and his curiosity were limited to the making of ads and that even in this field, he was not intuitively creative or given to flashes of inspiration.

In a 1967 newspaper feature in *The News and Observer* that focused primarily on McKinney's growing reputation for creativity, he was unable to present a coherent explanation of the inspiration for his creativity or the inner passions that might have fueled his desire to excel. Instead he repeated tired clichés such as "we're looking for the most efficient use of the dollars invested."

As he moved up to positions of authority in the advertising business, McKinney's approach to creating an ad was a dogged trial and error process in which it seemed, to some colleagues, he often ignored the best ideas – ideas inspired by history, literature, pop psychology or popular movies, areas in which McKinney was largely uninformed. Always, he wanted each ad to be a McKinney creation, with others relegated to the role of helpers. For art directors, who valued their own creative judgment as much as McKinney valued his, working with him could be tiresome and thankless.

Copywriters had fewer difficulties than art directors with McKinney, primarily, because of his great respect for a writer's fluency with words.

We did not know it at the time, but McKinney and I teaming up to create ads placed us on the cutting edge of what would soon become the accepted way of creating advertising at the most successful agencies on Madison Avenue.

The concept of putting a copywriter and an art director together for the purpose of creating ads became standard practice at Doyle Dane Bernbach (DDB), the agency that initiated and promulgated the creative revolution in advertising in the late 1950s and throughout the 1960s. At DDB, advertisements for all accounts were produced by a copywriter and an art director working as a team In the team arrangement the artist might suggest a headline; the writer might suggest a visual and the ad was conceived as a whole in the exchange between two disciplines.

Bernbach felt that a copywriter and an art director working together produced ad concepts in which visuals and text were better integrated. The combination of the visuals and words coming together formed a "third *better* thing."

As McKinney and I settled into the team approach in ad creation, I developed the habit of taking whatever project we were currently working on home with me when I left the office. With a wife and four small children wanting my attention, I really hoped I would not have to work at home, but I never knew when the phone would ring and McKinney would want me to write a headline for a picture he was looking at or envisioning, or would simply want to discuss a project. Many times, he would awaken me at one or two a.m. to discuss an ad. I never awakened *him* in the late night hours to discuss an advertisement.

McKinney's intensity was such that most members of the agency worried that he would "flame out" at an early age or worse, drop dead of a heart attack. We all wondered about his home life and were not surprised when his first marriage failed.

Mike Silver: A New York
Jew Goes Southern

Although Mike Silver came from New York, and I came from a North Carolina farm, our mutual background in broadcasting became a bond that quickly enabled us to become friends. Silver loved show business, and he and I shared a fondness for the comedy of Jack Paar, Alan King, Jackie Mason, Lenny Bruce and the writings of John Updike and Phillip Roth, topics of little or no interest to McKinney. Silver could tell jokes with a professional style and engage in banter with clients in ways that made them eager to share his company. McKinney lacked that ease with others.

Silver and I both enjoyed fishing and on many Sunday mornings, we would fish Neuse River, nearby farm ponds and sometimes the private lake at wealthy developer E.N. Richards' Pinehurst estate. Richards, an agency client, also owned a 42-foot yacht birthed at Morehead City that he rarely used. He was generous in allowing Howard, Silver and me to use the luxury craft.

Sitting on the banks of the Neuse River one Sunday morning, Silver said to me, "Grady, I am beginning to doubt that I am really a Jew."

"Why on earth would you doubt that you are Jewish?" I asked.

"Well," replied Silver, "I haven't been to Temple in years. I'm married to a Gentile. I have developed a southern accent, and here on Sunday morning, I am sitting on the banks of the Neuse River with a fishing pole in my hand. And I'm dammed certain that I'm not rich. I feel more like a backsliding Baptist."

Silver and I entered the advertising business with a different mindset than McKinney. We took our work in advertising seriously, but not obsessively. Both of us had curiosity and interest in all aspects of the communications industry. McKinney seemed fixated on advertising and the creation of print ads. He rarely showed much interest in the television commercials that we produced.

Early on, Silver was always complimentary of McKinney's work, although he seemed bemused and puzzled that anyone could be so obsessive about the minor details of ad-making. It was later in their working relationship that Silver came to dislike McKinney, but his dislike never seemed to be as intense as McKinney's dislike for Silver. Mostly, Silver sought to stay on friendly terms with McKinney and avoid areas of controversy that might ignite McKinney's anger. He was adept at defusing anger with humor.

Festering Resentment: Caught Between Two Friends

That McKinney and Silver did not really like each other often placed me in an awkward position, but I was determined early on not to be influenced by the attitudes they held toward each other, and to never repeat things one said about the other. I held to that position rigidly and it served me well.

As the weeks and months passed, the Howard Agency acquired new accounts, at what might be termed a "measured pace." The new clients were solid, well-established businesses that were very generally conservative and conventional in their approach to advertising and marketing.

McKinney was not interested in creating the kind of advertising the clients were accustomed to and with which they were comfortable. He had become infatuated with the "new wave" advertising being created in New York and yearned to be a part of the advertising revolution. Like McKinney, I was bored by the old ways of creating advertising. Together, McKinney and I set about to create edgy, hard-hitting advertising that attracted considerable attention.

When we entered our ads in regional and national competitions, we were pleasantly surprised when our work won numerous awards, sometimes sweeping the top honors in big cities such as Chicago and Atlanta and attracting the attention of New York ad judges. Howard was pleased with the awards, although he professed not to understand some of the approaches McKinney and I took in various ads. As he had with Silver and McKinney, Howard offered me an opportunity to be a part owner, and I accepted.

On a day-to-day basis, Howard seemed content to let others do the heavy lifting. He was not very interested in taking the agency on a rapid growth cycle.

He cautioned about the pitfalls of growing too fast. Silver agreed, and McKinney was infuriated. Howard liked to arrive at the office at mid-morning, leisurely read the Wall Street Journal, have a couple of cups of coffee and take an early lunch. McKinney, who was putting in 80 or more hours a week, began to seethe with resentment.

McKinney felt that Howard was irrelevant to the agency, and he would often suggest that the three of us should buy Howard's share and let him resign. Silver was not in favor of that plan and neither was I. Much of the agency client base was related to long-standing relationships that clients had with Howard. It was clear that the clients that had been with the agency the longest had complete confidence in Howard and were comfortable with others doing the actual work as long as Howard was involved. McKinney did not seem to grasp the subtle nuances of a business that is based largely on relationships and confidence. He felt that the quality of the work was the paramount issue in the advertising business.

In a small advertising agency with a limited roster of clients, ad writing quickly becomes repetitive. The continuing challenge is to produce ads that are better than the previous ones, and a few months later, produce another series of ads that are still better. It is a never-ending cycle of trying to top one's self, often for clients whose products and/or services are not very interesting to begin with and who don't appreciate the Herculean effort that must be expended.

After two years at the Howard Agency, I was ready for change. I was suffering from an ulcer and despite a desk drawer full of advertising awards, was profoundly bored. My move to the Howard Agency had provided no greater career fulfillment than my stints in television.

I never actually disliked ad writing. The problem for me was that there was very little that was inherently interesting in the content of the advertising that we produced. Working on some of the technical ads for clients such as ITT, Corning, the Aerotron two-way radio manufacturer and a mammoth technical manual and teachers' guide for Westinghouse watt-hour meters was especially onerous for me.

A survey conducted by the American Association of Advertising Agencies disclosed that 85 percent of all advertising was ignored. I had come to agree with the highly respected William Bernbach who observed that the public doesn't love or hate advertising. It is simply bored by it.

A Happy and Rewarding Interlude

Probably most writers, regardless of how satisfied they might be with their jobs, entertain the notion of becoming free-lancers, able to pick and choose their assignments, write at their own pace and gain fame and fortune. Alas, for most writers, that is a fantasy. Often, the freelance writer has to bear the expense of researching articles, including any travel and overnight expenses, and his negotiating ability with publications has traditionally been weak. In most cases, the free-lancer accepts what the publication offers – and is glad to get it. Nevertheless, for many, the dream endures, and some, with hope, fear and trepidation take the plunge.

A few days past my second anniversary at the Howard Agency, I decided to try my hand as a free-lance writer. It was a difficult decision. With four small children, it seemed foolish to leave a job in which I apparently was doing well, earning an above average salary. However, I felt that if I applied myself as diligently to free-lance writing as I had applied myself over nearly eight years, I could probably provide for my family. I was so bored with the clients at the Howard Agency, I felt that if I failed, I would prefer to go into another line of work, rather than to continue to write ads for the same group of clients over and over again with a new client providing a new assignment only rarely.

The Agency eased my transition to freelancing by asking me to handle on a freelance or contract basis a good bit of work that I was already doing.

The next three years were the most interesting and enjoyable years of my working life. To my great surprise, I found it relatively easy to replace my salary with freelance work for newspapers, magazines and a number of governmental and private sector organizations. Within a few months I was contributing articles on a regular basis to a number of publications. I established a good working relationship with both *The News and Observer* and *The Raleigh Times* that led to a permanent position on the *N&O* staff, a position that permitted me to continue many freelance assignments. I established relationships with the feature editors of *The Greensboro Daily News, The Durham Herald, The Rocky Mount Evening Telegram* and more than two dozen smaller, non-competitive papers. Within a relatively short period, my mailbox contained more than a dozen checks each month. I found a ready market for articles in *The State* magazine, numerous trade journals and outdoor publications, and the Howard Agency continued to provide a regular volume of freelance work.

The assignments that were offered to me were varied and interesting. The John Hardin Public Relations firm retained me to produce a half hour film on opportunities in the broadcasting industry for a Wake County Public School Career Day program.

An acquaintance with the public information office for the North Carolina Highway Patrol led to an assignment to adapt a book on Police Pursuit Driving written by then Patrol Sergeant Ed Jones to a half hour film which would be used in the Patrol's training program. The film attracted national attention, and resulted in a continuing relationship with the Patrol in which I wrote scripts for various highway safety films and speeches for the Patrol commanders.

During the production of the Police Pursuit Driving film, I met Carroll McGuaghey, news director for WSOC-Television in Charlotte. McGuaghey had agreed to narrate the Pursuit Driving film. He was impressed with the script, and after narrating the film, the station hired me to research and write a series of documentary films on North Carolina topics.

Over the next year, I became a roving reporter for the station, researching and writing scripts for a series of half-hour documentaries on topics such as Dr. Gaines Cannon, North Carolina's famed "Mountain Doctor;" a pioneering mental health program for young people operated by a Charlotte religious denomination; and the statewide service for unwed mothers. WSOC-TV's news staff produced the programs and they were aired in prime time, resulting in numerous awards for the series.

A year after McGaughey hired me, he left the station to form a film production company in Charlotte, and we remained friends until his untimely death. His successor had a different vision for TV news that did not include the long-form documentaries that McGaughey advocated.

As much as I enjoyed my interlude of freelancing, I realized that it would never provide the stability that was required to support a family. My position on *The News and Observer* staff provided a measure of stability and much of the satisfaction I had sought in my career, but considerably less money than advertising. Although I had diversified into several areas, I had never actually severed my ties to the Howard Agency. Throughout my years as a freelancer, I handled numerous projects for the agency. Howard, Silver and McKinney were always quite considerate of my desire to be engaged in things other than ad writing, and allowed me to pick and choose projects and assignments that were interesting to me.

Advertising's Creative Revolution:
A Political Campaign Revolution

In early 1964, a newspaper ad appeared in *The News and Observer* announcing the candidacy of Democrat Dan K. Moore of Webster for governor of North Carolina The ad was ordinary, and in layout and design, somewhat amateurish. The only person to notice the ad at the Howard Agency was copywriter Jim Johnston.

The Howard Agency hired Johnston, a native of Missouri, a few months after I left the agency to pursue freelance writing, and for a brief period he would play a significant role in the future of the Howard Agency as well as the future of North Carolina.

Congenial and easy-going, Johnston had an enormous talent for ad writing as well as a comprehensive understanding of the advertising business, assets that would lead him to the presidency of a national advertising agency. Unlike McKinney, Johnston never seemed to work hard. Many afternoons, he would take a nap on a couch in his office, much to McKinney's consternation. However, virtually all of his ads were award winners.

McKinney was awed by Johnston's ability to almost effortlessly come up with concepts for ads and to develop ad copy that seemed always on target. Johnston understood the driving forces that were behind what was then called advertising's creative revolution—the imperative for advertising to be less mundane and boring and to engage audiences at deeper intellectual and emotional levels that elicited positive responses. Johnston was as ambitious as McKinney, eager to achieve the maximum monetary rewards from a business in which monetary rewards were the major source of satisfaction. He just brought a more relaxed approach to the pursuit of his goals.

McKinney and Johnston never seemed to mesh as a team. Their relationship was more a contest in which McKinney tried to be the first to come up with *The Right Concept* for every ad campaign or individual ad. McKinney usually lost the contest, much to his frustration. More and more, McKinney seemed to be trying daily to top Johnston – to prove that he was his equal or better in creating memorable ads.

When Johnston clipped the Dan Moore ad and began urging Howard, Silver and McKinney to consider making a formal proposal to Moore to handle his political campaign, they were not interested. Their experience with political advertising had not been particularly pleasant. All three thought it unlikely that Moore could beat the two candidates already in the field, Richardson Preyer of Greensboro and I. Beverly Lake, Sr., of Wake Forest, the conservative candidate who had given Sanford a close and bitterly contested race four years earlier.

Johnston refused to give up. He continued to press for at least an opportunity to consider the Moore campaign. Finally, Howard and Silver agreed to let Johnston write a letter to Moore, suggesting a meeting to consider the possibility of the agency's handling his campaign.

Moore responded almost immediately to Johnston's letter. A meeting in Raleigh was arranged and the Howard Agency, after meeting Moore, agreed to handle his campaign. The arrangement between Moore and the Agency gave the agency a free hand in developing the advertising strategy and creating specific print and broadcast ads. It was the first time the agency had acquired a new client that agreed to what then were untested concepts in agency-client relations.

At the beginning it seemed the relationship between the Howard Agency and Dan Moore could not be successful. Moore was a former North Carolina Superior Court Judge with a firm judicial temperament, a mountain accent that emphasized his difficulty in speech making, and a middle of the road political philosophy. He was oblivious to the requirements of what the Howard Agency wanted to be a new model of political campaigning, one that used mass media in ways that were untried and untested. Moore and the small group of people around him were unaware of the enormous expenditures that would be required to mount a credible campaign against the very popular Richardson Preyer, who was supported by the Terry Sanford wing of the Democratic Party and fiery segregationist, I. Beverly Lake, who could deliver a spell binding speech.

In his initial campaigning, Moore was regarded by many observers, including the media, as politically clumsy, inarticulate and lacking in that indefinable trait known as charisma. Moore was all of those things attributed to him. However, to the general public Moore had a quality that overshadowed his shortcomings. He was the genuine article, the kind of candidate now described as "authentic."

As the chief advocate of a new style of advertising that resulted in advertising's creative revolution, Bill Bernbach stressed that in the crowded media climate, effective advertising had to "cut through the clutter" with an "interrupting idea dramatized with photographs that conveyed images of real people.

"The messages," said Bernbach, "should be simple and dramatic, sympathetic rather than strident, and, above all, convey candor and honesty."

Copywriter Jim Johnston embraced the Bernbach theory wholeheartedly and he employed it brilliantly by capturing the authenticity of Dan Moore in a full-page newspaper ad that showed a picture of a small boy sweeping a long hallway with a broom that was almost larger than he. The Ad headline read: "When Dan Moore was a boy, he was his School Janitor. Everyone wondered what he would grow up to be." Beside the picture of the small boy was the picture of now candidate-for-Governor Moore. The text of the ad simply listed the stellar resume of a man who had overcome childhood hardship to reach the top of his profession. The contrast between Moore and Preyer, heir to a family fortune and the rather strident professorial segregationist, Beverly Lake was startling and profound.

That ad set the tone for the entire Moore media campaign. Overnight it energized a significant number of voters who were not happy with Preyer or Lake and the dynamics of the campaign were immediately changed.

Moore and his small group of supporters were thrilled. The Howard Agency continued to have a free hand in developing the media campaign, and successive ads and television commercials continued to employ the Bernbach method of ad making.

Advertising could present the media image of Moore dramatically and forcefully. On the campaign trail, in personal appearance, the candidate was a work in progress. The paramount need was to provide him with personal communications skills without reducing that aura of authenticity that came through so vividly.

Mike Silver, who was assigned as account executive for the Moore campaign, escorted the candidate to New York where he sat for a series of photographs at Bachrach studios, world famous photographer of world leaders. The Bachrach photos presented Moore with a compelling believability that enhanced and reinforced the already favorable public perception of him.

While in the big apple, Moore underwent an intensive session with Betty Cashman, known by those who used her services as "the magic lady" for her ability to teach prospective public figures how to make speeches, respond to questions, reorder their body language and personal demeanor and in the process to become competent, confident and poised in public and on television and radio. Cashman had worked with many of the U.S. presidents and presidential hopefuls as well as heads of corporations and public figures from many walks of life. Moore, however, was the first candidate for Governor from North Carolina to avail himself of her services. She admitted that Moore was a difficult challenge, but the transformation she was able to make in him was truly remarkable.

The Bachrach photos were used in campaign literature, on billboards and posters and, of course, in newspaper and other print ads. At the Howard Agency, it was felt that Moore would not be effective in the typical TV ad in which the camera focuses on a head and shoulders shot of the candidate who attempts to speak directly to the voter. Instead, the agency retained the well-known, radio, TV and movie character actor Mason Adams to narrate what were essentially one-minute documentaries, showing Moore interacting with people, while Adams narrated scripts that outlined Moore's experience and position on the issues.

Adams had been the narrator for dog food along with other commercial products, and soon, the word went out that the Howard Agency was trying to sell Dan Moore the way manufacturers sold dog food.

Such techniques are now standard practices in political campaigns. However, for a state political campaign of 1964, the use of world class photography, speech training and Hollywood actors to narrate television commercials were a first. Indeed, for political campaigns throughout the country, the Howard Agency approach was a pioneering effort that attracted the attention of the national media, which published articles comparing the Moore campaign to the most sophisticated ad campaigns of the times.

Soon after the Moore media campaign was launched, Copywriter Jim Johnston decided to leave the Howard Agency for a job as creative director of Griswald-Edelsman in Cleveland, Ohio. In the two years that he had been with the Howard Agency, he had accumulated a number of advertising awards. He had used those awards as leverage in achieving a position at the larger advertising agency, and when the opportunity arose, he did not hesitate to make a change, although he said he was not actively pursuing a new job at the time he was offered the position. Johnston's career flourished at the

Cleveland agency. He was promoted from creative director to the presidency of the agency, and under his leadership, Griswald-Edelsman grew to become the world's 38th largest advertising agency.

Soon after assuming the presidency of Griswald-Edelsman, Johnston wrote to McKinney, inviting McKinney and me to join him at the agency in Cleveland. He pointed out that although the "winters are longer, the colors of autumn are just as brilliant as in North Carolina and spring bursts upon the land with the same intensity as it does in the Tar Heel state." Both McKinney and I declined the offer.

A few years after assuming the presidency of Griswald-Edelsman, Johnston recommended that the agency headquarters be relocated to Chapel Hill, North Carolina. When the agency's board refused to accept his recommendation, Johnston resigned and moved to Chapel Hill where he established a new agency with a roster of clients that included some of the most well-known names in corporate America. He later became one of a handful of advertising people installed in the University's Advertising Hall of Fame.

Johnston's abrupt departure from the Howard Agency left a large hole at a critical point and both Silver and McKinney urged me to rejoin the agency on a full time basis, something I was reluctant to do.

Instead of joining the agency full time, I agreed to devote whatever time was required to handle the Moore campaign and other agency writing chores. The truth is, the campaign had begun to consume most of the agency's time and effort, and many campaigns for other clients had been postponed. Both the agency and the newspaper agreed that I could continue my editorial relationship with *The News and Observer*, a relationship that had become very important to me. The agency also agreed to a substantial increase in compensation.

During the next several months, I plunged deeper and deeper into the Moore campaign, not only writing speeches and campaign material, but briefing Silver on governmental and political issues, areas in which he was not always fully informed.

He was, however, a quick study, and after a few minutes of briefing on such topics as the North Carolina Council of State and its responsibilities, he could discuss the issue with competence and confidence. At one point, on his way to a meeting, he dashed into my office and asked, "How many counties in North Carolina and what in the hell is the council of state?"

In 1964, professional political polls were reserved for the candidates for national office. With momentum building for Moore, the Howard Agency as well as the campaign advisors wanted to know just how effective was the media campaign – especially the use of expensive photography and actors. The Howard Agency retained Peter Hart, who was beginning to be as well-known as the Gallup organization, to conduct on-going polling for Moore in North Carolina. The initial polling data showed a surge in support for Moore, but not sufficient to place him in first place. Instead, the polls showed Moore in a solid second place position – precisely where he wanted to be. The Moore campaign strategy was to win a solid second place position and then in a runoff election, as the moderate, middle of the road candidate, be in a position to win either Lake's conservative voters who did not like Preyer, or Preyer's more liberal voters who would not vote for Lake.

The Richardson Preyer campaign apparently figured out the Moore strategy and set out to knock Moore out of second place. Preyer's advisors felt their candidate would be able to attract more of the Moore supporters than would Lake. Preyer dipped into the family fortune and began pouring money into his campaign. With expensive television and newspaper advertising and polling, the Moore campaign was feeling a financial pinch.

Moore's campaign manager was Joe Branch, a quiet spoken lawyer from Northeastern North Carolina. Also backing Moore was Lewis R. "Snow" Holding whose family owned controlling interest in First Citizens Bank & Trust Company. Branch asked Silver to join him in a meeting with Holding to explain the financial squeeze and to discuss ways of funding the Moore campaign. Silver asked me to join him, Branch and several other key Moore advisers in the meeting at First Citizen's offices on Martin Street in Raleigh.

Branch explained the problem resulting from Preyer's infusion of cash into the campaign. He then asked Silver to explain how we would use additional money to counter the Preyer effort. Silver went through the details of the media strategy, and when he was through, Holding asked two questions:

"If you get the money you say you need, will it assure a victory?"

Silver said he was confident that it would.

Holding pointed to the huge First Citizen's bank vault and asked, "do you suppose there's enough in there to pay for what you want to do?"

With funds assured, the Moore campaign organized a massive rally in Raleigh to assure supporters that Moore was indeed a viable candidate. Virtually every county sent a delegation, and the logistics were planned so that dozens and dozens of buses arrived in Raleigh to form a massive caravan that began at the State Capitol building and moved slowly down Fayetteville Street where the historic Memorial Auditorium was overflowing with supporters. When the 100 buses began moving past the old Sir Walter Hotel, the state headquarters for the Beverly Lake campaign, one of Lake's supporters recalled that he looked out the window, saw the huge caravan and rushed to a bathroom to throw up.

"I knew we were doomed," he recalled.

The Howard Agency arranged to film the caravan of buses, the mammoth rally at the auditorium which included an appearance by Marie Beale Fletcher of Asheville who had recently been named Miss America and endorsements from residents of counties throughout the state. In the weeks ahead, all of this film coverage was carefully edited and I wrote a script that became a statewide television show entitled *Tide of Victory*. The film was considered a major centerpiece in the victory that Moore eventually won.

As planned, Dan Moore came in a solid second in the first Democratic primary, eliminating the fiery segregationist Beverly Lake. In a runoff election marked by uncharacteristic personal attacks by Richardson Preyer, Moore almost coasted to an easy victory, picking up virtually all of the Lake vote as well as the large moderate vote that he had secured in the first primary. In the general election, which pitted Moore against Republican Robert Gavin, Moore won a lopsided landslide.

For those of us who had been directly involved in the media effort that propelled Moore from a little known former superior court judge to the state's highest office, the electoral victory was an exhilarating experience. Nothing we had done in the past came close to the satisfaction of winning a gubernatorial election. The victory and the work we had done to assure it made most of our other efforts pale by comparison. Not only did it set a new course for the State of North Carolina, the victory would set most of us who had been involved on a new direction in our careers. Being introduced to a potential client as "one of the guys that got Dan Moore elected" was a valuable embellishment to whatever other credentials were being offered. And it was long lasting.

A Promise Made, A Promise to Keep

At one point during the campaign, Silver had asked Holding about the possibility of handling the First Citizen's rather large advertising account. Holding responded by promising Silver that if Moore won the governorship, he would give the Howard Agency the Bank's advertising account. It was a promise that although not kept would play an enormous role in the lives of Jack Howard, Mike Silver and Charles C. Chick McKinney – as well as the future of the advertising business in North Carolina and the South.

When Holding made the promise to Silver to turn over the bank's advertising account to the Howard Agency if Moore were elected governor, he had expected the owner of the agency that was handling the bank's account, a family member, to retire. The family member decided to postpone retirement, placing Holding in a quandary.

In explaining his inability to make good on his promise, Holding was apologetic, but he told Silver that if he would be patient, there would be something far better for the Howard Agency in the near future.

Silver was skeptical of Holding's promise. As the months and years passed without Holding offering any new business, Silver and all of us at the Howard Agency largely forgot about his promise. There was a far more urgent matter to consider, an unstated, implicit, promise of the State's advertising account, based on the winning campaign the agency had conducted for Governor Moore. The account provided for an expenditure of more than a million dollars for advertising to promote tourism in North Carolina as well the promotion of the state for industrial development. In 1965, a million-dollar advertising account was a choice plum for a local advertising agency.

In the 1960 campaign for governor, the Bennett Advertising Agency had prepared and placed advertising for Terry Sanford who had won the election. The agency was "rewarded" with the State advertising account, and it was generally conceded by advertising professionals that the agency had not acquitted itself well in the handling of the account.

Politicians and editors had taken a skeptical view of handing over a large account as a plum simply for assisting in a political campaign. Despite the concerns being expressed, it was generally conceded that the Howard Agency, which had brought a candidate from back in the field to victory, was in a strong position to win the account.

The opportunity to work on the State advertising account interested me. The account provided a national forum, and the topic – which included the most interesting places in North Carolina – promised to be far more interesting than the current roster of accounts at the agency. McKinney and Silver used the high probability of the agency winning the account to lure me back to the agency on a permanent basis. The agency agreed, however, that I could manage my time in a way that would enable me to continue my position with *The News & Observer,* a position I thoroughly enjoyed and valued. In addition, I would be given time to pursue other interests as long as they did not interfere with the quality of the work I did for the agency. Finally, to close the deal, the Agency doubled my previous salary—a persuasive move that with a wife and four children, I simply could not reject.

In short, the Howard Agency was not terribly concerned with the number of hours that I spent behind a desk in its offices. What it required – indeed demanded -- was the kind of ads that attracted and kept clients -- and won awards.

Winning The State
Advertising Contract

In preparing its bid for the North Carolina state advertising contract, the Howard Agency was determined that its presentation would leave no doubt in anyone's mind that the agency was not up to the task. Over a period of several weeks, we reviewed the tourism and industrial development advertising that that had been done for the state in the past as well as that done for other states in the Southeast.

Our conclusion was that virtually all of the work was ordinary, that it lacked creativity and was most often not based on an understanding of the factors that influenced travel destination choices or the location of industrial plants. Virtually every state with beaches showed attractive girls in swimsuits, guys fishing and swimming. Those with mountains showed people gazing over mountain vistas. The pictures looked like snapshots taken on family vacations.

At the Howard Agency, we searched for information that people used in making decisions regarding vacations, and we found a number of studies that indicated that people on vacation liked to do the same things they did when not on vacation. They just wanted to do them in different and interesting places.

The Howard Agency presentation was a joint effort of virtually every staff member. Although my role was to write the presentation, it reflected the best thinking of everyone involved. It included sample print ads, sample television production, market and research studies all slickly packaged. To the Howard Agency, the size of the account, which would double the agency's billings, the prestige that it carried and the financial potential for the agency justified the effort.

The day of the presentation was one of high drama. The Bennett Advertising Agency made what appeared to be a desperate effort to hold on to the account and at the same time to justify the work that it had done in the past. Every member of the Howard Agency was in top form. To most observers, the contrast between the two presentations was profound and in granting the contract to the Howard Agency, it appeared that the State was quite willing to move into a new way of communicating with potential visitors.

Governor Moore appointed Willie York Chairman of the North Carolina Department of Conservation and Development and Bill F. Hensley as Director of the Travel and Tourism Division. York, who had a deep interest and extensive knowledge of North Carolina named himself chairman of the advertising committee. Hensley was a former FBI agent who had transferred to journalism and had earned high marks as sports information officer for N.C. State University. York had a mercurial personality; Hensley was even tempered. Both, however, were committed to a new standard of excellence in the travel and tourism advertising program for North Carolina.

In the celebratory mood following the Howard Agency's successful bid for the State account, Silver and I met with York to begin planning the first wave of ads. York began by congratulating Silver and the agency on acquiring the account.

"You fellows did a good job in presenting yourselves," said York.

Jokingly, Silver responded in a somewhat flippant manner. "Willie, you 'ain't' seen nothing yet."

Turning a stern gaze on Silver, York replied, "Listen young man, I know you think you and your team are hot stuff, but pay attention. You are going to make good on all those promises or I'm going to personally have my hand around your neck and my foot up your ass. I'm expecting great work that's nationally recognized. Make me and the State proud, and maybe I'll back off some.

"A lot of people are going to be watching what you do and what I do. I don't want them to have any reason to think we didn't make the right decision in hiring you."

York left no doubt in anyone's mind. The challenge was clear.

I immediately began a crash course on North Carolina by reading again Hugh Lefler's definitive book on the Tar Heel State and W.J. Cash's *Mind of the South.* In a search for perspective I consulted past issues of *The State* magazine and historical publications from the Division of Archives and History.

In a book entitled *The North Carolina Guide,* I struck a mother lode. The volume is a comprehensive description of virtually every place of interest in North Carolina and many interesting people. It was produced under the WPA's Writer's project, one of the New Deal programs designed to provide employment for unemployed Americans during the Great Depression. Not only was the information well researched, the articles were written by some of the best writers in North Carolina and the nation.

In creating our first campaign for the State of North Carolina, my goal was to redefine the state for a national audience by using well-known and *little known* bits and pieces of the state's history as well as lore and legend in compelling messages that could just as easily been subjects of feature articles. Our first series of advertisements were stories of odd and mysterious lights that rose in the night from a mountain valley, of folk music legends, of shipwrecks and stovepipe hat rebellions on the State's storied Outer Banks and of pirate gold and the swashbucklers who stole it during a colorful past.

In design, layout and text, the advertisements were unlike any that were being published by other states, and they created an ambience for the state that did, indeed, redefine North Carolina and set it apart from other states.

All of the ads were full pages in four colors that ran in national magazines such as *Esquire, National Geographic, Readers Digest,* and several other consumer magazines. Both Willie York and Travel and Tourism Director Bill Hensley approved of the ads and were delighted with the response they produced.

The North Carolina advertising campaign caught the attention of the national media and several articles in national magazines reported on the ground-breaking aspects of the campaign. One of the ads was included in a college textbook on effective writing entitled *Language In Uniform* by Morgan State College Professor Nick Aaron Ford.

Silver, McKinney and I were, however, nervous when we learned that Hensley had entered the North Carolina advertising campaign in the annual competition conducted by the National Association of Travel Organizations (NATO). Silver and I vividly recalled York's challenge to us, and we were not only pleased, but relieved, when the NATO judges selected North Carolina's campaign as the best in the nation. It was the first time North Carolina had won the prestigious award.

Over the four-year life of the contract, the relationship between the Howard Agency and the Department of Commerce strengthened as those of us involved spared no effort to produce the kind of advertising that not only would be effective for North Carolina, but would continue to win the regard and respect of everyone.

In addition to numerous magazine ads, we produced a number of items that promoted the state in unusual ways: a long-playing album of ghost stories from North Carolina, a small book on North Carolina's southern style of talking entitled *A Dictionary of The Queen's English,* both of which became collectors' items, a comprehensive economic profile of the state, booklets on industrial development opportunities in the State and novelty items such a "gee-haw whimmy diddle," carved from twigs by mountain craftsmen to demonstrate the dexterity of North Carolinians to industrialists seeking competent labor forces.

Perhaps the most ambitious project undertaken by the agency, other than advertising, was the publication of a travel book that described North Carolina and was sent to thousands of persons each year who responded to the advertising campaign and requested additional information.

The decision to replace a rather small, ordinary looking pamphlet entitled *North Carolina, Variety Vacationland* was not made lightly. For one thing, the cost of hundreds of thousands of copies was substantial. Moreover, the preparation costs were in addition to the cost of preparing and placing advertising. Several members of the State's advertising committee were in favor of updating the existing publication, an idea that none of us at the Howard Agency favored. Neither did Hensley. Toward the end of the second year of the agency's contract, the decision to publish a new volume was made, and I was given the assignment to write the book, an assignment I had looked forward to for some time. Art director John Gilbert was assigned to design the book and supervise the photography and production.

In writing the travel book, I wanted to continue the process of redefining North Carolina as a place of unique history and heritage as well as a place of extraordinary natural beauty. In selecting material to include in the book, I looked for the most interesting attributes of the state, and sought to write about them in a style that drew from literature, specifically, the writings of Thomas Wolfe, Henry David Thoreau, and popular contemporary writers such as Norman Mailer, Grace Matalous, author of *Peyton Place,* and the "new journalism" that was dominating non-fiction magazine writing. My goal was to blend literature and journalism into a new style of communication. I titled the book, *North Carolina, The Goodliest Land Under the Cope of*

Heaven, a phrase, taken from a line in a booklet written in 1584 by Arthur Barlow and Phillip Amadas, the two Englishmen who described coastal North Carolina after they visited the area.

Art Director John Gilbert commissioned some of the nation's top photographers to photograph the state's most scenic and dramatic attractions. Instead of small pictures of people fishing and swimming and playing golf, Gilbert used large dramatic photographs.

One of the most popular sections in the book was a series of folklore stories about craftsmen, odd historical events and strange mountain people whose deaths were recorded for 73 years by a man known as Uncle Jake Carpenter.

Our proposed text and design for the book received immediate and enthusiastic approval from York and Hensley, and after minor editing and design refinements, the book went to press with a run of 250,000 copies. Hensley, who had a wide circle of media contacts, sent copies of the book to travel writers and columnists at newspapers throughout the country.

Jim Henderson, a columnist for the *Virginia Pilot,* Norfolk's most widely circulated daily newspaper, was especially intrigued by the folklore stories, and gave glowing praise to the state for its new travel book, and a journalistic bouquet to me whom he generously noted was, in his opinion, the "best travel writer under the cope of heaven." Other travel writers and columnist also wrote glowing articles about the book and "its new style of travel writing." In subsequent years, *The Goodliest Land* travel book was reprinted and provided to the thousands of people who requested information about the Tar Heel State each year. Among states that competed with North Carolina for tourism business, *The Goodliest Land* set off a competition in travel book publishing that continues to this present.

The Howard Agency's success in helping elect Governor Moore, its award-winning advertising campaign for North Carolina and the other awards won by the agency in national competition created much conversation in the advertising community. The Agency seemed poised for bigger and better things.

My work on the North Carolina advertising account and other agency accounts as well as consulting positions I had accepted with the North Carolina Department of Motor Vehicles and The Governor's Highway Safety Authority and my editorial responsibilities with *The News and Observer* provided me with a full and diverse workload. However, we all realized that unless the Howard Agency signed a candidate for governor who was elected, the contract between the Howard agency and the State most likely would end after a new governor took office.

Whether or not to seek another candidate and thus attempt to hold the lucrative State advertising account became a topic of intense debate. McKinney, Silver and I were in favor of soliciting a candidate for the 1968 governor's race. Jack Howard was not inclined to take on another statewide political campaign. He felt that the Moore campaign had proven that it was extremely difficult for an advertising agency to provide a high quality of service to its regular clients during a highly contested political campaign. Although the Howard Agency had not lost any accounts during the Moore campaign, many long-time, valuable clients had expressed concern about the agency's future role in politics. As the majority owner, Howard's position regarding continuing political activity prevailed.

The Genesis of Political Consulting In North Carolina

The Moore campaign had been very profitable for the Howard Agency. In a few months, the campaign produced as much revenue as many clients provided in several years. It also pointed the way to a new "style" of campaign advertising that was more effective and more interesting than previous methods.

For those of us directly involved, the Dan Moore political campaign had been one of the most exciting projects undertaken by the agency. For McKinney, Silver and me, the possibility of handling a major political candidate's campaign outside the Howard Agency was appealing. McKinney and I discussed forming a one-client agency that would handle candidates for high political office. At the time, the era of political consultants had not evolved in the country and certainly not in North Carolina.

McKinney, who had Republican sentiments and contacts, went so far as to make a personal presentation to Republican Jack Stickley, a candidate for Governor in the Republican primary campaign. Stickley was opposed by Jim Gardner, who had defeated the venerable Harold Cooley for Congress in the Fourth Congressional district. Stickley was supported by many old line Republicans from the western part of the state, He was, however, overshadowed by Gardner, and unable to raise the budget that McKinney had proposed, Stickley declined McKinney's proposal.

When J. Melville (Mel) Broughton, a Democrat who had served as chairman of the Democratic Party under Governor Moore and whose father had been both Governor and Senator, let it be known that he was considering running in the 1968 Democratic primary, Mike Silver and I discussed ways in which we might put together an organization outside the Howard Agency to handle his campaign. After considerable thought, Silver decided it would not be in his best interest to be involved in such an undertaking. After considering how much time he had spent on the Moore campaign, he realized it would be a disservice to the Howard Agency to attempt such a project.

My conversations with both McKinney and Silver had given me much food for thought. Silver encouraged me to consider establishing an agency to handle political clients, and promised that he would be available to provide assistance and pointers that he had picked up during the Moore campaign. McKinney was not opposed to the project, and promised to assist in ways that did not interfere with his work at the Howard Agency.

If Broughton were successful in winning the governorship, we would have an "inside track" to retaining the State advertising account at the Howard Agency or winning the account at the firm that handled the Broughton campaign.

At *The News & Observer,* Robert Upton, a reporter and freelance public relations practitioner, and I often discussed starting a new kind of service that combined advertising, public relations, publishing and film production. Evenings in the *N&O* newsroom while waiting for the first edition of the paper to be printed, we would kick around ideas for the kind of agency that we envisioned.

When Broughton formally announced his candidacy to seek the democratic nomination for governor, I suggested to Upton that he and I make a proposal to handle all aspects of the Broughton campaign. In 1968, no North Carolina candidate for governor had ever hired a single organization to manage all aspects of his campaign – speechwriting, publicity, press relations, polling, and advertising. The Dan Moore campaign had come closer to that model than any other.

Our plan, which represented a first in political campaigns, posed a huge and bold challenge for two people who had no staff, no offices, except the studies in our respective homes and no experience in handling such a large and demanding undertaking. I was 33 years old. Upton was a few years older.

Although I had gained experience in the hard-fought and successful Dan Moore campaign, and Upton had some political experience in lesser campaigns, neither of us truly understood what we would be letting ourselves in for in our proposal to handle all aspects of the communication needs of a statewide political campaign for the state's highest office.

Moreover, we had not fully assessed Broughton's chances for victory. It was later that we learned that among many Democrats and most of the media it was almost a foregone conclusion that Bob Scott would win the Democratic Primary. He had served as Lt. Governor for the previous four years, getting along well with Governor Moore, the democratically controlled legislature and key members of Moore's inner circle.

Scott had had four years of high visibility in the media, a ready-made campaign organization that had come together in his successful campaign for Lt. Governor and the remnants of his father's old organization known as "Kerr Scott's branch head boys." Scott was folksy and likeable with a common touch that served him well on the campaign trail.

Too late we learned that although Broughton might have made a good governor, he was an awful candidate. Shy and awkward in public, he seemed to dislike and even dread any interaction with voters. He was unable to engage in the kind of small talk that enabled a candidate to get through a day of meeting many people.

Tall and physically fit, Broughton could present a favorable first impression that quickly dissipated within a few seconds of awkward conversation. Broughton had a credible resume: corporate lawyer, son of a former governor and senator, well-connected "old Raleigh" family, service to the Democratic Party as its former chairman and service to the state on the State Highway Commission. On paper, the candidates appeared to be evenly matched. On the campaign trail, the odds heavily favored Scott.

For decades, right-of-center Democrats had prevailed in most North Carolina elections. Melville Broughton Sr., Greg Cherry, William Umstead, Luther Hodges and Dan Moore reflected the dominant mood of the state and its slightly conservative political tilt. The election of Kerr Scott in 1948 had been a shock to what was known as the Democratic Party's "old guard," and many of the more conservative members of the faction feared that Bob Scott would be in the mold of the liberal and unpopular Terry Sanford.

The moderate-conservative faction recruited Broughton to run for Governor to assure that the old guard's political philosophy would continue in the tradition of Dan Moore. His decision to run had caused domestic strife at home. His wife, Mary Ann, had recently given birth to their second child, and their daughter, several years older than the new addition, in the turbulent teen years, was resentful. Mrs. Broughton did not think it was a good time for her husband to be away from home on the campaign trail. We did not know it at the time we made our proposal, but Broughton was not just a reluctant candidate, he was a resentful one.

Although Upton and I were both registered Democrats, neither of us considered ourselves either liberal or conservative. We were "no prefix democrats."

With no offices and no staff, we were surprised and pleased when Broughton's campaign manager, Jim Mason of Laurinburg, agreed for us to make a proposal. We did not know who the members of the committee would be, but I set to work drafting what I thought would be a compelling proposal and winning strategy for the candidate as well as for our fledgling, largely non-existent organization.

A Winning Pitch

The Broughton campaign decided to receive proposals from firms interested in handling the account in the first few days of 1968. Upton and I were scheduled for a mid-afternoon presentation, the last in a series of proposals.

As most candidates for statewide office did in the 1960s, Broughton had rented a suite of rooms in the Sir Walter Hotel, then one of Raleigh's better hotels, for his campaign headquarters. We were asked to meet with the campaign committee in one of the rooms where we would make our presentation.

Members of the committee, in addition to Jim Mason, were Harold Makepiece of Sanford, who had been the personal secretary to Governor Luther Hodges, Akers Moore, the owner of a commercial printing company in Raleigh, and Robert Broughton, the brother and law partner of the candidate.

Our presentation required slightly less than an hour. We acknowledged that this would be our first venture, but we did not disclose that at the moment, Upton and I constituted the entire organization. Our proposal provided for a package of services required for a statewide campaign, a publicity person to travel with the candidate, a speech writer to research and write all speeches and statements, writers and graphic artists to write and design all campaign literature, news releases, and television, radio, outdoor, and newspaper advertising and supervision of all professional polling.

Although we were not required to do so, we outlined a political strategy that essentially replicated the successful campaign of Governor Dan Moore, whom all present knew, admired and had supported. When we finished our presentation, we were asked to wait for the committee to meet with the candidate.

Outside, the weather had taken a nasty turn. Black clouds began to darken the southwestern sky. To experienced North Carolina weather observers, it looked like we were in for a heavy snowfall.

An hour passed, then another. The sky continued its ominous darkening. I lived 10 miles out in the country. I had ridden to the meeting with Upton, leaving my car with my wife and children. If snow began to fall, traffic would be awful, and I did not know whether I could get home. Still, we waited, wondering whether we had been forgotten.

As we paced the floor, frequently watching the sky outside, snow began to fall, fine, icy flakes that rattled the windowpanes. In the street below, the tires of cars began to spin. Still, no sign of the committee members or the candidate.

Outside, darkness fell, and the streetlights came on. The air was white with the driving snow. Around seven p.m. Mason and Makepiece returned to the room with the news. Our proposal had been accepted. The fee that we had proposed for our services – an amount we had been prepared to negotiate down – was accepted without question. Upton and I stood to make more money from January to May than we had ever before earned.

Upton and I were grinning at each other, when Mason gave us reason to lose our smiles. "The candidate has a speech to make tomorrow morning at 7 a.m. here at the hotel," said Mason. "He is going to speak on the economic needs of North Carolina and his ideas for meeting them. Because of the weather, he was wondering if you would like to have the use of one of the offices here which is equipped with telephones, typewriters, etc."

Upton and I exchanged worried looks. Neither of us was prepared for this immediate assignment, although we had given the impression that we already were up to speed and ready to take on immediate work. We just did not expect an assignment this quickly. Moreover, Broughton had given us no information as to what he might want to say in his speech, no insight as to what he viewed as the state's paramount economic needs. Indeed, we had not been introduced to the candidate. Neither Mason nor Makepiece had any thoughts on the matter.

Upton and I asked for a few minutes to discuss the project. Upton said he had no ideas, had not even given it a thought. I felt that if we failed at this initial challenge, the account could easily be in jeopardy before we even signed a contract. I also was confident that I could put something together if I could get back to my study in my home, where I had many reference works from which to draw.

Outside the snow had piled up, making driving difficult. Upton was not sure he could get to my house safely and return. Mason called on Dennis Ducker, Broughton's driver who said he had snow tires and was confident he could get me home safely. Around 8 p.m., Ducker, Broughton and I drove through the snow to my house. Broughton and I had a chance to become formally acquainted, but despite my questions, he gave no indication of his views on the state's economic needs. "That's what I hired you for," he said. "You know that I'm not a liberal, don't you?"

I wondered how I would get the speech to Broughton by 7 a.m. through several inches of snow on an unplowed country road. Broughton said he would have Ducker pick up the speech at 5:30 a.m. and deliver it to him at the hotel so I would not have to try to get into the city in the snow.

A Night to Remember

By the time I arrived at my home, it was past 9 p.m. I had not eaten since early morning, and my head was spinning with the good news about acquiring the Broughton account and the worry about preparing a major speech on such short notice.

My wife, Marie, congratulated me on the acquiring the account, hustled up a quick meal and got the children off to bed.

As she finished the bedtime ritual, I said, "If I am able to get this speech written tonight, my draft will need to be typed cleanly so it can be read. Will you be able to retype it for me?" It was not an unfamiliar request. Marie, an excellent typist, was accustomed to typing speeches and my rough drafts of articles, film scripts and other materials.

Marie decided to go to bed and catch a nap and be ready to get up and type the speech when I completed the draft. I repaired to my study and began to gather material that I hoped would be useful in preparing the speech. I assembled a batch of material, which included a draft of a speech given several months earlier by State Treasurer Edwin Gill. Gill was considered to be the wisest of the wise men in state government in financial and economic matters and a Broughton supporter so I felt comfortable in relying on his writings in the preparation of the Broughton speech.

As I slipped a sheet of paper into my old manual typewriter, the room – indeed the whole house -- went dark. The mixture of ice and snow had caused limbs to fall on power lines, causing a major power outage. Not only was the house dark, the heating system, operated in part by electricity shut down.

Fortunately, we had a couple of oil lamps filled with kerosene, and our house had a large fireplace just a short distance from my study. While Marie lighted the lamps, I scurried outside to the woodpile, gathered snow covered logs and as much dry wood as I could find and built a fire in the fireplace.

By the glow of two oil lamps and the warmth of a fireplace, I furiously wrote, snatching thoughts and phrases from multiple sources. Fortunately, I had prepared speeches for Dan Moore on economic matters as well as many industrial development ads for North Carolina and several brochures that dealt with economic issues. In my role as a consultant to the Highway Safety Authority, I had learned about the importance of good roads to the state.

By 4 a.m., I had a draft with which I felt reasonably comfortable. I awakened Marie, and she began to type a clean version of my draft. I decided to take a nap, but having consumed several cups of black coffee boiled in a pot in the fireplace, I was unable to go to sleep.

About 5 a.m., the electricity was restored, the furnace began warming the house, and I began reading the speech I had written in the previous hours. Promptly at 5:30 a.m., Dennis Ducker rang our doorbell. His were the first tire tracks in the snow on the road outside our home. I handed him the speech, asked him about the road conditions, and sent him off.

The speech that was en route to Raleigh was the first of more than 50 such speeches and statements that I would write over the next four months. Broughton never offered a suggestion regarding the content or the style of any of them. He never commented positively or negatively about any of them. He simply read them – not very well.

Facing Reality

Within a few days of acquiring the Broughton for Governor campaign, Upton and I, with the help of my wife, Marie, acquired a suite of offices near the campaign headquarters and equipped it with essential furniture and equipment. That was the easy part. Finding competent people willing to join our venture brought us face to face with the reality of our task. Many of the people we wanted to hire were unwilling to leave secure positions for what could be temporary jobs of only a few months.

We looked to family members and friends. My brother, Macon, had expressed an interest in moving back to Raleigh, and I was able to persuade him to leave his job as city editor of the *Sanford Herald*, and handle the task of writing daily news releases and communicating with the growing Broughton campaign organization. Graphic artist John Gilbert, a former colleague from the Howard Agency, agreed to handle the campaign graphics on a freelance basis and Marshall Lancaster, a former colleague and writer at *The News & Observer*, signed on to travel with Broughton, but after a couple of trips and exposure to Broughton's prickly personality, decided to return to the newspaper, leaving us with a rather difficult task of finding a replacement.

The main problem in attracting a staff was the lack of permanence in all the positions. If Broughton won the primary, jobs would extend through the general election, and if he were successful in the general election, there was a good chance of well-paying and interesting jobs for four years. There was, alas, no certainty in any of those scenarios.

After a diligent search, we were able to hire veteran WRAL radio news reporter Tom Tucker, as the traveling publicist for Broughton, and after promising my wife, Marie, a fur coat and a new car. I was able to persuade her to join our group for the period of the campaign, a position that extended over the next several decades. She was able to recruit her best friend, Jean Woodall, a well-qualified secretary, to handle much of the clerical work. The addition of my nephew Donald to run errands and help with mailings and a professional media-buying specialist completed our team. We were ready to win an election.

A Frightened and Reluctant Candidate

In my first strategy session with Broughton, I realized that our job was going to be more difficult than we had anticipated. Broughton did not appear confident of his ability to win against Scott. His early efforts to organize a statewide campaign organization had left him with serious doubts about his chances to win the nomination. A few meeting with newspaper editors and radio stations news directors had left him distrustful of the media. Although he had hardly begun campaigning, Broughton appeared to be exhausted. His sentences were punctuated with long, weary sighs.

Seeking to gain an understanding of the vision that Broughton had for the state, I asked him why he was seeking the office of governor. His hands began to tremble, and he looked at me as if I had offended him. No answer was forthcoming. The meeting ended with very little information from Broughton.

As I considered his attitude, I came to believe that Broughton had agreed to the requests of those who urged him to seek the office of governor, then realized just how difficult the task would be and was overcome with something close to panic. Not only did Broughton look tired, he looked *scared*.

Also troubling was Broughton's attitude that many people were not just supporting another candidate but that they were actively against him.

Before retaining us, the Broughton campaign had printed cards and handbills that depicted the candidate as a humorless, stiff and rather pompous man with the personality of a stick. Someone had made the decision to use his full name, J. Melville Broughton, Jr., in his campaign materials. The photograph that depicted a stiff, humorless man with a name that reminded one of

Victorian England did not captivate voters. Moreover, it soon became apparent that Broughton could not deliver a speech with any believability. The first time I heard him speak, I was appalled. He read the words on the page as if he had never seen them before, much less believed – or even understood -- them. At the end of each sentence, his voice would trail off as if he were too tired and too bored to continue. If Dan Moore needed help in speechmaking, Broughton needed a total makeover.

I asked Mason to let us give Broughton the same treatment given Dan Moore: a photo session with Bachrach in New York and speech coaching with Betty Cashman. Mason was all for the idea, but Broughton was reluctant. He actually liked the picture that we thought was so awful, and he said he had been successful in addressing juries and saw no need for speech coaching. Moreover, Broughton did not want anyone to know that he needed speech coaching.

With the help of Mason, we persuaded Broughton to go to New York for the photo and coaching sessions. After setting up the appointments, he and I caught the last flight out of Raleigh-Durham around 10 p.m. and arrived in New York about 11:30. We checked into our hotel, for a night's sleep before the busy day that lay ahead.

Early the next day, we went to the Bachrach studios, where a very personable photographer worked magic. The set of proofs he provided for our review was startling. No longer did Broughton appear stiff and pompous. He looked like a candidate from central casting. Betty Cashman worked her magic, too. Over the course of several hours, she enabled Broughton to replace the tired, bored persona with a more assertive, uplifting way of delivering a speech. On the flight back to Raleigh, Broughton seemed buoyed by the experience. When he saw the campaign literature and the advertising campaign, he seemed even more encouraged.

As a young man, Broughton had been the driver for his father's campaign for Governor. Typical of the times, the senior Broughton had campaigned by crisscrossing the state, east to west, north to south, stopping in at country stores, courthouses, sheriff's offices and civic clubs to chat with people, make talks and solicit votes. In the television age, such personal campaigning was not essential as it had been in earlier times. We tried to dissuade Broughton from taking on the rigorous and exhausting task of daily driving and meeting with small groups. Instead we wanted to concentrate on using resources to keep him in the media and organize speaking engagements before large groups that would attract maximum media coverage.

Broughton insisted on a daily grueling schedule of driving, stopping and meeting with small groups. He was determined to visit each of the 100 counties in North Carolina, although he would have been better served to concentrate his efforts in the populous Piedmont Crescent, the band of cities and small towns that extended from Raleigh to Charlotte and contained more than 75 percent of the State's total population.

On the grueling trips, Broughton was accompanied by Dennis Ducker, his driver, and Tom Tucker, his press relations associate. At his campaign stops, Broughton insisted that both men accompany him as he went into various places of business. He developed a habit of introducing both of them, which in retrospect was not necessary and resulted in a tragic/comic episode.

Entering a place of business, Broughton, a tall, patrician type man would introduce both of the men accompanying him. The introductions went something like this: "Hello, this is Dennis Ducker and this is Tom Tucker, and I'm Melville Broughton, candidate for Governor. Apparently Broughton never realized the humor in such an introduction until he and his small entourage were leaving and he overheard a customer in the store say, "It was nice to meet Mr. Ducker and Mr. Tucker, but who the hell was that tall man in the middle?"

An Angry Man Grows Angrier

When Broughton returned to Raleigh, he immediately summoned Upton and me to his office and demanded that we replace Tucker. With an even shorter time span before the primary, we knew it would be an impossible task to find a replacement. We decided that our best move was for Upton to take on the task of traveling press liaison.

Tucker had performed well as traveling media liaison. He had established rapport with many local radio stations that had carried his news reports when he worked for WRAL, which also owned the Tobacco Radio Network. Through Tucker's daily phoned-in reports, Broughton was achieving a good bit of name recognition. Tucker was well known to the major newspapers and got along well with reporters. He did not deserve to be terminated, but Broughton insisted that he be replaced.

Upton was an easy-going, competent news writer and public relations professional who understood the dynamics of the news business as well as anyone. He handled press relations for Broughton so effortlessly that Broughton thought he was not doing anything. Broughton began immediately to complain to me about Upton. He wanted him replaced. I reminded Broughton that Upton was a full partner in the business, and that I had no intentions of trying to force him out. Moreover, with the difficulty we already had experienced, I was not confident that we could find anyone to take the job of traveling press liaison. Upton stayed, and Broughton fumed.

Money Troubles

In Raleigh, Broughton's state campaign headquarters were well organized and well run by Ed Woodhouse, the office manager, Jim Mason, campaign manager, Harold Makepiece, Treasurer and a group of Broughton's long-time friends and associates who constituted an advisory group. Volunteers from both the Moore and Lake campaigns worked in the offices.

Although the tension was always high – as it usually is in a statewide political campaign -- the office ran fairly smoothly -- at first. As we had promised, we launched the Broughton media campaign with a statewide outdoor billboard campaign that was intended to increase Broughton's name recognition. We were to follow that with a statewide television campaign that was to set forth Broughton's main campaign issues – issues to which he had given very little thought. As the first wave of television ads was completed, we planned a statewide newspaper advertising campaign that fleshed out what we had devised as *the Broughton 10-point program for progress*. That's when we ran into the first major problems.

The television and newspaper campaigns were, to be sure, going to be expensive. But the Broughton campaign assured us that the money was available – or would be available. Based on the assurance of Mason who said he had conferred directly with Mel and Bob Broughton, we proceeded to implement our recommendations.

We produced a series of television commercials as well as a series of large-space newspaper ads. With the help of media placement consultant Nat Hale, we planned an ad blitz on all the major television stations, and sent the Broughton campaign a bill for the television time.

No check was immediately forthcoming. I stressed that the television time had to be paid for in advance or the expensive commercials that we had produced would not be aired. As customary in the advertising business, I had signed the contracts for the television time, and the payment would be made by our agency with funds provided by the campaign. At that point in our business, we had no funds for an expensive television campaign.

I again called Mason, reminding him of the need for the funds. Again he assured me that there was no problem. However, no check was received. In television contracts of that era, the agency of record that contracted for the time became liable for the payment – even if the candidate did not pay the agency. There was, however, a provision in the policy that allowed the agency to cancel the contract 72 hours in advance of its start date and avoid becoming liable for the payment.

As the deadline drew near, I drafted a telegram canceling the entire schedule, and waited. It had become apparent that the Broughton campaign could not or would not pay for the television time. In our office, anxiety was high. Everyone knew that our agency would be liable for the payment if the Broughton campaign did not pay.

Television ad salesmen began calling repeatedly seeking the advance payment. Some even came to my office, hoping to pick up a check. I told Mason that if the television schedule were cancelled, the impact on the campaign would be serious. It would signal that it was out of money, and it would be more difficult to get campaign contributions from potential contributors. Mason continued to assure me that the payment was on its way.

As the 72-hour deadline approached, I made one final phone call, and again received a promise of payment but no actual payment. I called my wife Marie into my office, handed her the telegram I had drafted and asked her to personally see that it was sent immediately to all of the television stations.

The cancellation of the statewide television ad campaign had a predicable effect. The news media played the story big, implying that the Broughton campaign was in serious trouble. We tried to put the issue in its best light, but the damage to the campaign was significant. Neither Broughton nor anyone in his office offered any explanation as to why payment was promised right up to the moment that I cancelled the ad campaign.

I could reach only one conclusion. The Broughton campaign was willing to allow me to incur financial ruin rather than deal with financial issues in an honest manner. From that point on, my attitude toward the campaign, the candidate and those associated with it changed. I knew that my first obligation in dealing with the campaign was to protect my interest and the interest of our new organization.

The cancellation of the television advertising and the accompanying media attention and speculation exerted a profound effect on Broughton's already sour and prickly demeanor. His temper, already on a hair trigger, became more fierce and more easily aroused.

Eventually, funds were raised to purchase television time, but never in a coordinated approach that was followed by a carefully planned newspaper campaign. With little money for paid advertising, we directed our efforts to the publicity and personal appearances by the candidate to reach voters.

Broughton's weekly itinerary was established by Mason and Woodhouse. When Broughton returned to Raleigh on the weekends, we would provide him with speeches and statements that were tailored to the needs of the upcoming week. In addition, we would film excerpts from the more significant speeches and send them on a timed basis to television stations serving the areas in which Broughton was appearing.

Broughton's lack of involvement in the content of his campaign messages was a matter of constant puzzlement. Completely disengaged from the larger aspects of his campaign, Broughton became more and more involved in its minutia. On the campaign trail, he would fly into rages at the slightest problem. He constantly seethed with anger, much of it directed toward Upton. Some of it was directed at people he felt were not supporting him or who were not supporting him as vigorously as he thought they should. Oddly, Broughton never directed his blazing anger at me. His verbal attacks on Upton as well as the complaints he made about him were unfair and undeserved, but Broughton never apologized.

Broughton began to carry around a notebook. At one meeting, he announced that the notebook contained the names of people he would get even with when he was elected governor. Shades of Richard Nixon and his enemies' list.

Could It Get Stranger
Than This?

Upton and I urged Mason and Woodhouse to keep Broughton off the road for a rest period. Upton stressed that the groups Broughton encountered during his travels were usually small, and during a week, didn't add up to more than a few dozen people.

We proposed that Broughton limit his appearances to large events, carefully arranged for maximum impact, and on a weekly basis hold a news conference in Raleigh where the State's major media were concentrated. We called several members of the press corps in Raleigh and asked them if they would be interested in attending regular news conferences at which they would be given opportunity to question the candidate at length. Many of them were enthusiastic about the prospect. Mason and Woodhouse supported the proposal. Broughton went along reluctantly.

Thus began one of the strangest series of episodes of my political experience.

Based on the news cycles in which Monday is traditionally a slow news day, we decided that Monday would be the appropriate day for Broughton to hold his weekly news conferences. On Wednesday preceding the Monday, we sent out a written notice to all of the media. On Friday, we followed up with phone calls, which confirmed that most of the media represented in Raleigh would attend.

On Friday, I prepared what I believed to be a newsworthy statement for Broughton to deliver and briefed him on questions that I thought he might get from reporters.

At 7:30 a.m. on the following Monday, I received a phone call at home from campaign manager Mason. "Broughton asked me to call you and let you know that he would not be able have the news conference that you scheduled," said Mason.

"Is he sick?" I asked.

Mason did not answer. Instead he merely reiterated that Broughton would not be available for the news conference. I called Upton. We decided that since I could not truthfully explain why Broughton was not going to hold the news conference, it would be better for Upton to simply call and tell the media the conference had been cancelled, and that he would call back when it was rescheduled. We did not know, however, whether it would be rescheduled.

When I arrived at my office, I called Mason and asked for more details. I explained that we needed to tell the media why the conference was cancelled. Mason said bluntly, "I don't know why he cancelled. He is at his mother's house. Let's drive over and talk with him."

At Mrs. Broughton's home, Mason and I found Broughton lying on a couch in the den. Periodically, he would emit a loud groan or grunt. When Mason and I went into the den, the copy of the statement he was to have delivered was lying across his chest. Broughton seemed to be in physical pain.

When we asked why he had cancelled the news conference, Broughton said between loud grunts, "I just couldn't do it. Just couldn't do it."

I asked if he was dissatisfied with the statement.

"No," he said. "I just couldn't do it."

We agreed to tell the media that Broughton was suffering from "campaign fatigue" and was going to rest a few days and would reschedule the news conference for the following Monday.

On the following Monday, the previous Monday's scenario repeated itself -- an early phone call from Mason, my call to Upton, Upton's cancellation of the news conference. On five successive attempts to conduct a news conference, Broughton failed to appear.

Mason, his patience exhausted, described the situation as follows:

"The SOB has got the grunts again. He's lying on his mama's couch whining. He's 46 years old and he needs his mommy."

Back On The Campaign Trail

Unable or unwilling to confront the news media in Raleigh, Broughton decided to return to the campaign trail, stopping in at country stores, talking with small groups of farmers and others. These daily travels which included sleeping in motels, eating on the run and facing what seemed to be a losing campaign made Broughton's disposition bizarre, subject to screaming tirades that often were laced with profanity over trivial matters.

One of our tasks was to provide the news media with a weekly schedule of Broughton's travels. The schedule was generally carried by the Associated Press and published in most of the daily newspapers – especially those serving areas to which Broughton was visiting.

One Sunday morning about five a.m., I was awakened by a phone call from Broughton. He was in a state of high rage. After a meeting in Roanoke Rapids, Broughton, unable to sleep, had arisen, picked up a copy of the first edition of *The News & Observer* and did not see his weekly schedule that usually appeared on Sunday. At first, he raged at me, accusing me of not sending it to the paper. Then he quickly turned his anger on the newspaper, ordering me to purchase a half hour of television time on WRAL-TV so that he could make a half hour address in which he said he was going to "call out" Jonathan Daniels, the editor and part owner of the paper.

While I listened to Broughton's rant, Marie who had awakened picked up the paper at the end of our driveway, opened it to the political section and there was Broughton's schedule – as usual. I told Broughton that apparently, he was not scheduled in any of the areas covered by the paper's first edition and, therefore, the paper chose to include the schedule in the second and final editions, thus reaching those areas where Broughton was schedule to visit.

That information did little to calm Broughton. He was in such a rage I became concerned about his mental stability. I tried to get him to change his mind about the purchase of a half-hour of television time. Viewer studies showed that half hour speeches by politicians attracted few viewers. The production was often stressful on the candidate, and in Broughton's case, I did not feel that he could speak effectively for a half hour. Moreover, his decision was being made in a fit of anger over a perceived slight that had not occurred.

Although *The News & Observer* supported Bob Scott in the Democratic Primary, the paper had been even-handed in its news coverage of the campaign. The sister paper of the *N&O, The Raleigh Times,* supported Broughton editorially, and editor Herb O'Keef wrote strong editorials supporting Broughton.

Broughton refused to take my advice regarding the half-hour televised address. With the assistance of Broughton's friends, attorney Ken Wooten and Akers Moore, I was able to persuade him not to begin a media fight with *The News & Observer* and instead to use the half hour for a more positive address that might actually help his campaign. Despite our best efforts, the half-hour production came off as a rather boring event that probably attracted very few viewers. Broughton thought it was going to assure his victory.

Ethical Dilemmas

With each passing day, Broughton appeared to be less stable emotionally. Upton and I discussed our dilemma: What was the proper course of action? We had a firm contract to use our best professional skills and energies to assure the success of Broughton in the Democratic Primary election. However, we had come to believe that Broughton's behavior made him unfit for the job. Indeed, we thought he was mentally unbalanced. Should we resign? Could we legally resign inasmuch as there was no escape clause in our contract?

We concluded that inasmuch as we lacked credentials for diagnosing mental instability, we should soldier on, doing our best, seeking to avoid confrontations with Broughton over the trivial matters with which he seemed more and more obsessed.

In April, 1968, when civil rights leader, Dr. Martin Luther King, was assassinated and cities throughout the nation erupted in flames as outraged black people rioted, political campaigning came to an abrupt halt in North Carolina and other states.

Candidates hurriedly returned to their homes and campaign offices for their own personal safety as well as in recognition of the need for the nation to absorb and deal with what appeared to be a national catastrophe.

Broughton was campaigning near the coast when we learned of the assassination. Mason and I quickly determined that Broughton should return to Raleigh. However, when we made contact with him, he was determined to continue, seemingly oblivious to the historic significance of the King assassination and its potential for disorder in North Carolina as well as the larger cities of the country.

When he finally returned to Raleigh, Broughton fumed during the several days that the state and the nation collectively sought to catch its breath, calm anger and fear and restore order. Broughton contended he was wasting valuable campaign time that would be more productively spent on the campaign trail.

In the aftermath of the King assassination, the ad-hoc campaign committees that were supporting Broughton published ads which depicted raging urban fires. The stark headlines on the ads claimed that only Broughton could deal with the race violence and restore order. We urged Broughton to ask the maverick groups not to run ads that sought to capitalize on a national tragedy. He declined. The ads troubled many people inasmuch as urban discord in black communities was virtually non-existent in North Carolina as Governor Dan Moore dealt with the issue calmly and decisively, defusing the anger and preventing the kind of disorder that occurred in larger cities.

More Money Troubles

The contract between the Broughton campaign and the firm of Jefferys-Upton Associates provided for four equal payments for our services to the campaign. Three of the payments were made on a timely basis, and the final payment was due two weeks prior to the primary election date.

As the due date for the final payment approached, Mason suggested that the campaign wanted to defer the final payment until the campaign was over. Robert Broughton raised the question of whether we had fulfilled the terms of our contract. We quickly provided proof that we had fulfilled the terms more than adequately. Still, the campaign wanted to delay the final payment – one fourth of our total compensation – until after the campaign.

Remembering how the campaign had been willing to allow us to incur financial ruin earlier in the campaign by not telling us that funds for an expensive television ad campaign were not available until we could have become financially liable, we quickly and unequivocally rejected the notion of waiting until the campaign was over for payment.

Mason suggested that the campaign might delay payment and require us to initiate legal action to collect what was owed. Broughton did not participate in the conversations regarding the final payment.

Upton and I agreed that legal action was not our best approach. I drafted a two-page statement, setting forth our concerns regarding Broughton's mental stability. I documented with dates and times the instances in which Broughton had behaved in a manner that made one doubt his stability, including Mason's own comments regarding Broughton and the strange episode in which Broughton would call news conferences and not show up.

Mason reacted with alarm.

"Bring us the payment or you'll see this statement in every newspaper and on every television station in the state." I said. "Pay us and we will continue to work as hard as we possibly can right up to the last minute."

The next day, we received the final payment and we continued our efforts for the next two weeks. Despite the difficulties that we had experienced, it appeared that as the campaign drew to a close, Broughton would accomplish his goal of receiving sufficient votes to call for a run-off election. Polling indicated that Bob Scott would come in first, Broughton second and Reginald Hawkins, the only black candidate in the race, third. Broughton would have another month in which to make his case, and with the race only between two candidates, his chances would be better, funding might be more readily available and he might actually win.

The End of The Campaign

Near the end of the campaign, I received an urgent phone call from attorney Ken Wooten, a long-time friend of Broughton's and one of the wiser, more informed advisors to Broughton. Wooten had supported our efforts throughout the campaign and often was a voice of reason on a number of tense occasions.

Wooten wanted to offer advice regarding the statement that Broughton would make when the returns were in. We were confident that Broughton would be in a solid second place position, able to call for a run-off, if he chose to. Wooten had learned that Raleigh attorney Tom Ellis, who later would play key roles in the election of Jesse Helms and other conservative candidates to national office, had become an advisor to Broughton, and he was concerned that Ellis, a strongly conservative lawyer, had drafted a statement for Broughton to make that sought to associate the votes of black citizens with Scott. In short, said Wooten, "Tom Ellis and his group are going to try to use Broughton's statement to hang the black vote around Bob Scott's neck and damage him in the General election. This won't be good for Broughton. It won't be good for North Carolina," said Wooten.

Inasmuch as Broughton never offered input into speeches and statements, I proceeded to draft two statements: one that contemplated the unlikely event that he came in first; and one that contemplated a second place finish. I ran them by Wooten who said he thought both struck the proper tone. I turned the two statements over to Mason, who also expressed approval. Broughton never commented.

On the night of the primary election, the vote resulted in the expected outcome: Bob Scott in first place; Broughton in a solid, but not commanding second place; Reginald Hawkins, in third and out of the race.

Broughton had secluded himself away from the media until the outcome of the election was certain. None of us knew what he might say--or given his reluctance to face the media--whether he would say anything at all.

As we all waited in anticipation, Broughton came to speak to his supporters and to the media. His statement was harsh, filled with racial overtones and rather strident. It was not the statement we had provided to him. Members of the media looked at Upton and me in astonishment. My friend David Murray, who had served as Scott's press relations person during the campaign, turned to me with a puzzled look. Murray and I had worked together in the past, and throughout the campaign ran into each other in the Sir Walter Hotel, headquarters for most statewide candidates. We commiserated over the stresses of the campaign and on occasion, both of us had agreed that we hoped the campaign, if it went to a runoff, would not become bitter and involve personal attacks.

In response to Murray's puzzled look and reporters' surprised glances, I shook my head to indicate that I had not written the statement. They didn't appear to believe me.

In his statement, Broughton neither called for a run-off nor conceded to Scott. The issue hung in the air, causing concern among Democrats. At the presidential level, Richard Nixon would battle Democrat Hubert Humphrey in what would be a down-to-the-wire photo finish campaign. In North Carolina, the Democratic candidate for governor would face the fiery conservative Republican Jim Gardner who had proven his campaign skills by knocking off the venerable Fourth District Congressman Harold Cooley. A hard-fought, divisive run off would not serve the Democratic Party.

In the crowded, smoke-filled rooms of the Broughton campaign, the debate raged. The coterie headed by Ellis and the more conservative faction urged a replay of the divisive, racially tainted campaign in which Raleigh Attorney Willis Smith defeated former UNC President Dr. Frank Porter Graham, who had been appointed to the U.S. Senate seat held by Broughton's father, J. Melville Broughton, Sr., when he had unexpectedly died in office before completing his term. The more moderate voices urged Broughton to face the reality of the difficulty he would face. Scott's first place vote, and Hawkins' vote, which would be expected to lean toward Scott, created a mathematical reality in which Broughton could not prevail. Basing his campaign on the racial issue following the assassination of Dr. Martin Luther King would intensify racial discord in North Carolina that would last well into the future.

If Broughton chose to call for a run-off, our contract with him required us to provide the same services provided in the first primary without further compensation. Considering the odds against Broughton and the additional effort and expense we would incur, Upton and I hoped Broughton would decide against a runoff. In addition, we had no stomach for the kind of campaign the conservative faction contended would be required for Broughton to prevail. Finally, we did not think Broughton was up to the challenge of a hard-fought run-off election. The rages and anger would only intensify and where it would lead we could not predict.

One of Governor Moore's closest advisors was Ralph Howland, former Associated Press Bureau Manager, public relations director for Chatham Mills, and more recently Commissioner of the Department of Motor Vehicles. During my tenure as a consultant to the DMV during the Dan Moore Administration, Howland and I had become close friends, and as the Broughton campaign weighed its chances in a run-off campaign, I received a call from Howland.

We chatted about the campaign briefly before Howland told me he had some news that I might want to get into the papers. Governor Moore, said Howland, had called Broughton and personally asked him not to seek a runoff—that if he did and ran a race-tainted campaign, he would announce his support for Scott. Broughton had promised the Governor that he would not call for a run-off, but would endorse Scott and call for Democratic Party unity. Broughton is going to wait a few days before he makes the announcement, said Howland.

"Do with this information what you think is best," he said.

I quickly saw an opportunity to accomplish several goals: bring the Broughton campaign to a definite end, clear up the misconception that I had been involved in the drafting of Broughton's race-baiting statement that already was causing discord in the state and perhaps strike a positive blow for the Democratic Party.

Placing a call to the *N&O*, I invited political reporter Russell Clay, a former colleague, to my office for what I promised would be a major scoop. He quickly accepted, and when he arrived, I offered him a deal.

"I will give you the best political scoop of the week, if you will include a paragraph in the story that I suggest. The information I provide will be accurate and will reflect on no one but me."

Clay thought it over briefly and agreed. I told him about Governor Moore's call to Broughton and Broughton's promise to Moore. Clay was pleased to get the scoop. He had been pressuring the campaign for an answer regarding the runoff.

The paragraph I wanted in Clay's story simply stated that the Jefferys-Upton firm had no role in the divisive statement made by Broughton on election night. When Clay's story was published the next day and picked up by the Associated Press, the Broughton campaign came to an end. I received a number of phone calls, expressing approval that I had not been involved in the ugly statement made by Broughton.

In the days following the Clay story, Broughton and Scott joined hands at the Sir Walter Hotel, with Broughton endorsing Scott and pledging his support to his candidacy. Scott defeated Gardner in the General

Election, and in 1970, Broughton, after a lifetime as a Democrat, switched his party registration to Republican.

As the Broughton campaign was dissolving, I received a call from Broughton. He asked me to join him and Mason in Mason's office at the Sir Walter Hotel. I had wanted to meet with Broughton to officially close out our contract, but I did not know what to expect from a candidate who had seemed so full of anger throughout the campaign.

Both Broughton and Mason were more relaxed than I had seen them in months. Both rose to shake hands with me, and after a bit of small talk, Broughton told me he was quite satisfied with the work I had done for him. He said he realized early that it was going to be difficult for him to win, but that our effort in his behalf could not be blamed.

He said he would be pleased to recommend me for other projects, and he thanked me for our work. Mason echoed Broughton's sentiments. Thus our relationship ended as it had begun, cordially and respectfully.

During the campaign, we had accumulated a large file of information on Jim Gardner, the presumptive Republican candidate for governor, on the chance that if Broughton won the primary the information would be useful in the general election.

Gardner was, indeed, the Republican candidate, but we had little use for the file we had accumulated. A few days after Broughton's endorsement of Scott, I called Scott's press aide David Murray, I told him about our file, and also told him I would be available to assist the Scott campaign in any way I could.

Murray asked me to turn over our files to Scott campaign Manager Roy Sowers, and he asked me to begin preparing a series of speeches for Scott on various issues that would be available when the general election campaign resumed. With our frenetic work load ending abruptly, I was glad to have something to do. By immediately offering my support to the Scott campaign and actively working on assignments for the candidate, I was welcomed into the campaign and following Scott's victory, I was awarded the contract to handle the statewide communication program for the Governor's Highway Safety Program throughout the Scott administration.

After a few weeks of rest and relaxation, Upton and I decided to move our offices to a smaller, less expensive location and organize our business as two independent, but cooperating firms. Ralph Howland, Commissioner of Motor Vehicles, asked me to resume my consulting work with the DMV, and the Howard Agency asked me to return to my copywriting chores.

After a month of trying to juggle the various pieces of my disjointed career, I decided to devote full time to building a business not entirely dependent upon a political candidate. Almost as soon as I made the decision I was confronted with other options, all quite intriguing.

A Strange Chain of Events

The phone call from Mike Silver was a shocker. "I've quit the Howard Agency," he said. "McKinney threatened to kill Jack (Jack Howard, the owner) and he's out, too. He trashed the place before he left."

I was so taken by surprise that for a moment, I thought Silver might be joking. I replied in what I thought would be taken in the same vein. "Darn," I said. "I resign and the place goes to hell in a month."

Silver didn't laugh. "I'm serious," he said. "It's a damn mess. It started when McKinney tried to get me to join him in forcing Jack out of the agency. It went downhill from there, and McKinney exploded. There's no way we can get back together."

As we continued to discuss the implosion of the Howard Agency, Silver brought up the subject of our joining together in an agency. He mentioned bringing John Gilbert, the art director at the Howard Agency who also free-lanced for me, into the business. Silver was confident that he could move several clients from the Howard Agency to the new agency. It was certainly an offer worth considering and I told Silver that I wanted to think about it a day or so.

Before Silver and I could again discuss his proposal, I received a call from McKinney. I didn't mention what Silver had told me, and neither did McKinney. Instead he asked if he could come out to my house on Sunday morning to discuss a project. I quickly agreed.

On Sunday, McKinney, accompanied by Harry Jacobs, the award-winning art director at the firm of Cargill, Wilson and Acree in Richmond, arrived about mid-morning. McKinney was bubbling with excitement. He said he and Jacobs were going to form an advertising agency, the kind he and I had often discussed, and he wanted me to join them.

McKinney, like Silver, said he was confident he could persuade several Howard Agency clients to move to the proposed new firm. Jacobs said he also could bring clients.

Both offers were tempting. I did not relish the idea of taking clients from the Howard Agency, but I realized that was a common practice in the business, and that many successful agencies had been formed the way McKinney and Silver were proposing.

What kept me from accepting either offer was the knowledge that for the foreseeable future, all of my creative energy and writing ability would be expended in creating ads. I wanted more diversity in my work.

While I was mulling over the two offers, a major news story appeared in the local papers. It said that a new advertising agency formed by Charles C. McKinney and Michael Silver, former principals in the J.T. Howard Advertising Agency, had been selected to make a presentation for the multi-million dollar account for the Atlantic States Bankcard Corporation, which was introducing Master Card throughout the nation.

The new agency would be called McKinney and Silver. Within hours after the story appeared, Silver called me and related the following:

Louis (Snow) Holding, president of First Citizens Bank, who had played a major role in the Dan Moore campaign for governor and who had reneged on his promise to give the Howard Agency the First Citizens account if Moore won, had delivered a far more valuable gift – the opportunity to acquire the Master Card account.

Although Silver had left the Howard Agency, Holding was agreeable to Silver making a presentation for the account if he could put together an organization capable of handling it. Silver assured him he could.

Although Silver and McKinney had not spoken since the Howard Agency implosion, Silver called McKinney at his home, told him of the offer, and the two former adversaries quickly mended fences and formed the agency. Silver wanted me to join the new agency as a third partner, a move I was not really prepared to make without further consideration.

Silver's call was soon followed by a call from McKinney who reiterated that he wanted me to become a part of the agency. During the next several days, we continued the discussions. Considering the animosity that existed between McKinney and Silver and the stresses that were sure to accompany the new account, I decided to decline their offers.

The McKinney and Silver agency won the Master Card account, a predictable event given Holding's major role in the decision, and over the next weeks and months was successful in moving most of the Howard Agency clients to the new operation. Howard was left with the Occidental Life Insurance Company and Southern National Bank.

Within a few days, art director John Gilbert, production manager Minnie Lee Wellman and copywriter Jan Karon left the Howard Agency for McKinney & Silver. Howard called me and asked me to prepare ad copy for the two accounts that remained with him. Virtually alone in the suite of offices once occupied by a full staff, Howard appeared lonely and somewhat pathetic. I felt an obligation to help him during this troubling period.

McKinney and Silver rented an impressive suite of offices in the upper floors of what was then one of the better business addresses in downtown Raleigh. With the Master Card account and most of the Howard Agency accounts, the new agency was off to a splendid start. A full staff – that, interestingly, did not include Harry Jacobs – was recruited. The new agency sent news releases to the local press and to the national trade press, announcing that it was the fastest growing agency in North Carolina.

In a stream of news articles over the next several years, McKinney & Silver was consistently identified as North Carolina's largest and fastest growing agency. Whether that was true remains uncertain. Reporters never challenged the statement although Silver once told me that the agency inflated its billings in news releases – "just like every other agency does," he said. What was certainly true is that McKinney & Silver flourished, acquiring the North Carolina State advertising account as well as several national accounts, winning advertising awards and in virtually every way fulfilling McKinney's dreams of success.

Although my contact with McKinney was infrequent over the coming years, Silver and I talked often by phone and frequently ran into each other during the course of daily activities.

Silver was pleased with the rapid growth of McKinney & Silver, but unhappy with his personal situation at the agency. McKinney had been named president and CEO, and thus was the more dominant figure at the agency. Silver sought to discharge his responsibilities without incurring McKinney's wrath. Until his death from cancer, Silver never received a fair share of public recognition for his contributions to the formation and success of the agency. All of the media attention was focused on McKinney. Today, the name, Silver, has been dropped from the agency, and it is known merely as the McKinney Agency.

Silver often told me he would have much preferred a different arrangement, but that he was locked into the partnership. As McKinney & Silver grew, the agency took on a third partner, Howard Rockett, a talented advertising man who specialized in the effective positioning and branding of companies and organizations.

After a few years with the agency, Rockett retired early to play golf, only to return a few years later to establish a new agency that sought to compete with McKinney and Silver. Rockett's new agency flourished for several years, only to fall victim to a sharp decline in advertising during one of the nation's periodic recessions. Unable to emerge from bankruptcy, Rockett's agency was liquidated.

McKinney & Silver experienced down cycles as the advertising industry waxed and waned, but it always persevered. At one point it lost several important accounts, including an airline, the state of North Carolina tourism account and others over the period of just a few days. However, it hung on and managed to recover by acquiring a stable of new accounts.

News stories about the agency never disclosed the way the McKinney & Silver Agency got its start, never asked how two unemployed ad men who did not like each other were able to win an account that was sought by some of the nation's most successful agencies. Had Silver remained at the Howard Agency, it would have been the Howard Agency that had the competitive edge in the competition for the account, and advertising history in North Carolina and the South might have been quite different.

Media people wondered what Howard would do – whether he would seek to rebuild his agency or retire. He chose the former, hiring Howard Merrill, staffing up with copywriters and art directors, and in a relatively short period, his agency was on solid footing. Later, Howard transferred controlling interest in the firm to Merrill, and the agency was renamed Howard Merrill and Partners. The firm remains in business and apparently is quite successful.

Moving On

Following the Scott inauguration, Ralph Howland resigned as Commissioner of the N.C. Division of Motor Vehicles and joined the firm, now known as Grady Jefferys and Associates, and in a relatively brief period the agency acquired an impressive array of clients that included Ringling Brothers, Barnum and Bailey Circus, Independent Insurance Agents of North Carolina, The Governor's Highway Safety Program, the North Carolina Rate Administrative Office, the North Carolina Soft Drink Association, Dillon Supply Company, Continental Trailways, the Self-Service Gasoline Dealers Association, the Roanoke Island Historical Society, the North Carolina State Bar and N.C. Bar Association which operated a public information division known the Lawyers of North Carolina, the University of North Carolina Highway Safety Research Center, the United Way of Wake County, the North Carolina Association, Long Term Care Facilities and a Wilmington real estate cooperative.

Many of those firms and organizations remained clients for many years, some for decades. Their communications needs and opportunities resulted in a continuous, diverse and interesting volume of work that included publishing, film production, public relations consultation, advertising and marketing.

One of my more enjoyable assignments was the production of movies—films of 20 to 60 minutes in length that explained public issues, technical procedures or promoted various travel destinations. In 1969 and again in 1982, our firm was selected to produce films promoting travel to North Carolina. Our 1969 production entitled *The Goodliest Land* and our 1982 production entitled, *North Carolina: A Special Kind of Splendor* were huge successes in attracting tourists to

North Carolina and were significant creative and technical achievements for our firm. Together the two films reached audiences totaling more than 100 million people, and both were recipients of national awards. *The Goodliest Land* was the recipient of a Bronze Medal in the New York Film Festival, and *A Special Kind of Splendor* was the winner of a Cine Golden Eagle Award, the nation's highest award for non-theatrical films.

As the only full service public relations firm in Raleigh that also provided film production, custom publishing and advertising services, we enjoyed a long period in which we had little, if any, competition.

In 1980, my youngest son, Shayne, joined the firm as a producer/director and by the turn of the century, our firm had produced several hundred films, television programs and video productions and an uncounted number of television commercials. With the introduction of affordable video cameras and digital editing, the competitive climate changed dramatically over the years.

Starting A New Magazine

The first time I saw an issue of a publication entitled *Atlanta,* I was intrigued by the concept of a slick magazine devoted to reflecting the better side of a city. In the mid-1960s, during my freelancing years, Jay Allen, a former employee of *The News & Observer* and other publications, and I had sought to begin a similar publication in Raleigh. The Raleigh Chamber of Commerce, unlike the Atlanta Chamber, was reluctant to provide the circulation support we needed. Moreover, neither Allen nor I at that time had the financial resources to launch the publication. However, I had never given up the hope that I would be able to start such a publication.

By 1969, Upton and I agreed that we could come up with the funding to launch the magazine – with or without the Chamber of Commerce's support. When we informed the Chamber of Commerce that we were going ahead with the publication, it surprised us by enthusiastically endorsing our project and pledging the support we needed in distributing the publication to members.

In the spring of 1969, we published the first edition of *Raleigh,* subhead, *Community Communications for The Capital City Area.* It was an immediate hit.

We recruited a number of contributors who were enthusiastic about the project, and the advertising community supported the magazine from the very first issue.

Unlike many publications that struggle financially during the first three years or so, *Raleigh Magazine* began as a profitable operation. The magazine took on some of the toughest unresolved issues in the community – slums that nestled close to downtown in an all black and blighted area known as Southside, the divisive issue of how to expand the Raleigh-Durham Airport, and for the Capital City, an insightful article about lobbying, by a professional lobbyist. The serious articles were balanced with articles about the city's entertainment scene and personal profiles.

Upton and I basked in the overwhelmingly favorable comments that were made about our new project, and we were determined to make subsequent issues even better.

With the flow of work in our office, the demands of the film projects I had taken on and the responsibilities of publishing *Raleigh Magazine*, we decided to take on an additional associate, Robert Jones, a North Carolina native who had recently worked for the Staunton, Virginia Historical Society.

Unknown to either Upton or me, the Raleigh Chamber of Commerce submitted the first year's editions of the magazine to the American Chamber of Commerce Executives (ACCE) as an entry in a national judging of chambers of commerce publications. In the competition with 300 city magazines from throughout the nation, *Raleigh Magazine* was declared "the most outstanding publication of its kind in the nation."

What should have been one of the most satisfying accomplishments of our new firm became a major point of contention. In the structure of our organization, Upton and I operated independently of each other. I acquired clients that were designated as clients of Grady Jefferys and Associates, an unincorporated business, and Upton did the same under the business name of Upton and Associates. We also had a few clients that were the joint clients of Jefferys-Upton. Under the terms of our arrangement, each of us could retain the other for work on our individual clients, and both of us could retain Jones for work on either joint or individual accounts.

I was satisfied with the arrangement, but Upton was not. He was not pleased that a majority of the new clients had been signed as Grady Jefferys and Associates' clients, and that this had produced an imbalance that was not in his favor. Our new associate, Jones, was not satisfied with the arrangement either. He had not been successful in bringing in new business, and although Upton had clients, he was not satisfied with the rate of his growth.

The issue was brought to a head by the national recognition accorded to our new publication and was resolved when Upton and Jones offered to buy my share of *Raleigh Magazine.* They said they planned to spend full time on the magazine.

Inasmuch as the publication had been profitable from the outset and in view of the national prestige it was enjoying, I was not inclined to sell my share of the magazine. After all, I had worked on the concept and its business plan far longer than anyone, and I felt a paternal interest in it. It also appeared to have the potential of growing and becoming a long-term and valuable asset.

Upton and I, through our respective attorneys, negotiated for several weeks before reaching a satisfactory resolution. The last offer from Upton and Jones was to extrapolate from the first year's income and profits to determine what the maximum profitability of the publication would be over a seven-year period. That became the purchase price.

I accepted the offer, which was substantial, and Upton and I dissolved Jefferys-Upton, and he and Robert Jones became the publishers of *Raleigh Magazine.* I was saddened when, after only three additional issues, the magazine ceased publication.

Its early success and sudden failure seemed to place a curse on the concept of a "city magazine" for Raleigh. Attempts by others to resurrect it over the years proved to be futile, although other publications for niche audiences have enjoyed success. For me, the downside of the buyout was, in addition to the loss of the magazine, a contract agreement that prohibited my beginning any publication that would directly compete with *Raleigh Magazine* for a period of five years.

The initial success of *Raleigh* magazine provided the incentive to launch a number of other publications over the years, a weekly newspaper, specialty publications and newsletters, but I was interested in more general interest publications, and I impatiently waited for the five-year period to expire.

Politics and More Politics

My involvement in the Dan Moore for Governor Campaign had been one of the factors that enabled Upton and me to acquire the Broughton for Governor Campaign. Inasmuch as the Broughton campaign was not successful, I wondered whether it would be a negative influence on my ability to work in future campaigns. I soon learned that the Broughton campaign was a favorable factor. Over the next four decades, I would participate at a professional level in 44 additional political campaigns -- for candidates for the U.S. Senate, Congress, the office of Lt. Governor, the State legislature, State Treasurer, State Superintendent of Public Instruction and candidates for Mayor and city and county councils, County Sheriff, Supreme Court justices and district judges.

In addition, we managed media for a dozen campaigns in support of United Way as well as for other fund raising efforts, North Carolina's implied consent law, tax issues, self-service gasoline laws, highway safety, drug abuse programs, municipal bond issues and changes in the State' system of choosing judges.

All of the campaigns were high intensity efforts with more victories than losses. All, however, were filled with suspense and dramatic highlights. In several of the campaigns unexpected controversy, conflict between candidate and consultant and bizarre behavior provide a perspective on politics and politicians that often was shielded from public view.

The 1970 Fourth District Congressional Race

As U.S. Fourth District Congressman Nick Galifianakis, his wife, Louise, my wife, Marie, and I walked into the studios of WRAL-TV; we were met by Jesse Helms, operations manager and *Viewpoint* commentator.

Helms had not supported Galifianakis, but was courteous and gracious, congratulating Galifianakis on his substantial victory earlier that evening over Republican Jack Hawke and telling Mrs. Galifianakis that he knew she must be proud of her husband. Mrs. Galifianakis viewed Helms guardedly. We had driven to the television station from the Sir Walter Hotel on that November evening so that Galifianakis could make a brief victory speech that would be shown on the late evening news.

WRAL-TV News Director Sam Beard was in the studio to interview Galifianakis, and as they were preparing for the taping of the interview, I remained nearby to provide any assistance that the Congressman might need. Helms, noting that Mrs. Galifianakis and my wife, Marie, were at loose ends, suggested that they accompany him to an upstairs viewing booth and watch the proceedings.

As the three went up the stairs, with Helms' arms about the shoulders of the two women, Mrs. Galifianakis said to Helms, "Jesse, why were you so against my husband in this campaign?"

Helms protested. "Ms. Louise, you know WRAL-TV doesn't take sides. We have to cover the news."

"Mrs. Galifianakis' response was loud and blunt. "Jesse Helms," she said, "You're just an old asshole and you've always been an asshole."

Helms took the insult in good humor. "You don't mean that, Ms. Louise," he said. "I know you don't mean that."

"Yes, I do," said Mrs. Galifianakis. "You know you're an asshole."

My wife, Marie, seemed to be having some difficulty. Later she told me she didn't know whether she was going to faint or "fall apart with the giggles."

Helms never lost his composure and certainly not his temper. Quite likely, it was the first and only time in his adult life that anyone had spoken to him in such a manner. Certainly it was the first time a U.S. Congressman's wife had spoken to him in such a coarse and blunt manner. However, Helms remained the courtly gentleman he always appeared to be in one-on-one situations and continued to chat and joke with the two women.

As we left the studio, Beard was finishing his chores for the late night show. Someone suggested that we go to a restaurant for hamburgers and coffee. I asked Beard if he would like to accompany us. He said he would, and the five of us drove to the Your House Restaurant, one of the few restaurants in Raleigh that stayed open late in 1970. As we approached the restaurant, Galifianakis turned to me and said, "I've got something I want to tell you. And it's very important.

"I am tired of having to spend so much time every two years in these really tough re-election campaigns," he said. "I have decided to run for the Senate."

All of us, including Galifianakis' wife were startled by the announcement. During the burgers and coffee, we discussed Galifianakis' decision at length, the pros and cons of challenging incumbent B. Everett Jordan in the Democratic Primary and the likely Republican candidate.

Beard and I informed Galifianakis of the rumors we had heard regarding Helms switching from the Democratic Party to Republican and running for the Senate.

"I hope he does," said Galifianakis. "I would rather run against Jesse Helms than anyone I can think of." A chill ran up and down my spine at the thought of a senate campaign between Galifianakis and Helms.

Galifianakis proposed that he put me on monthly retainer until the 1972 campaign period began, and I agreed. Over the coming weeks, I continued to hope for any candidate other than Helms. I feared that Galifianakis, spending most of his time in Washington, was unaware of the growing numbers of people, both Democrats and Republicans, who for a decade had found common ground with Jesse Helms.

Around countless television sets throughout a large section of North Carolina, entire families -- many lifelong Democrats -- gathered each evening in respectful silence as Jesse Helms expressed his daily "viewpoints" on the issues of the day. Even my father, a Franklin Roosevelt Democrat, never missed a Helms broadcast. The passions Helms engendered were remarkable. I also feared that Galifianakis did not fully grasp the kind of campaign that Helms might run and which, indeed, he did run in 1972.

Flashback: A Few Months Earlier

Jack Hawke, young Republican candidate from North Carolina Carolina's Fourth Congressional District, was obviously angry. Addressing a group of Raleigh newspaper and television reporters, he held up a large newspaper advertisement and accused his opponent, incumbent Nick Galifianakis of lying.

Hawke said the ad, which stated that he was a New Jersey native who had lived in North Carolina for only four years was untrue. Setting the record straight, Hawke said he had lived in the Teel Heel State a total of *six* years.

Watching the exchange on a television set, a group of Galifianakis supporters that included Russell Walker, Margaret Sugg, Marshall Lancaster and Barbara Fletcher, the granddaughter of A.J. Fletcher, burst into laughter. I had been trying to get the news media to question Hawke about the short time he had lived in North Carolina, but until now, it had not become an issue. In preparing a newspaper ad that we called a frank and honest comparison between the two candidates, I had deliberately misstated the length of time Hawke had lived in North Carolina.

Hawke had taken the bait and denounced the newspaper ad as untrue. In doing so, he called attention to the fact that he was not a native of the area and, indeed, had lived in the state for a very short period compared to most candidates who sought elective office in 1970. We quickly issued a statement from Galifianakis apologizing for the error. I took the blame.

Hawke's public complaint about the ad's misrepresentation of the length of time he had lived in North Carolina amplified the very point that I had sought to make -- that Jack Hawke was a modern day "carpet bagger" from New Jersey who had come south to run roughshod over southern folk.   The ad and the news conference altered the dynamics of the Fourth District Congressional campaign by placing media focus on the fitness of newcomer candidate Hawke for the office of U.S. Congressman and requiring him to be defensive for the remainder of the campaign. With Hawke on the defensive, Galifianakis had the opportunity to focus on the more positive contributions he had made in Congress.

In 1970, Galifianakis was in his second term in Congress, and as an incumbent, who prior to winning election to Congress, had served for a number of terms in the North Carolina Legislature, should have been looking forward to an easy re-election campaign.

A highly likeable attorney, Galifianakis was a second generation Greek American who was perceived by many North Carolina conservative Democrats as being too liberal for the district. Therefore, every Galifianakis campaign had been an uphill struggle. His name, which he jokingly told voters he could not spell until he was in the seventh grade, was an impediment among some voters. It was, however, his perceived liberal political views that many Democrats said they opposed.

Galifianakis was more moderate than liberal on most issues. As a representative from Durham, Galifianakis was dependent upon support from the black community to win elections. It was his support of issues that were favored by black voters that caused some white voters to view him as "too liberal," code words for being too sympathetic to black issues. Hawke had seized on voters perception of Galifianakis as a liberal with a foreign sounding name as his two major issues.

Despite the liberal label that his opponents tried to hang on him, Galifianakis was perceived to be a political "giant killer." In his first campaign for Congress, he ran as a candidate in the Fifth Congressional District against Smith Bagley of Winston-Salem, handsome, well-connected scion of the Reynolds tobacco fortune who had been considered a shoo in for the Democratic nomination and a rising star in the Democratic Party.

Outspent ten to one by his well-heeled opponent, Galifianakis stunned the political world by defeating Bagley with a significant margin of victory. In his next campaign, Congressional districts had been redrawn, and Galifianakis' district was now the Fourth District, the same district that had been represented for decades by the venerable Harold Cooley who had lost his seat to Jim Gardner, a young conservative who had given up his seat to run for Governor and had been defeated in the 1968 election by Robert Scott.

Galifianakis has faced light opposition in the Democratic primary, but he and his staff were concerned about his Republican opponent. Shortly after moving to North Carolina, Hawke had played a pivotal role in Gardner's successful upset of Cooley and now was seeking to succeed Gardner as the Fourth District Congressman.

A skillful politician who has remained active in North Carolina politics for decades, Hawke in 1970 was a young, aggressive and determined candidate. He had unleashed a fiery campaign in which he had successfully cast the campaign as a referendum on Galifianakis' perceived liberalism. Galifianakis had a grudging admiration for his young opponent. "If he wasn't a Republican trying to get my job, I might even want to hire him," said Galifianakis after engaging Hawke in a spirited debate at the North Hills Shopping Mall.

Among Galifianakis' staff was Marshall Lancaster, a former *N&O* colleague who had been a freelance writer for *The Raleigh Magazine* while I was part owner of the publication. Lancaster was young, but savvy about politics.

In the past, Galifianakis had been successful without the use of outside professional help. He counted on the strength of his personal campaigning to see him through. Lancaster was confident that the campaign against Hawke would be an entirely different kind of campaign in which the effective use of media would play a major role. He had seen how Gardner had used the media with both paid advertising and a schedule of almost daily news conferences to achieve high visibility for his campaign and a free forum for airing his views on issues of the time.

Lancaster suggested that I meet with Galifianakis and make a proposal to handle his campaign, much the way we had handled the Broughton campaign. I knew Galifianakis slightly and was aware of his skill as a campaigner, which had been noted in some news stories in the district. I agreed with Lancaster that the campaign with Jack Hawke would be tough and perhaps unlike any of his past campaigns. I also was aware of Hawke's campaign skills, and I did not take him lightly. His early campaign effort was resonating with the voters.

Galifianakis was good at connecting with voters, even those who initially were opposed to him. He could often walk into a room in which most of those present were opposed to him and leave with most of them supporting him. His was a rare gift.

However, Galifianakis was not effective in the rough and tumble of politics. He did not like to criticize his opponents and he was often unwilling to respond to political attacks from his opponents. He would frequently dismiss highly damaging attacks by saying he did not "want to dignify them by responding."

Those of us who had been involved in political campaigns as techniques evolved with improving technology had learned, sometimes the hard way, that a political attack made on television and in newspapers that was not quickly and effectively answered was regarded as true by most voters. Modern campaigning had created an imperative for candidates to be quick and nimble, able and willing to monitor the opposition and respond to its actions vigorously and forcefully.

Galifianakis also had an ambivalent attitude toward television advertising. In the past, black and white television had not been kind to his craggy face. He thought television created a negative impression of him and he was concerned about it.

In 1970, the "60s youth revolution" was still in full mode, and many candidates were concerned about the impact of the so-called "youth vote" in the 1970 election. Some political writers had predicted that the election would turn on the youth vote, but the more realistic studies of voting history indicated that young voters did far more talking than voting. In general their voting records paralleled their age groups. About twenty percent of 20-year-olds actually voted. The percentage of voters went up proportionally to age, with older voters outvoting younger ones by a wide margin. In virtually every election, it was the older generations that actually decided the outcome.

In 1970, Richard Nixon was in the second year of his first term of office, and there was concern about Republican gains in Congress. In our proposal to Galifianakis and his supporters, we proposed a three-pronged strategy that virtually ignored the youth vote and concentrated instead on appealing to older voters, with whom Galifianakis connected very well; an emphasis on the benefits that had come to the Fourth District as a result of Galifianakis' efforts in Congress, and his support for the burgeoning environment movement.

We crafted a campaign around the slogan, "Now, More Than Ever, We Need Nick In Congress." (The slogan was appropriated by the Nixon campaign in 1972) It included well-designed large space newspaper ads, dramatic outdoor billboards, and slick television commercials. The television commercials depicted Galifianakis in settings such as a country store, where he played checkers with senior citizens, at the Falls of Neuse where funds had recently been appropriated for the construction of Falls Lake; with Presbyterian Church members who were in the process of establishing Capitol Towers, a HUD-subsidized residential facility for the elderly; and with his wife and children in warm family interaction.

While television ads presented the softer and personal side of Galifianakis, newspaper ads challenged Hawke forcefully in ways the young republican had not anticipated. The multi-pronged approach caught the Hawke campaign off guard. It had been anticipating the kind of personal campaigning that had marked Galifianakis' previous campaigns.

Hawke's campaign was not prepared to mount the kind of advertising effort that Galifianakis was conducting. He resorted to daily charges made in news conferences and statements issued through the media. We were prepared for that kind of attack and responded quickly and forcefully. Howard Jones, the publisher of the Warrenton weekly newspaper, who had taken a temporary leave from the paper to work for Galifianakis, said the ferocity of the exchanges made him feel like he "was caught between two big cannons firing away at each other." Jones said the campaign was just too fierce for him. He returned to the quieter pace of Warren County and weekly newspaper publishing.

Galifianakis had initially been concerned about his ability to raise the money necessary for a high intensity media campaign. As the campaign got underway, however, the contributions to Galifianakis were quite adequate, and again the Hawke campaign was caught off guard in its belief that Galifianakis would not be able to easily raise campaign contributions.

A Mess of Pottage on
A Saturday Night

On a Saturday night, several days before the November election, I received a phone call from Mike Payne, a *News & Observer* reporter who later became a district judge. Payne was calling to inform me that Mel Broughton, a 1968 Democratic candidate for Governor and former chairman of the North Carolina Democratic Party, had issued a statement endorsing Republican Jack Hawke. He wanted to know if the Galifianakis campaign had a response.

Broughton and Hawke had timed the announcement well. Their statement would make the well-read Sunday edition. Late on a Saturday evening, they figured Galifianakis would be hard pressed to offer a strong rebuttal, especially since Broughton's defection to the Republican Party was a complete surprise.

I asked Payne how much time we had to respond. He told me what I already knew – the paper's first edition deadline was rapidly approaching. The best we could hope for was to get a response in the second and final editions, editions that would, however, cover the Fourth District.

My telephone calls to Galifianakis, Walker and Sugg were futile. Everyone was out, and it was long before the invention of cell phones. I figured that as a last resort, I could make a statement on Galifianakis' behalf, expressing disappointment at Broughton's defection. As I was contemplating the statement, I recalled that Gene Simmons, the chairman of the State Democratic Party, had been friends with the Broughton family, more specifically with Broughton's father, the former Democratic governor and senator. I was certain that a statement from a long time Democrat, current chairman of the party, and friend of the Broughton family would be more helpful to Galifianakis than a comment from me or anyone associated directly with the campaign.

I was unable to raise Simmons on the phone, but was able to reach Chuck Barbour, the Executive Secretary of the Democratic Party who worked closely with Simmons. I explained the problem to Barbour, who told me he had no idea where Simmons could be reached.

Barbour said he had seen Simmons earlier in the evening, leaving an event in Orange County. "I think he was asleep in the back of a friend's car at the time," said Barbour.

I asked Barbour if he thought he could reach Simmons and get him to make a response to the Broughton endorsement of Hawke. "He won't be able to make a statement," said Barbour. "You draft the statement you think is needed, and I will see if I can find him and get him to approve it."

I went to my typewriter and began to draft a statement. I tried to put myself in the frame of mind of a long time Democrat who was disappointed in the defection of a fellow democrat with whom he had historic ties.

My opening paragraph read, "Tonight, Mel Broughton traded his Democratic heritage for a mess of Republican pottage. His friends are disappointed and saddened, and his father, the former Democratic governor and senator must be spinning in his grave."

The statement went on for a few hundred words along that vein. When I completed the draft, I called Barbour, who said he had not been able to reach Simmons.

Barbour liked the statement. He authorized its release as a statement from the chairman of the Democratic Party.

In the next day's *News and Observer*, the Simmons response captured the headline and the lead, and Broughton's endorsement of Hawke was moved lower down in the story. All day, I kept expecting to hear from Simmons admonishing me for releasing a statement that he had never seen. He never called.

A few days later, I asked Barbour what Simmons's response to the statement had been. "Gene thought he had made a damn good statement," said Barbour, "but he said he couldn't remember how he had come up with that line about the 'mess of Republican pottage.'"

Unhappy with the impact the Broughton statement had made in the newspapers, the Hawke campaign purchased time for Broughton to tape a two-minute statement for airing in prime time on WRAL-TV, the dominant station in the Fourth District. Again, Hawke and his campaign advisors sought to catch Galifianakis off guard. We learned of the pending statement when Jesse Helms, then the station's director of news and public affairs and operations manager, called, saying he felt obligated by television's fairness doctrine to inform us. Helms' call was received at approximately 5 p.m., leaving the Galifianakis campaign less than four hours to come up with a response.

When we informed Galifianakis, he didn't seem to be troubled by the news. Instead, he gave us the private telephone number of Luther Hodges, the popular former "businessman governor" of the state who had served as Secretary of the U.S. Department of Commerce during the Kennedy administration.

"Governor Hodges is standing by to help in any way he can," said Galifianakis to everyone's surprise. The former governor answered our phone call promptly and immediately agreed to drive from his home in Chapel Hill to the WRAL-TV studios and tape a response to the Broughton endorsement of Hawke.

I asked Hodges if he wanted us to prepare a statement for him. "You can put some ideas on paper if you wish, and I'll look at them," he said. We quickly arranged for the purchase of a two-minute statement as well as the production costs for taping, rushed the payment to the station and arranged to meet Governor Hodges when he arrived.

Hodges greeted the station personnel cordially, sat down at a table in the studio, quickly read over the material we had drafted for him, made a number of changes, drafted several paragraphs with a big magic marker, and then laid the material aside. When the cameras were turned on he made, without looking at notes, what was unquestionably the most effective statement in behalf of Galifianakis that had been made during the entire campaign. Again, the Broughton endorsement has been eclipsed.

As the campaign made its way to conclusion, I became confident that Galifianakis would emerge victorious. Russell Walker and Galifianakis had concerns, mainly regarding Randolph County that was then in the Fourth District. The county traditionally voted overwhelmingly Republican, and although we conducted a strong advertising campaign in the county, we did not have reliable polling to indicate the outcome. All would be decided on Election Day.

On the evening of November 2 the Galifianakis election suite at the Sir Walter Hotel began to fill quickly – a good sign, indicating confidence among his supporters.

As the vote count began to be reported, Galifianakis surged ahead, establishing a comfortable lead that he sustained throughout the evening. As I encountered Galifianakis in the election suite, my first words were, "Nick, you're winning. You're way ahead."

"Are you sure?" he said. "Are you really sure?"

As we discussed the vote count, WRAL-TV announced that the Associated Press had called the election for Galifianakis. It was relatively early in the evening and there was no doubt regarding the outcome. Galifianakis had emerged victorious. Hawke had been soundly defeated.

As it turned out, the re-election of Nick Galifianakis was not the most significant outcome of the election. The trouncing of Jack Hawke damaged him profoundly as a potential candidate for high office in North Carolina. Although Hawke made another run for Congress in 1972, he was defeated by Ike Andrews and would never again be a candidate for office, but rather a crafty and formidable strategist for other Republican candidates.

Apparently, Galifianakis had decided well before the election that if he were the winner, he would seek the U.S. Senate seat. Thus, the 1970 victory proved to be the catalyst for his campaign for the U.S. Senate and the entrance of Jesse Helms as a candidate for political office. The political landscape was about to be altered in North Carolina and the nation.

1972: A Historic Election For North Carolina And The Nation

The 1972 general election in North Carolina was an event of historic proportions not only in the Tar Heel State, but also for the nation. For the first time in the 20th century, a Republican was elected Governor of the state, and the election placed in the U.S. Senate Jesse Helms who for the next 30 years wielded significant influence as the foremost voice of conservatism in that august deliberative body.

Helms' election gave birth to the National Congressional club, a fund-raising and influential arm of the Helms campaign organization that would play key roles in many future elections. Ronald Reagan credited Helms and the Congressional Club for keeping alive Reagan's presidential aspirations when they delivered North Carolina's primary vote for him at a crucial moment when many thought he was finished.

In the U.S. Senate, Helms quick mastery of that body's arcane rules of procedures could stall legislation, impede the appointment of federal officials, insert amendments in bills that if voted on would cause mischief in the reelection of fellow lawmakers and stall important legislation that he opposed. The former TV commentator quickly became the nemesis of both moderate Republicans and Democrats.

As he rose through the years to important positions as chairman of the Senate Agriculture Committee and later as Chairman of the Senate Foreign Relations Committee, Helms' influence shaped some of the nation's most important political debates as well as the nation's policy.

For example, the Helms-crafted proposal for the buyout of federal tobacco quotas throughout the flue-cured and burley tobacco-growing regions has altered forever the economic landscape in thousands of communities. As chairman of the Foreign Relations Committee, Helms occasionally worked cooperatively with the Clinton Administration's Secretary of State Madeleine Albright. Helms expressed admiration for Albright, but most often he disagreed with her position on foreign affairs. Although the two maintained cordial relations, Helms seldom supported Albright's position.

The Helms political ascendancy might well have been set in motion by that fateful decision of U.S. Congressman Nick Galifianakis to challenge incumbent Senator B. Everett Jordan, a traditional Democrat from Saxaphaw, N.C., who was appointed in 1958 to fill out the term of Kerr Scott who died in office. Jordan had served North Carolina reasonably well and was known mostly for his ability to gain federal benefits for his state.

In his memoirs, Helms said he considered Jordan, then a fellow Democrat, a good friend. He indicated that if Jordan had won the Democratic primary he might not have switched parties and entered the U.S. Senate race. Helms, however, had been a harsh critic of Jordan in his "Viewpoint" commentaries, accusing him of protecting former President Lyndon Johnson against accusations that Johnson had used his senate position to enrich himself. It is doubtful that Jordan, having endured Helm's criticism, considered Helms a friend. Helms transition from conservative Democrat to Republican was probably inevitable.

When Galifianakis announced his intention to challenge Jordan, he was most definitely an underdog. Although he was well known in the counties that had formed the fourth and fifth congressional districts, he was virtually unknown in the counties far removed from the Raleigh-Durham and Winston-Salem-Greensboro areas. Despite Helm's criticism, there was no compelling reason for voters to eject Jordan from his Senate seat. His strong advocacy for the construction of a reservoir that took farm land from a number of people in Chatham County had angered farmers who did not wish to lose their land and had prompted opposition from environmentalists who contended that the water from the Haw River would be so polluted it would be unfit for any worthwhile purpose.

When Galifianakis announced his candidacy, Jordan was 75 years old and suffering from cancer. By today's standards, Jordan's age would not have been a factor. His health, however, was of concern to those who were aware of his problem. Galifianakis' principal task was to convince Democratic voters that Jordan's age had caused him to become "out of touch" with the current and future needs of North Carolina and the nation. It also was important that voters become aware of his health problem. Everyone agreed, however, that these issues were too sensitive to be dealt with in a direct manner. They had to be addressed in a way that would not cause a backlash among older voters, a group that had provided crucial support to Galifianakis in his victory over Jack Hawke.

After wrestling with the problem for many hours, we decided on a media concept that said simply, "Galifianakis for the Senate. It's Our Future!" We spread that message in every county of the state through outdoor billboards that did double duty. The billboards introduced Galifianakis to voters who did not know him and subtly reminded everyone that Jordan, at 75, suffering from cancer, did not have a lengthy future. The message resonated, and Galifianakis began immediately to move up in the polls.

Always popular with the media, Galifianakis quickly won newspaper endorsement from many of the daily newspapers and was the beneficiary of almost universally favorable news coverage. The news media zeroed in on Jordan's age and health and Galifianakis was able to devote his advertising entirely to positive messages about the future direction of the country, including an end to the Vietnam war.

As the primary drew near, Galifianakis continued to gain ground. However, the presence of two little known candidates on the ballot, J.R. Brown and Eugene Grace, denied Galifianakis a clear victory and enabled Jordan to call for a runoff. In the second primary, Galifianakis extended his lead, and when the votes were counted, Galifianakis defeated Jordan by 55 percent to 44 percent, a lopsided, almost landslide, victory.

In the Democratic gubernatorial primary, Greensboro businessman Hargrove (Skipper) Bowles, the father of Erskine Bowles, who served as President Clinton's Chief of Staff, easily won the democratic primary defeating his two challengers, Lt. Governor H. Patrick Taylor and Wilbur Hobby, head of the statewide AFL-CIO organization. In the Republican primary, a quiet-spoken mountain lawyer and legislator named James Holshouser defeated Jim Gardner who was seeking the office of Governor for the second time.

Bowles won the Democratic primary with a massive media blitz orchestrated by Walter DeVries, who had played major roles in three successful campaigns of Michigan Republican Governor George Romney as well as in Romney's administration. DeVries held masters and doctorate degrees in political science and social psychology from Michigan State University. In addition to serving as a professor of political science at Michigan State, he was a Fellow of the Institute or Politics in the Kennedy School of Politics at Harvard University.

DeVries was just another academic until he and co-author V. Lance Terrance, wrote *The Ticket Splitter: A New Force In American Politics.* Jim Perry of *The Wall Street Journal* wrote that DeVries and Terrance "have brilliantly destroyed generations of conventional wisdom about how America votes and why they vote as they do. The *Ticket-Splitter* has opened new vistas in political research techniques and strategies."

Earlier, DeVries had established a political consulting firm, DeVries and Associates, offering public relations, polling and media production as well as campaign consulting, essentially the same menu of services provided by our firm. DeVries' book, with the national media attention it was receiving, was a major asset to him in attracting clients. In addition to claiming new and ultimate wisdom regarding voter behavior, DeVries represented himself as the ultimate pollster, who specialized in predicting the outcomes of elections through the use of videotaped focus groups, a rather new technique at the time.

Those of us who had been in the political trenches before and experienced firsthand the vagaries of voter choices regarded DeVries' thesis with interest, but cautious reservation, a decision that proved to be sound. Bowles, however, viewed DeVries as a political genius and, according to many who were involved in the campaign, slavishly followed DeVries' advice as the Michigan professor led him straight down the garden path to defeat in the general election.

Gearing Up For Helms: A Summer Of Discontent

Galifianakis' lopsided victory over Jordan lulled both him and his Washington staff into a false sense of confidence regarding the fall election. Early polls showing Galifianakis with a 20-point lead over Helms supported their belief that an easy and certain victory lay ahead.

Helms had easily won the Republican primary, defeating Jimmy Johnson and Bill Booe, hardly breaking a sweat in the process, although he said he was surprised when he won. Those of us who knew Helms well were worried from the outset. In Washington, Galifianakis and his staff could not appreciate the strong public support that Helms had received through his "Viewpoint" editorials that appeared on WRAL-TV as well as a statewide network of radio stations that were a part of WRAL radio's Tobacco Radio Network. Throughout North Carolina, Helms was far better known than he admitted.

In one day's mail, Helms received 15,000 letters from North Carolina citizens, urging him to run for the senate. The letters also contained $20,000 in small contributions.

I urged Russell Walker, Galifianakis' campaign manager and Margaret Sugg, his top congressional aide who handled many of the details of his candidacy, including fund raising, to allow us to conduct "opposition research" on Helms.

As a champion of banking interests in North Carolina that often were diametrically opposed to the interests of average citizens, as the owner of substandard housing in one of Raleigh's most decrepit slums, as an opponent of government programs such as the tobacco allotment or quota system that had enabled thousands of tobacco farmers to survive and prosper and with a record of opposition to most programs of value to the poor and elderly, Helms would have been vulnerable to the kind of attack ads that would come to dominate political advertising.

Galifianakis vetoed any type of negative advertising. He said that if Helms attacked him, he would simply dismiss the attacks as "not deserving of a response." Throughout most of the summer of 1972, Galifianakis led Helms in the polls by impressive margins, thus reinforcing the notion of an easy victory.

Meanwhile, Bowles continued to flood the airways with the same kind of advertising he had done in the primary. In 30-second commercials, Bowles would appear, surrounded by a group of "average citizens" and make an earnest statement, looking directly into the camera. The similarity and frequency of the commercials had begun to wear on the nerves of many people, including Bowles' supporters.

Associated Press writer Reece Hart wrote that the Bowles televisions ads reminded him of "syrup being poured over a barrel of sugar." The ads are just too sweet," said Hart.

Bowles' ads were just part of multiple problems that North Carolina Democrats would soon face. Posing potential future trouble was Bowles' refusal to seek the support of Taylor and the rather large Taylor faction. He arrogantly contended that he did not have to accommodate Taylor, but rather that Taylor should come to him.

The late Harlan Boyles, long-time State Treasurer, recalled that following the first primary, Lt. Governor Taylor had left over campaign funds amounting to well over $100,000. Taylor supporters met with representatives of the Bowles organization, prepared to turn over the unspent funds to Bowles. The only request the group made was that Taylor supporters, many of whom held positions in State government, would be treated as good solid Democrats and not subjected to dismissal or harassment because of their support for Taylor.

Bowles received the offer from Taylor with disdain, contending that he did not need the support of Taylor or his organization. The Taylor organization, angered by the Bowles' attitude, encountered a much friendlier reception when it approached Republican Holshouser, who gratefully accepted the funds and support of the Taylor organization. As the general election neared, the rift in the Democratic Party remained unmended.

In the gathering clouds that were to create the perfect storm for Tar Heel Democrats, the national Democratic Party nominated George McGovern of South Dakota, a far-left liberal who was totally out of step with North Carolina and mainstream America, to challenge incumbent Richard Nixon whose popularity had increased since his narrow victory over Hubert Humphrey.

Throughout the summer, Helms did little public campaigning and no advertising, providing further evidence that the campaign was going to be a walk in the park. Shortly after Labor Day, the Galifianakis campaign felt the first shock waves of the Helms' assault. It came in the form of a full-page newspaper advertisement that in excruciating detail began to dissect the Galifianakis record in the State legislature as well as in Congress. The ad appeared in all of the State's major newspapers. The Helms campaign had adopted the slogan that said simply: Jesse Helms. *He's one of us.* The harsh implication of that slogan could not be denied inasmuch as it was directed against a first generation Greek-American. It appealed to the worst side of North Carolina voters.

Decades later, attorney Charles (Chuck) Neely, a Helms supporter and member of the Tom Ellis law firm chuckled as he recalled the slogan. "It was probably the most important phrase in the Helms campaign," he said.

In his memoirs, Helms presented the campaign in an entirely different manner. "We ran on the issues and where we stood," he wrote. "We certainly never wasted our resources on the kinds of attacks some people have suggested, including the false charge that we made our opponent's proud heritage an issue."

In the weeks following that first ad, the Helms organization unleashed wave after wave of newspaper ads critical of virtually every aspect of Congressman Galifianakis and carefully setting forth Helms' positions on issues sure to resonate with conservative Tar Heel voters. Carter Wrenn, a key figure in the campaign, once referred to that kind of campaign advertising as "spreading grain on the ground for the goats."

While the Helms' newspaper ads were pounding on Galifianakis, the Helms' television ads presented an entirely different view--images of Helms at tobacco markets, at "down east" social and church events and with small businessmen. The Helms' ad campaign presented the dual sides of a man who was considered a southern gentleman, courteous and helpful, but who was unrelentingly merciless in engagements with political adversaries.

To the dismay of those who saw what was happening, Galifianakis refused to punch back. At times, it seemed he did not even attempt to deflect the blows the Helms' campaign was delivering.

When the Galifianakis campaign became active after Labor Day, much of his congressional staff came to Raleigh to work in the campaign. Accompanying them was a young man named Lance Brisson, the only son of Frederick Brisson and the legendary movie and stage star Rosalind Russell.

Brisson had connected with the Galifianakis campaign as a result of his being named a Congressional Fellow. He had achieved that position by virtue of a rapidly rising career in journalism. He had worked for the *Los Angeles Times* and his freelance article on California political corruption had been published in *Look* magazine, one of the nation's most popular publications with a circulation of several million subscribers. Brisson's Hollywood connections and the recent publication of his article in one of the nation's most important mass journals had given him a kind of celebrity status that impressed the Galifianakis staff. He was inexperienced in politics and especially lacking in understanding of North Carolina political mores. Nevertheless, he was free with his advice to the Galifianakis campaign, and on most issues, he and I did not agree.

As I struggled to persuade Galifianakis to take a more aggressive position against the Helms onslaught, Brisson, working inside the Galifianakis campaign, offered advice that to me seemed counterproductive for Galifianakis. A good bit of tension existed between Brisson and me, but Galifianakis never seemed to be aware of it or even aware that conflicting strategies were being contested within the campaign.

As Helms' campaign surged, my advice to the Galifianakis campaign seemed to be more and more disregarded. At one point when the Helms' campaign advertising was attacking Galifianakis, I prepared a series of counter ads for publication in all of the major media markets in North Carolina. Campaign Chairman Walker approved of the ads and the expenditure, and the ads had already been sent to the papers when we were instructed to cancel them.

With no means of answering the Helms' onslaught, I became dispirited regarding the entire campaign, but we soldiered on doing the best we could for a candidate who deserved much better support than he was receiving.

As the campaign drew to a close, DeVries, the highly regarded consultant and pollster, issued glowing predictions regarding the campaign. The DeVries predictions were completely at odds with what we could easily perceive. Even Galifianakis' mother who, in the past, had correctly predicted Galifianakis' victories, and whom we had come to believe possessed psychic powers regarding the outcome of her son's campaigns, was unwilling to predict a victory.

"I have seen no sign," she told my wife, Marie. "We must pray."

On the evening of November 7, 1972, the old Sir Walter Hotel was filled with voters awaiting the outcome of the elections. Much of the attention was focused on the governor's race that, based on DeVries' polling, had led most Democrats to expect a Bowles' victory.

As the election returns came in, the outlook for both Bowles and Galifianakis looked uncertain. At an early hour, Helms surged into a lead, and Holshouser began to edge out Bowles. DeVries came out from his hotel room to talk to supporters. His confidence was still intact. He predicted that the vote would "see-saw" for a while before Bowles took a lead, based on the votes from eastern North Carolina. With Bowles a resident of Greensboro with business and family ties in the state's Piedmont, DeVries' prediction did not seem to make sense to many Democrats. As the night wore on, his theory of a vote surge from eastern precincts that would take Bowles to victory proved false.

Just before the vote count became conclusive in Holshouser's favor, Bowles made an announcement from his room over the hotel speaker system. "I'm going to win this election – even if it is just by one vote," he said, his voice filled with something much like panic. A few minutes later, it was all over for Bowles and Galifianakis. Both were defeated.

Galifianakis made a gracious concession statement, thanking his supporters for their efforts, and promising to remain active in politics. Unlike Bowles, Galifianakis did not experience disappointment that some might have. He had not expected to win.

Bowles returned to his business interests, and Galifianakis returned to the practice of law, a bit of lobbying and teaching. Republican Holshouser prepared to become the first Republican Governor of North Carolina in the 20th Century, and Helms prepared for the 30-year tenure he would enjoy as "Senator No" and "Mr. Conservative" in the U.S. Senate. His political organization, the National Congressional Club, would become a campaign powerhouse that would introduce some of the most toxic campaign techniques of modern times, techniques that eventually spread across the nation and which continue to poison the political atmosphere.

Young Democrat Jim Hunt, running for Lt. Governor, was victorious. Thus the 1972 campaign, with the election of the first Republican Governor and Senator in the 20th century, changed the political landscape in North Carolina and set the stage for what would become two of the most successful political careers in North Carolina – Democrat Jim Hunt and Republican Jesse Helms.

The election also cast doubt on the DeVries theory of the ticket splitter being the key to future elections. DeVries, however, continued to believe fervently in his theory.

A dozen years later, in 1984, Hunt and Helms would wage political war with each other in an epic political battle for Helms' senate seat in which Hunt would suffer his first and only political defeat.

For me, the 1972 election, as important as it was for North Carolina and the nation, was just one of many adventures in decades of dealing with political issues and political candidates. There were many more campaigns, generating more stories that I never promised not to tell.

An Ugly Episode in
A Deal Gone Bad

As I shoved the head and shoulders of the short fat man out the sixth floor window of the Sir Walter Hotel, my associate Jay Allen urged restraint.

"Don't do it, Grady!" he exclaimed. "It's not worth it."

I ignored Allen's words of caution. Much younger and much bigger than the short fat man, I had easily muscled him from behind his desk to the nearby open window. Tightening my grip on his neck, I said, "You see that street down there. I want a certified check for $60,000 TODAY or I'm going to splatter your fat ass all over the sidewalk, and Jay and I will swear that we saw you in the window and tried to keep you from jumping."

It was a raw and brutal moment, reflecting the full extent of the anger and frustration that a political campaign can generate and the poisonous relationships that can develop between candidates and consultants. My brutish behavior would have made a Mafia loan shark enforcer proud, but it was necessary. There is nothing more vaporous than a political "campaign committee" after the candidate has lost. Attempting to collect a debt from a politician is most often an exercise in futility. The cases can drag on indefinitely while the person seeking payment receives nothing, and, indeed, incurs additional legal expenses as he seeks to collect a just debt. I had neither the time nor the inclination to pursue the debt through Byzantine-like legal channels. I decided on a more direct way.

Certainly I had no intention of throwing anyone out of a sixth floor window, but I did not want the object of my anger, State Representative Allen Barbee of Spring Hope, North Carolina, to know that I would not carry out my threat. Barbee was a candidate for the office of

Lt. Governor, running in the 1972 democratic primary campaign against fellow Democrat Jim Hunt.   He had been my client since the late autumn of 1971.   After approving a statewide television advertising campaign, Barbee had deliberately given me a bad check in the amount of $60,000, not an insignificant sum in 1972. It was only after I had deposited Barbee's check, then, wrote checks on my office account to pay for the television campaign in advance, as required by television stations, that I learned that Barbee's bad check was a premeditated effort to avoid payment for the television time. By the time I was aware that Barbee's check had bounced, many of the television commercials had already been aired on the stations, and I was stuck with the $60,000 bill.

Barbee had initially denied that the check was bad. Then he contended that although he had approved the ads, he was not satisfied with them and did not think he should have to pay for the television time.   The bad check was the final straw in a relationship that had started off well, but had quickly gone bad.

In 1972, when Democrat Jim Hunt, then a young lawyer with political ambitions, but largely unknown throughout North Carolina, announced his candidacy for the Lt. Governor's office, I would have liked very much to handle his media campaign.   However, he had made other arrangements, and I was already deep into Congressman Nick Galifianakis' campaign for the U.S. Senate.   When State Representative Allen Barbee approached me, my associate Jay Allen and I decided that we could handle both campaigns, with Allen taking the lead in the Barbee campaign and I taking the lead in the Galifianakis campaign.

Barbee seemed like a solid, decent man. He had been referred to our firm by my former boss and good friend, Woodrow Price, the managing editor of *The News and Observer.* A successful businessman in Spring Hope, North Carolina, Barbee was a "big fish in a small pond." His major business was supplying high school and college class rings and caps and gowns for graduates. He, his wife and daughter lived in a handsome old two-story house near the center of the small eastern North Carolina town.

Although he had been successful in winning election to the North Carolina Legislature, Barbee was intimated by the prospect of running a statewide campaign. He also was ignorant regarding the complexities and nuances of media advertising. In our initial meetings, He seemed quite willing to place himself in our hands. Supporting his candidacy was a small group of friends from Spring Hope, Nashville and Rocky Mount. Among them was former U.S. Congressman Tim Valentine of Nashville, who had been a key figure in the Dan Moore campaign for Governor. This "brain trust" was also responsible for raising campaign contributions.

The autumn of 1971 was too early to begin a media campaign, so our early efforts were mostly aimed at helping Barbee acquire an office staff and obtain as much publicity as possible without purchasing advertising. For his campaign coordinator, we recommended Jim Perry, an affable and competent young man who had gained some valuable experience in the Broughton campaign. Perry was eager to take on the responsibility of coordinating a statewide campaign. We began preparing 'position papers' from which we developed statements and speeches, and it was then that we learned that Barbee was not a spellbinding speaker. We worked with him diligently with very little success.

Most of the media attention in the Democratic primary campaign for Lt. Governor was devoted to the fast rising Jim Hunt. Early on, the major newspapers dismissed Barbee as not a credible candidate. He found it tough slogging as he went about the state seeking to generate support. By early December, he was panicky.

With the attention of most people focused on Christmas and the holidays, we felt there was little reason to hope that the situation would change without a major effort. We recommended to Barbee an expenditure on television sufficient to purchase a highly visible schedule of commercials in which he would appear, announce simply that he was a candidate for Lt. Governor, but that political advertising was not appropriate during the Christmas season, and he merely wanted to wish everyone a Merry Christmas and Happy New Year.

The unusual campaign had a startling effect. Barbee's popularity rose immediately. The campaign attracted news coverage and favorable editorial comments in the very papers that earlier had dismissed his candidacy. In Rocky Mount, the Barbee supporters began to organize a massive hometown kickoff rally for Barbee at the landmark Parker's Barbecue restaurant. One of the goals of the rally, scheduled for mid-January, was to raise $25,000, which would be presented to the candidate following the formal announcement of his candidacy.

In preparation for the big event, I wrote what I thought would be an appropriate speech to launch his campaign, stressing Barbee's legislative experience, his eastern North Carolina roots and his desire to be a positive force in assuring the passage of laws beneficial to all of North Carolina.

All the major media were alerted, and I was pleasantly surprised when the *N&O's* chief political reporter, Roy Parker, Jr., called and asked if he could ride with me to the rally. Parker's willingness to personally cover the rally indicated his paper's renewed interest in a candidate it had previously discounted.

Several people had reviewed Barbee's speech and had given it thumbs up approval. Barbee was given a copy about a week in advance of the rally so that he could become very comfortable with it. He had suggested no changes.

My wife, Marie, my associate Jay Allen, reporter Roy Parker and I arrived at the restaurant a bit early for the rally, but a crowd already was gathering. By the time of the rally, the big restaurant was packed. We joined the small group of men who comprised the Barbee core supporters. Barbee was not in sight, so I immediately asked, "Where is the candidate?" I wanted to see him, wish him well and attend to any final details regarding his speech. No one in the group answered. Finally, one of them informed me that Barbee was in a private room "getting ready for his speech." Clearly, there was some concern among the Barbee inner circle.

After a few minutes of awkward silence, Barbee's finance chairman asked me to accompany him to the private room where Barbee was preparing for his announcement.

Meanwhile dinner was being served, music was playing and the head table was filling up. A warm, festive mood permeated the crowded restaurant.

In the private room where he was presumably preparing for the most important speech of his political career, the mood was anything but festive. Barbee was half dressed, clearly intoxicated and unwilling to make an appearance. Several people whom I did not know were encouraging him to drink coffee, eat barbecue and to get ready for his speech.

I asked Barbee if he had his speech, and he assured me that he did. I returned to the table to join my wife, Jay Allen and Roy Parker. At the head table, Tim Valentine had already begun his speech, an eloquent and rousing endorsement of Barbee. By the time he was finished, the roomful of Barbee supporters was ready to go out and beat the bushes for the candidate.

I wondered whether Barbee would appear, and if he did, what kind of impression he would make. I had come to wish that Roy Parker had declined the invitation to attend the rally.

Following Valentine's introduction, Barbee lurched from the private room, clutching a rolled up sheaf of papers, the speech I had prepared. I was glad to see he was fully dressed. Without acknowledging Valentine or the large crowd, Barbee went directly to the podium and began reading the first page of his speech, slurring most of his words.

An embarrassed quietus settled over the room. Barbee finished the first page and continued reading, but clearly something was wrong. The speech made no sense. After reading a few sentences, Barbee stopped and explained. "I got the pages mixed up," he said. "Let me start over." And he did, reading the first page again.

Before he finished the second reading of the first page, he throat dried to a crisp, and his words squeaked out of his mouth like fingernails rubbing across a blackboard. Barbee looked around for water and found none. Like a man stranded in the desert, he gasped, "water, I need water." No one near the head table offered assistance. My wife, unable to bear his distress looked frantically for a pitcher of water. No luck. She began to grab partially filled glasses from the tables and pouring the contents into a larger glass, she rushed to Barbee's aid. He was immensely grateful. The large crowd had grown restless. Some began to leave. Barbee's finance chairman, an executive with Planters Bank, looked at me and exclaimed, "The son of a bitch has let us down." He rose and left the room. I noticed that Parker, the N&O political reporter, was not taking notes. I was profoundly glad.

Barbee rambled on through the speech, and by the time he finished, the room had emptied. On the 50-mile ride back to Raleigh, none of us spoke of the event. We chatted about insignificant things, never mentioning the awful political debacle we had witnessed.

The next morning, *The News and Observer* carried a brief story, mentioning only that Barbee had appeared before a hometown crowd to announce his candidacy for Lt. Governor. Journalists do have compassion.

Later we learned that instead of the $25,000 the hometown folks were going to donate to Barbee, they presented him the bill for the restaurant tab.

Returning to his campaign office in the Sir Walter Hotel, Barbee was apologetic. He said he felt a "few drinks" would calm his nerves so that he could appear before the large crowd without appearing to be nervous. "I messed up," he said. "I took too many drinks."

In view of the bad start, we felt that an aggressive promotional campaign was needed to maintain the momentum that Barbee had achieved prior to the rally disaster. We also agreed that Barbee needed the services of Betty Cashman, the speech coach whom we had employed for other candidates. Barbee was enthusiastic about a trip to New York for speech coaching.

Over the next several days, we produced a series of television commercials for Barbee, presenting him as a folksy, but compassionate candidate who would work for the best interest of the average citizen. We contemplated an expenditure of roughly $10,000 in each of North Carolina's six media markets for a total television purchase of $60,000.

Barbee issued a check for the expenditure, and he and Jay Allen left for New York and a session of speech coaching with "the magic lady."

Near midnight, I received an urgent phone call from Jay Allen in New York. Barbee was in his hotel room, drinking heavily and demanding that Allen procure a prostitute for him from the 'ladies of the evening' strolling in the street below.

My response required no thought. "Don't do it," I told Allen. "No matter how insistent he becomes, just don't do it."

Allen told me later that he left the hotel, walked around the city for a while and when he returned, Barbee was asleep. Barbee never mentioned the incident. He completed his speech coaching, and he and Allen returned to Raleigh.

Shortly after he returned, I received a phone call from Barbee's campaign coordinator, Jim Perry, whom we had recommended for the job. Perry began the conversation hesitantly. "I don't know whether I should be telling you this," he said, "but I overheard Mr. Barbee saying that the check he gave you was no good, and that he did not plan to pay you for the television commercials."

Something in Perry's voice had alerted me, and I had turned on the recording device that was connected to my office phone. We continued the conversation and Perry reiterated that Barbee was planning to stick our firm with a $60,000 television bill.

In the next day's mail, I received the bank notice advising me of the insufficient funds in the Barbee campaign account. It was later that day that I confronted him in his office. Finding him alone, I decided on rather extreme measures, but they worked. Under threat of serious bodily harm, Barbee made some phone calls and arranged to have a cashier's check drawn on Planter's National Bank in Rocky Mount for $60,000.

My wife, Marie, drove to Rocky Mount the next morning and cashed the check.

Less than a week later, Barbee's attorney, Lee Smith, sent me a letter advising that Barbee was suing me for breach of contract. By that time, all of the television commercials had been run and, thankfully, paid for. Smith suggested that he and my attorney meet to discuss some type of resolution. I called my attorney and friend, Bill Hoke, and Smith. Hoke and I met in Smith's office. Unknown to Barbee, Smith and I were well acquainted. Both of us had been retained by the North Carolina Soft Drink Association. Smith provided legal advice, and I provided media and advertising counsel.

I suggested to Smith that before we went too far in our discussion we should listen to the tape I had brought to the meeting. I played the recording of Perry's conversation with me in which he disclosed that Barbee had planned to stick us with the $60,000 television bill.

"I think we are done here," said Smith. We shook hands, left the meeting and I concluded all my involvement with the Allen Barbee campaign. On the night of the Democratic primary election, the Sir Walter

Hotel was crowded as usual. Jim Hunt won the nomination handily. Fairly early in the evening, I saw Barbee, with a cardboard box of papers making his way through the crowd, apparently leaving early. He appeared to be intoxicated.

School Desegregation:
A Never-Ending Problem

In 2011, the Wake County School Board in Raleigh ignited a minor firestorm when a slate of four Republicans gained control over what had historically been a non-partisan body charged with setting policy for North Carolina's largest school district. The firestorm erupted when the dominant Republicans set out to change the school system's method of assigning students from one based on busing to achieve socio-economic diversity to one based on the concept of neighborhood schools. It was a continuation of the strife that had been a part of public education in Wake County for four decades.

Early in 1971, two rising young Raleigh businessmen, Bob Southerland and Ronnie Shavlick, came to our office somewhat embarrassed and unsure as to why they were there. Turns out they had been advised by someone at *The News and Observer* to seek us out for assistance in helping them manage a campaign to merge Wake County and Raleigh City schools into a unitary system.

Shavlick, was a former N.C. State University basketball star and owner of a growing office maintenance business, and Southerland, a bank vice-president. The two young businessmen had been recruited to head up what would become a highly contentious issue throughout Wake County. They had participated in a news conference to announce their appointment as managers of the campaign, and unfortunately for them, they had not been prepared for the strong emotions that the referendum would generate or the robust media attention they would attract. In short, they said their news conference had been an embarrassing mess. They had been advised to seek professional help.

In 1971, Wake County schools were almost all white, while the Raleigh city schools were becoming predominately black. Many white parents, confronted with the option of sending their children to a predominately black school or moving to the county had opted for moving.

Compounding the problem was Raleigh's refusal to consider a county request for merger a decade or so earlier when city schools were considered far superior to county schools because of the stronger funding base for the city schools.

City business leaders, fearing the white flight and the resulting deterioration of the city school system would be bad for business, were the principal promoters of the merger. They had selected Shavlick and Southerland, two up and coming young businessmen to head the campaign. Neither had political experience and neither was prepared for the intensity of the campaign they had agreed to head.

Both men, however, were intelligent, quick studies, and over the next several weeks, equipped with the tools they needed and instruction in how to use them, righted the campaign and acquitted themselves well as they led a strong effort to present persuasive cases to the public. No one however, had anticipated or fully appreciated the polarization that the merger of the two school systems would engender when opponents pointed out that the City of Raleigh's main goal in seeking merger was to send inner city black children to predominately white schools in the county.

Feelings ran high as the campaign came down to the wire. Despite the strong feelings on both sides, it appeared that the merger would be approved in a county-wide referendum. With the cooperation of WRAL-TV, a prime-time panel discussion of the merger issue was broadcast on the station a few days before the vote.

The chairman of the Wake County Board of

Commissioners was Waverly Akins of Fuquay-Varina, whom most people believed would be an effective advocate for the merger.

Akins had served ably on the County Board and as its chairman. He was considered to be a rising star in the Democratic Party, and no one believed in his future political stardom more than Akins, himself.

During the live television broadcast, however, Akins gave a short answer to a question that proved to be damaging to his political future and disastrous to the merger issue. When the moderator asked Akins if the merger would result in an increase in property taxes, Akins replied, "It certainly will." Supporters of the merger gasped in astonishment. The issue of tax increases had been carefully kept out of the debate during the tough campaign that mostly centered on racial issues.

In the referendum, the merger of Wake County and Raleigh City Schools failed by a mere handful of votes. Akins never seemed to understand that his short answer that might or might not have been an accurate statement had torpedoed the work of many people over several weeks. He never took responsibility for it, and never seemed to be bothered by the failure of the merger. Many wondered if he had purposefully dropped a stink bomb on the campaign to derail it at the last minute. We never found out for sure.

The merger of the two school systems never won public approval. A non-binding resolution to merge the two systems was rejected in 1973 by a three to one majority. In desperation, city officials appealed to the State Legislature and won legislative approval to merge the systems in 1976.

Many people were upset with Akins, and he acquired a reputation as being arrogant and vain. When he ran for the office of Lt. Governor, even his mother said she would not vote for her son "because he was just too vain." Akins was not elected.

Decades later, the Wake County School System won praise in national forums for its plan of using the income status of the families of students as a basis for determining which schools the children would attend. The term income status was a code word for minority students and many parents were unhappy with the system, its massive busing of students and the large number of minority students that were bussed to some of the schools outside the inner city. They expressed their displeasure by voting in a slate of candidates that promised a return to neighborhood schools, a promise that failed to materialize. Four decades after the first attempt to merge the two school systems the legacy of those early failed attempts to win public approval for the merger of the two systems continued to haunt Wake education leaders. Many schemes have been implemented to achieve the original goal of creating some kind of acceptable racial balance in the schools without causing the wholesale loss of support for public education from white parents. The struggle goes on without a satisfactory resolution.

Herbert Hyde's Old-Fashioned Campaign for Lt. Governor

State Representative Herbert Hyde looked at me as if I had called his mama a bad name. "No way in hell am I going to go around begging people for money to finance my political campaign. I never have, never will."

Hyde's response was to my question regarding how his fundraising was proceeding. At first, he seemed not to understand my question. I explained that most campaigns had to solicit funds to pay for media, travel and other expenses associated with a political campaign.

It was hard to believe that a veteran legislator, an accomplished lawyer and a long-time political activist did not understand the need for political fund-raising campaigns. However, Hyde's position seemed definite and inflexible. When I presented him cost figures on billboard advertising, printing costs, newspaper advertising and the biggest expense of all, television advertising, he dismissed my presentation. Instead, he told me bluntly that he had about $50,000 to spend. "When we spend that, we'll quit spending," he said.

When Hyde had called me to discuss handling his campaign for Lt. Governor in 1976, I was delighted. I had admired him for some time, finding his frequent comments on key issues to be not only thoughtful, but refreshingly candid.

Hyde, a Buncombe County lawyer, cast in the mold of the late Senator Sam Ervin, came across as folksy, plain spoken and funny. Educated at Western Carolina University, Hyde was a Root-Tilden Fellow at the New York University School of Law where he earned a J.D. degree. His folksy manner concealed a razor sharp intellect, a rapier wit and a gift for story telling similar to that of Will Rogers and Mark Twain.

The late Thad Stem, the winner of North Carolina's Gold Medal for Literary Excellence, wrote that "Herbert Hyde must be an anachronism. During a depressing era when many lawyers and legislators seem to be posed as commercials for golfing equipment, Herbert 'projecks' around churches, schoolhouses, reunions, shaded streets, tobacco warehouses, mountain coves and pumpkin patches."

In 1976, when virtually every candidate for state or national office frantically sought money for radio, television and other media, Hyde expected to run his campaign by continuing to "projeck" around churches, reunions, tobacco warehouses, etc.

Unless one is extremely wealthy, a personal expenditure of $50,000 seems quite significant, more so in 1976 than now. However, $50,000 was hardly enough to operate a campaign office for several months. Inasmuch as Hyde was definitely not going to seek contributions, he desperately needed a revenue stream to keep his campaign viable and make it competitive. His chief opponent was Jimmy Green, a hard-boiled traditional politician who had no reservations when it came to soliciting campaign contributions.

Earlier, Hyde had given me a collection of speeches he had made at various venues across the state. I had read some of them, finding them, thoughtful and interesting, extremely engaging, provocative and in many cases quite funny. In virtually every speech, there would be an amusing nugget that illuminated the human condition and the paradoxes of life.

Sometime prior to announcing that he would seek the Democratic nomination for Lt. Governor, Hyde had addressed the legislature from the floor of the House of Representative to make an impassioned and hilarious appeal to exempt Swain County from a bill that would make it a misdemeanor to use profanity on public streets. Hyde's eloquent defense of a person's right to "cuss" when suitably vexed demolished the bill and attracted national attention.

Back in my office, as I pondered ways of raising money for Hyde's campaign, it occurred to me that people might be willing to pay for a recording of Hyde's famous defense of cursing and that voters who supported him would be willing to purchase a collection of his "wit and wisdom" if carefully edited and published in a small book.

Hyde liked the idea and we proceeded to make inexpensive recordings of his "Defense of Cussing" speech, which radio station WPTF had conveniently recorded on high quality tape. I culled through Hyde's collection of speeches and statements, deleted extraneous material and wrote elongated editor's notes to set the stage for each speech. I titled the book *Genuine Hyde*, with a subhead that read *A Collection of the Wit and Wisdom On the Important Issues Confronting North Carolina by One of Today's Most Engaging Men of Letters and Politics*.

As Hyde traveled the state, 'projecking' at reunions, tobacco warehouses and other, more significant forums, he carried stacks of the recordings and the small paperback books. The two items produced a revenue stream sufficient to pay for all of his travel, food and motel expenses, leaving the $50,000 for more important expenditures.

Prior to making a media buy to increase public awareness of him, we needed to know just how well known Herbert Hyde was throughout North Carolina. Reluctantly, he agreed for us to conduct a statewide poll to determine the information we needed.

The results of the poll were startlingly disappointing. Except for Buncombe, Swain and a few other far-western counties, Hyde was virtually unknown to the voters of North Carolina.

When we presented the results of the poll to Hyde, he glanced at the summary, flipped through a few of the pages and tossed the document into the wastebasket. "I don't give a damn about polls," he said. "We'll find out how many people know us on the day after the election."

The casually dismissed poll had cost him slightly more than $6,000.

Most of Hyde's $50,000 budget was quickly exhausted by expenditures for outdoor billboard advertising, printed campaign materials and a modest statewide radio blitz. Hyde maintained a vigorous personal campaign schedule, amusing audiences throughout the state with speeches in which he proclaimed that he was "proud to be a politician, that the hell with the issues," he was "running on his personality." He delighted audiences with snappy one-liners in which he declared that he was "born in a log cabin that he built himself," that growing up in the depression he often had "breakfast in the persimmon tree down by the creek,' and that his oldest son should not be called "destructive, simply because at four years of age, he could tear up an anvil with his bare hands."

While other candidates for Lt. Governor sought to embellish the importance of the office, Hyde was brutally candid. "There really isn't much to the office of Lt. Governor," he said. "He has two duties under the constitution and one statutory duty. He is required to preside over the Senate. I've noticed that just about anybody can do that. He also sits as a member of the Board of Education. I've checked those folks out and found that just about anybody can do that. He is also a member of the Indian Commission. I haven't checked that, but I bet just about anybody can do that.

"Now, I'm running for the office of Lt. Governor of North Carolina, and I don't have much to recommend me." He said his chief qualification was that he was honest and a loyal Democrat and would work hard for the people.

Hyde's candid and engaging style on the significant issues of the day as well as his record of consistently defending freedom of the press earned him the editorial endorsement of virtually all of the state's newspapers.

In the Democratic primary, Hyde lost to Jimmy Green, who, with virtually no newspaper endorsements, won a lopsided victory.

How did Green win? With the support of the vast Democratic "machine" effective at that time, but in disarray in 2012.

The Campaigns for Sheriff:
Solid Citizens vs. Bloc Voters

Who would have ever thought that the two-word phrase, *solid citizens,* could ignite racial anger and tear at the fabric of a city that had taken pride in its moderate approach to racial matters?

In my role as media consultant, I had included the phrase in a post-election statement for Lester Kelly, a veteran Wake County Deputy Sheriff who was running against former professional football star, John Baker of the Detroit Lions. Kelly was white. Baker was black.

The campaign to elect the successor to long time Wake County Sheriff Robert Pleasants had been spirited and close. It was the first time since reconstruction days that a black candidate had so aggressively confronted a white candidate in Raleigh and Wake County, North Carolina.

Both men were Democrats, and the outcome of the Democratic Primary would, as usual, determine the next Sheriff. In 1978, Republicans had not won an election in Wake County since the turn of the 20th century.

Kelly had led Baker in a three-man race, but had not captured the required 51 percent of the vote. Baker had the option of calling for a run-off, and when interviewed by the media following the counting of the votes, he announced that, indeed, he would call for a run-off.

Black voters throughout Wake County had voted overwhelmingly for Baker, whose father had broken racial barriers when he became the first black police officer in Raleigh, the State Capital. In the election night interview, Baker was asked about what the media termed "bloc voting by black citizens." Baker said he was proud to have the bloc vote and was counting on receiving it again in the run-off election.

The media had descended on Kelly's campaign headquarters at the Brownstone Hotel on Hillsborough Street, and I was sequestered in a crowded cubbyhole of a room furiously writing a statement for Kelly. His supporters yelled suggestions at me to include in the statement. I had heard Baker's reference to his bloc of voters, and realizing that he was referring to black voters. I sought a counter argument that would balance the scales. "It's true," I wrote, "that John Baker can count on a bloc of voters, but I am confident that I can count on a bloc of 'solid citizens' to return to the polls in a runoff election." A half dozen people in the room, including Kelly, read the statement prior to Kelly's reading it to the media. No one saw any racial overtones in it. Up to that point, the issue of race had not been publicly mentioned.

The *Raleigh Times* reporter immediately seized on the phrase, solid citizens. "Are you implying that Baker's voters are not solid citizens?" he asked. *The News and Observer* reporter followed with similar questions. After denying that he intended any racial connotation, Kelly tried to concentrate on his goal of "creating a new standard of excellence in law enforcement."

In the warm hotel room, under the hot lights set up for television cameras, Kelly began to sweat. The reporters continued to press him. Unable to concentrate under the adverse conditions, Kelly began to simply say "no comment" to some of the questions. The reporters might or might not have known that Kelly was only weeks into his recovery from a serious heart attack, but they pressed on. Kelly's oldest son, seeing his father's distress, threatened to thrash the *Raleigh Times* reporter. He literally had to be restrained.

The next day's papers focused almost entirely on the solid citizen phrase and their belief that it implied a racial insult aimed at the black voters who had overwhelmingly voted for Baker. For the month-long second primary, the papers pounded on that theme, almost to the exclusion of anything else.

An analysis of the votes cast in the first primary for sheriff, showed that Kelly had won the support of most of the rural areas of Wake County, and white voters who lived in areas now defined as inside the beltline. Newcomers to Raleigh, those principally in Northern and Western suburbs, had given a majority of their votes to Baker, exacerbating tensions between "old Raleigh" white voters and the newcomers that continue to this day.

Without the constant negative news reporting and the unfavorable editorials, Kelly would have probably won the election. Among his main obstacles early on were his boss, long time Sheriff Robert Pleasants, a fixture in local law enforcement for some 20 years, and his health problem. Pleasants had been battered in the press for his administration of the local jail and his friendship with former Alabama Sheriff Jim Clark, who was a supporter of white citizen's councils.

Kelly, a Raleigh native, had spent his entire career with the Wake County Sheriff's Department. He had risen through the ranks, attended the FBI Academy and was well regarded throughout the community. He was a steady, decent man who understood the role of the sheriff's office better than virtually anyone and sincerely wanted to make it a more efficient and effective agency of county government.

As a political candidate, Kelly had a secret weapon – his wife, a gregarious redheaded nurse who, during many years at Rex Hospital, had assisted hundreds, perhaps thousands of new mothers through the joys of childbirth. In almost any gathering, the mention of her name resulted in stories of her consideration and kindness to those sick or giving birth.

Until Baker threw his hat into the ring, Kelly had a clear path to the position of sheriff, an office he had aspired to as Pleasants grew older and neared retirement.

Kelly was not entirely free of some problems, however. He was still smarting from media criticism of his handling of an incident in which, a resident of rural Wake County just outside the city began firing shots in his neighborhood from his home where he had barricaded himself. In a nearly week-long standoff, the resident was fatally wounded, and Kelly, who, as chief deputy, had been in charge of the operation, was blamed. A subsequent investigation cleared Kelly of any wrongdoing, but a cloud hung over his head, obviously troubling him greatly.

Although Sheriff Pleasants had fallen out of favor with the local press, he was popular with the people. Kelly expected a prompt endorsement from his former boss that would have solidified a broad base of support. Instead of giving his loyal deputy his blessing, Pleasants dithered for weeks, giving coy answers when asked whom he would support.

From the moment Baker announced his candidacy, the two local papers virtually anointed him, providing a steady stream of positive coverage and unrelenting negative news coverage of Kelly. Pleasants' unwillingness to provide an unequivocal endorsement and the continuing negative press coverage took a toll on Kelly. Although only in his early 40s, Kelly suffered a serious heart attack, severely limiting his campaign activity.

When he was released from the hospital, Kelly contacted our firm, and we agreed to handle his media campaign. Kelly and I were the same age, and growing up in the Raleigh area in the 1940s and 50s, we had much in common. Although we had not known each other as youths, we had many mutual friends and acquaintances and had similar experiences in the Capital City. Moreover, we liked each other immediately and enjoyed each other's company.

With friends throughout the law enforcement and legal community, Kelly had no trouble putting together a competent team of advisers and supporters who, understanding the limits that his health had placed on his personal campaigning, raised significant sums of money for an extensive media campaign.

Kelly's campaign office manager and staff were charged with graciously declining the numerous requests for Kelly to appear at public events, without disclosing his health problem. Kelly would often spend a good bit of time just "hanging out" at our office where we took care to shield him from the media as his damaged heart mended.

Sheriff Pleasants eventually endorsed Kelly, half-heartedly, almost as if he were unable to find positive things to say about his chief deputy who had served him so ably over the years.

Despite one of the most intense media campaigns ever mounted for sheriff, Kelly could not overcome the unrelenting power of the two dominant newspapers that were unalterably against his election and in favor of Baker. Becoming Wake County's first black sheriff, Baker made history in 1978 with his election. He served ably until he was defeated by Republican Donnie Harrison.

The papers wrote that they believed the election of a black sheriff would "send a message" that Raleigh and Wake County had transcended the politics of race and were truly an enlightened community.

Along with the Willis Smith, Frank Porter Graham campaign for the U.S. Senate, the Hunt-Helms campaign for the Senate and the Helms - Gant Campaign for the senate, the Wake County Sheriff campaign of 1978 ranks as one of the most bitter political campaigns of its times.

The coverage of and editorial commentary about the Wake Sheriff's campaign and candidate Lester Kelley as well as that of candidates for the Wake County Board of Commissioners and the State Senate exacerbated hard feelings many voters in Raleigh already had regarding both *The News & Observer* and *The Raleigh Times*. In the coming months those hard feelings festered and resulted in a movement by conservative Democrats to challenge

the news and editorial dominance of the two papers.
(More about that in a later chapter).

Taking A Hit For
The Attorney General

When Robert Morgan asked us to handle the media for his 1972 re-election as attorney general of North Carolina, it was like an early Christmas gift. As perhaps the most popular public official in the Tar Heel State at that time, his re-election was a virtual certainty.

"If Robert is not caught with a dead girl or a live boy in some embarrassing situation, extremely remote, of course, he has nothing to worry about," said one local political observer. A domestic problem of some consequence did, however, lie ahead for the popular attorney general, and it would involve me in ways that I never envisioned.

In his first term, Morgan had transformed a moribund office into an efficient, smoothly functioning operation that championed consumer issues and appeared to be a consistent protector of the citizenry. After only one full term, many people were clamoring for Morgan to run for Governor. Others believed he was destined for the U.S. Senate.

Morgan's re-election budget was not huge, but was quite adequate for what was certainly going to be an easy ride. Moreover, he had a solid record of achievement in North Carolina, not only as Attorney General, but as a veteran member of the North Carolina Legislature, where he had been a champion of East Carolina University and its desire to achieve university status and create a medical school, issues dear to the hearts of eastern North Carolinians.

The campaign slogan we developed for his re-election was a simple, but powerful, affirmation of Morgan's record in office: "Promises Made; Promises Kept." Morgan's opponent was not one to create concern. He was a college professor with an odd name, whom Morgan could dismiss by telling audiences that "he is a decent man, but you probably did not know that *he is an anthropologist."* Those who did not understand the term assumed the worst.

Along with campaign posters, newspaper ads and radio commercials, we prepared a campaign brochure that provided a brief biographical sketch of Morgan, a list of his achievements, and his agenda for the next term. – standard, non-controversial campaign materials. For the brochure, we wanted a series of family pictures, including, of course, Morgan's wife Katy.

We had taken pictures of Morgan, and when we asked him about setting up a photo sessions with his wife and children, he immediately told me had a picture of Mrs. Morgan that he thought was appropriate for the brochure. He reached into his desk and brought out a framed photo of his wife, a perfectly nice picture, but obviously one that probably was taken 25 years earlier.

"Are you sure your wife would want to use *that picture?"* I asked. "It looks a bit dated."

"It's her favorite picture – and my favorite, too," Morgan replied.

Reluctantly, I accepted the photo, and included it in the brochure we were designing.

A local printing company had offered Morgan a good price on printing campaign materials, and he had instructed us to deliver the materials for the brochure ready for printing to the firm.

A few days later, several thousand of the finished brochures, with the photo of Mrs. Morgan nicely displayed, were delivered to our office then located about three blocks down the street from Morgan's office and about five blocks away on the same street from his campaign headquarters, staffed largely by volunteers who took vacation from their regular jobs to work in his campaign.

Late on a Friday afternoon, Morgan called our office and said he was headed to a political dinner. He wanted to take with him a number of the newly published brochures to pass out at the dinner.

When he stopped by the office, he looked at the brochure, admired the layout, text and pictures and took a bundle of about 100 copies with him. Later that evening, I was somewhat surprised to receive a phone call from Morgan at home. Usually, cheerful, always cordial and considerate, he uncharacteristically began to chastise me for putting "that picture of my wife" in the brochure. I started to protest, but realized that Morgan was in trouble with his wife and was blaming me for what he had suggested and approved. I let him continue and when he finished, I quietly asked, "What do you want me to do with the brochures?"

He did not answer, immediately, but after hanging up the phone, he called me back and in a whisper said, "Take those brochures down to the campaign headquarters and tell them to begin mailing them out. I can't afford to reprint all of those brochures."

We delivered the brochures early Monday, and the campaign volunteers began mailing them to voters. On Monday, Morgan was in and out of his office, carrying out his duties and perhaps getting in a little campaigning at the same time. Unknown to him, Mrs. Morgan had decided to visit Raleigh for some shopping. Around lunchtime, she stopped in at her husband's office in the Justice Building, hoping to join him for lunch. Morgan was out of his office. One of the members of his staff suggested that he might be at his campaign office, a short distance away.

Mrs. Morgan went to the campaign office and discovered the volunteers busily mailing the brochures with the picture that she did not want included. She became upset.

Soon, I received a phone call from Morgan, chastising me even stronger for allowing the brochures to be mailed out. When he finished, I inquired, "Do you want me to pick up those that have not been mailed out?"

"No," he said. He added, however, that he wanted me to make things right with Mrs. Morgan.

I met her, apologized profusely, and asked her if she and the children would come to Raleigh again, and let us spend several hours in a photo session at scenic locations around the city. She agreed, but obviously remained angry with me.

My associate, Jay Allen, spent several hours with Mrs. Morgan and the Morgan children, acquiring a very nice set of photographs. We quickly redesigned the brochure, and delivered the print-ready materials to the printer in Fuquay. He quickly printed a couple of hundred copies of the brochure--enough for Mrs. Morgan to pass around.

Back at the Morgan campaign headquarters, the rest of the original brochures were quickly mailed and all signs of them were eliminated.

Mrs. Morgan never quite got over her peevishness with me. On election night, when her husband won an overwhelming majority of the vote, she barely acknowledged my presence.

Several years later, when my stepfather died, Mrs. Morgan attended the wake, mainly out of consideration for my stepsister who lived near her. She was still somewhat put out with me.

I have no way of knowing for sure, but I have long suspected that Mrs. Morgan's anger at me, for something her husband did, prevented Morgan from retaining my firm for his U. S. Senate campaign. He had virtually assured one of my associates, Ralph Howland, that if he ran for Governor or Senator, our firm would be retained. He ran for and was elected to the U.S. Senate in 1974. We were invited to make a proposal, but our firm was not selected. We never learned the reason.

I haven't seen Mrs. Morgan in several years. She might still be mad at me.

Keeping The Motor Vehicles Commissioner on Message

Almost immediately after taking office, Governor Dan Moore began an aggressive effort to enact the 10-point highway safety program that had been a cornerstone of his campaign. The 1965 General Assembly had enacted into law the Governor's recommendations, and the current need was to explain the new program to the motoring public.

To accomplish this, Moore appointed Ralph Howland, a former Associated Press bureau chief, as assistant commissioner in charge of safety promotion. Until then, the DMV had functioned with only one assistant commissioner, the long-tenured Joe Garrett. From 1953 until 1965, the position of Commissioner of Motor Vehicles was held by Edward Scheidt, a former FBI agent who set and demanded high standards of performance throughout the DMV. At that time the DMV included the State Highway Patrol.

However, eight months into the Moore administration, Scheidt abruptly resigned, leaving an opportunity for the Governor to fill a key post involved with an important part of his program for the state.

While the Governor pondered the appointment of a new commissioner of motor vehicles, he named Assistant Commissioner Joe Garrett as interim commissioner. Although a highly competent administrator who had kept the DMV running smoothly for years with a high morale among the employees, Garrett was not the promotion-minded executive that Moore wanted in the post.

The Governor thought he had found the right person in Pilston Godwin, a Gates county lawyer and former legislator with strong ties to the Democratic Party in eastern North Carolina.

Assistant Commissioner Howland asked me to become a consultant to the DMV to assist in promoting Governor Moore's safety program and help coordinate the publicity effort for the governor's newly formed Highway Safety Authority. My position was unusual, inasmuch as I had no specific office hours and reported to the Governor's Office. As I settled into my position, Charles Dunn, assistant to Governor Moore said that one of the things the Governor expected of me was to keep the Governor informed regarding activities at the DMV and to keep everybody on message. He wanted a coordinated approach in the public information program to avoid some of the controversy that had erupted in the past over such programs as auto inspections, driver licensing exams and mandatory liability insurance.

Many of the people with whom I interacted at the DMV viewed me with a wary eye. Motte Griffith, a former *Raleigh Times* reporter and the new director of the agency's public information office reportedly told friends that he "never knew whether I worked for him or he worked for me."

In the period following enactment of the safety program, Governor Moore accepted a number of invitations to speak on one of his favorite topics. On those occasions, he wanted to include new developments and refinements in the program that would achieve headline coverage in the daily papers.

Commissioner Godwin liked headlines, too. On several occasions, Godwin would make a speech just ahead of Governor Moore, stealing the headlines and relegating Moore's speech to lesser attention. The Governor passed the word that Godwin was not to make a speech about highway safety without first clearing it with the Governor's office regarding both the timing and the content. In addition, he instructed the Commissioner that he wanted me to write all highway safety speeches by all DMV officials.

My first meeting with Godwin for the purpose of writing a speech for him was tense. Godwin was at least two decades my senior, an experienced lawyer who had made countless speeches, often speaking extemporaneously. He was not happy with the restrictions that were being placed on him. And he was less than impressed with me.

He was cordial, but stern, explaining his preferences in speech making and stressing that he did not want it to be too flowery with words that the audience might not understand.

After clearing the speech with the Governor's office, I turned it over to Commissioner Godwin. He thanked me, but did not read it in my presence. About a week later I received a note from the Commissioner. It was brief. Please draft me another speech for and he named the group. He made no suggestions. Over the next two years, I wrote numerous speeches for Godwin. He never criticized any of them or offered suggestions.

After a couple of years in the office, however, Governor Moore appointed Godwin to a Superior Court judgeship, and named Assistant Commissioner Howland to the Commissioner's post.

On numerous occasions over the next years, I encountered Judge Godwin at State Bar and Bar Association events. He was always warmly cordial as we reminisced about our cooperative effort.

Missing Washington

Highway Patrol Sergeant Bill Huskins was determined to take a shower before he and I scurried to the Raleigh-Durham Airport for an early morning flight to Washington, D.C., for a meeting with a motion picture laboratory where the final editing and processing would be completed on a half-hour documentary film on Highway Safety.

We both needed showers. The two of us had worked throughout the night at the Division of Motor Vehicles Building on New Bern Avenue to complete what is known as "rough cut" of the film we were producing. Looking at my watch, I was certain that there was not enough time for me to drive home, shower, shave, change clothes and get to the airport in time to make the flight. Huskins, a world-class procrastinator, had, in my opinion, dithered too much and too long during the entire production period.

Completing the project was a high priority assignment for both of us from the office of Governor Dan Moore. Failure was not an option.

In running for governor in 1964, Moore had made traffic safety a cornerstone of his campaign. He had advocated the adoption of a 10-point plan to reduce the skyrocketing carnage on the state's streets and highways. At three years into his administration, his plan had been largely adopted by the Legislature and the Division of Motor Vehicles and had been successful in reducing deaths and injuries from motor vehicle crashes.

The state's news media had been reluctant to give the highway safety story great prominence. Governor Moore, as well as the many state troopers and others involved in the program, were frustrated. Charles Dunn, one of Governor Moore's top assistants at the time, had asked me to recommend a strategy for bringing public attention to the accomplishments and the need for continuing public support for all facets of the Governor's highway safety program.

I had recommended that a number of corporations that had a vested interest in highway safety be solicited for contributions to pay for the production of a half-hour documentary film as well as for its broadcast in "primetime" (evening hours) in every television market in the state. Dunn and Governor Moore liked the idea, and letters over the Governor's signature were dispatched to about a dozen corporations, all of which quickly responded with sufficient contributions to accomplish our goal.

Through his own initiative, Sgt. Huskins, a career state trooper, had carved out for himself what at that time was a unique position – official Highway Patrol Photographer. As a trooper stationed in Charlotte, Huskins, had developed an interest in photography, and a sincere desire to help reduce traffic crashes. Without public funding, he purchased a 16mm motion picture camera and when he was summoned to a wreck scene, he would film the carnage and after completing the on-scene investigation, rush the film to a nearby television station. The station would process and edit the film and from information provided by Huskins, include the footage in their newscasts.

With Charlotte getting extraordinary coverage of Highway Patrol efforts, Huskins' superiors recognized a good thing and assigned him to Raleigh and gave him the title of official patrol photographer. He spent much time filming and taking pictures of routine patrol activities, but his efforts paid off in increased awareness of the Patrol's efforts to reduce traffic deaths and injuries.

Early on, Huskins and I developed a good working relationship during the production of a training film for the patrol on police pursuit driving, and public information films on the introduction of chemical testing for driving under the influence, the use of radar, Vascar and other traffic control techniques.

Having never worked in media, Huskins, although very professional in his production techniques, had never appreciated the unrelenting deadline pressure of television.

When the decision was made to produce a documentary on highway safety and broadcast it on a statewide television network, I had purchased the "primetime" half hour time periods, and as a bonus, most of the stations had agreed to air the program in non-primetime hours. They did, however, require that the program be completed and provided to them well in advance of the broadcast dates so that their program department could review it for editorial and technical issues. I had promised that the programs would be delivered as requested.

What I perceived as Huskins' procrastination during all phases of the production had eliminated our margin of safety. Time was so short that any adversity could cause us to miss our deadlines.

Huskins resided at the time at the Beckana Apartments on Glenwood Avenue. When he insisted that he had to take a shower before leaving for the airport, we decided that I would rush home, freshen up and meet Huskins at his apartment an hour before our Eastern Airlines takeoff time.

I dashed home, washed my face, changed my shirt, kissed my children, and my wife drove me to Huskins' apartment. I arrived with a full hour left to drive to the airport. Huskins was not ready. While I paced the floor, looking frantically at my watch, he leisurely shaved and dressed in a newly pressed Patrol uniform. As we climbed into his patrol cruiser, I noticed that we had less than 15 minutes to get to the airport, park, pick up our boarding passes and take our seats. It was a near impossibility.

As Huskins wheeled the high-powered cruiser into the street, he turned on its siren and blue light and put "pedal to the metal" as the saying goes. Despite the high speed, the time ran out. As we were turning into the road leading to the airport, I said to Huskins, "We're too late. We missed the flight."

"Don't worry," he said, "I'll call the tower and tell them to hold the plane." Using his two-way patrol radio, Huskins quickly established radio contact with the Raleigh-Durham airport tower. "This is Highway Patrol Sergeant Bill Huskins," he said. "How about holding the Eastern flight to Washington? We are scheduled to be on that flight, and we're running a bit late."

"Look up to the northeastern sky," said the tower operator. "The plane is in the air."

"Can you call it back?" asked Huskins.

"I probably couldn't do that for the President of the United States," said the tower operator. "You will have to catch a later flight."

Catching a later flight that would get us to the nation's Capital in time to meet our appointment with the film lab proved to be impossible. No flights were leaving until late in the day.

As we tried to determine how we might get to Washington, Huskins mentioned that the Highway Patrol kept two planes at the Raleigh-Durham Airport. I immediately called DMV Commissioner Ralph Howland and explained our problem. I asked about the possibility of having the Patrol fly us to Washington.

"No problem," said Howland. "The two Patrol pilots hardly ever have much to do." A couple of phone calls later, and the two Highway Patrol pilots arrived to service one of the two small planes and ready it for the flight to Washington.

Both men appeared competent and confident. They seemed pleased to have the assignment.

Soon, Huskins and I were comfortably seated in the rear of the single-engine Piper airplane, the two pilots reviewed charts, and soon we were in the air. Instead of a flight time of slightly less than an hour, we were told we would be flying for about two hours. As the flight smoothed out and the engine droned on, both Huskins and I nodded off, with a reminder to land us at

Alexandria, Virginia, a few miles south of the Capital, where we would take a cab into downtown Washington.

Despite our late start, it looked like we would be able to make our appointment, complete the work and I would be able to return home on a late afternoon flight. Huskins planned to spend the night and assist with some of the technical work.

When we were awakened, we were not approaching the Alexandria airport. We were over an area of farms and woodlands. Both pilots had worried expressions on their faces.

"I thought we would have seen the Washington Monument by now," said one of them. "According to our flight plan we should have seen Washington some time ago."

"We must have picked up a headwind," said one.

The plane continued its flight for another 15 minutes. Still no sign of Washington or the Alexandria Airport. Another 10 minutes, and we still were over farms and woodland. No sign of any city at all.

The two pilots conferred with each other in hushed tones. Huskins and I could not hear what they were saying. Finally, one of them exclaimed, "Ah, there it is, the airport."

All of us were relieved. The co-pilot called the airport on the radio, requesting landing permission and a taxi into Washington. The airport person responded with puzzlement. "A taxi into Washington?"

"This is the Alexandria Airport, isn't it?" inquired the co-pilot.

"Why no," said the airport guy. "You are 75 miles north of Washington, in Maryland."

The two pilots said nothing. They looked at each other with worried expressions. The landing went smoothly. No other traffic was in the area. As our plane pulled up to stop, Huskins and I began to gather our materials and exit the plane. The pilot said sternly, "Hold on, guys. You're not leaving this plane until we get a promise."

"What kind of promise?" asked Huskins.

"You've got to promise that you will never tell anyone about this as long as we are working for the North Carolina Highway Patrol. We would never live down the embarrassment of missing Washington, D.C. You gotta promise."

Huskins and I gave our word. Neither trooper is employed by the Highway Patrol, but I still feel honor bound not to disclose their identity.

We had a long taxi ride into Washington, but we were able to complete the production and deliver the documentary films to the stations in time to meet the stations' broadcast schedules. The program was well received throughout the State.

Everyone Was Wrong
Except The Chairman

Rumors had been circulating around the halls of the legislature for several days regarding the scheduled committee hearing on the bill to repeal a special tax imposed on soft drinks and soft drink products.

The chairman of the House Finance Committee that was charged with considering the bill was Rep. Dwight Quinn, a veteran Democratic legislator from Cabarrus County. Quinn was known to be an opponent of the bill. Some legislators said they had heard him say that he was not going to let the bill out of the committee with a favorable report.

Quinn was not the only legislator opposed to the bill. The bill that established the soft drink tax had caused controversy when it was proposed by Governor Bob Scott and enacted by the 1969 session of the General Assembly as a part of a tax package that also included the first ever state tax on cigarettes in North Carolina. Since its enactment, the North Carolina Soft Drink Association, the trade group representing all of the soft drink bottlers in the Tar Heel State had worked diligently for its repeal.

In 1971, the Association retained our firm to plan and administer a public information program designed to persuade the public to voice its disapproval of the bill. The campaign, which included massive television and radio exposure as well as newspaper advertisements and displays at the major supermarkets and grocery stores had been expensive, but highly effective in mobilizing public support. Thousands of letters, cards, and phone calls had poured into the legislators' offices, overwhelming their office staffs. Many representatives were ready to "say uncle" and repeal the tax just to relieve themselves of the burdensome communications with voters.

Opposition to the bill had come from the North Carolina Association of Educators and, strangely, from the North Carolina AFL-CIO. Wilbur Hobby, head of the labor union had been vocal in his criticism of what he called the "slickly packaged, Madison Avenue campaign" to influence public opinion. In the face of the statewide media campaign in behalf of repeal, the teachers' and the labor union's opposition had been largely neutralized.

As the day of the hearing approached, Sam Whitehurst, the executive director of the Soft Drink Association and a former legislator, was cautiously optimistic. He had counted votes on the House Finance Committee and was reasonably sure the bill to repeal the tax would receive a favorable report. He had not counted on the intransigence of Committee Chairman Quinn.

In the North Carolina General Assembly's committee system, an unfavorable vote by the committee considering a bill has the effect of eliminating its consideration by the full house and senate. Thus, an unfavorable vote by the House Finance Committee would prevent repeal of the soft drink tax.

On controversial bills, where the outcome is not certain, the committee vote is filled with drama. Supporters and opponents and their lobbyists fill the room to observe the proceedings and to provide moral support to the legislators who are voting for their respective positions.

When the House Finance Committee convened to take up the Soft Drink repeal legislation, the committee room was packed. Every inch of wall space was filled with supporters and opponents. After some dithering and housekeeping chores, the committee took up the soft drink tax repeal bill. Supporters and opponents were given opportunities to speak for and against the bill, and then the vote was scheduled.

Although everyone expected the vote to be close, Chairman Quinn asked for a voice vote, of ayes and nays. When the voice votes were cast, Quinn ruled that the nays were in the majority, although virtually everyone thought otherwise. A legislator rose to request a show of hands, and Quinn agreed to a recount.

Virtually everyone, including the recording secretary, thought the repeal bill had received a favorable report, enabling it to be voted on by the full legislature. Quinn ruled that the bill had received an unfavorable report. Numerous legislators requested a third recount in which those in favor would stand and then those opposed would do likewise. Quinn rejected that request and ruled that the bill had received an unfavorable report.

One could feel the anger in room, but there was nothing that those who believed Quinn had deliberately miscounted the vote could do. As chairman of the committee, he had absolute authority, and as his actions proved, he was willing to exercise it to achieve his predetermined goals.

The Great Elephant Walk
And Other Circus Stories

On a quiet Saturday afternoon, Dave Mobbs, advance man for Ringling Brothers and Barnum and Bailey Circus, and I were considering ways of gaining some last minute publicity for the upcoming performances in Raleigh of "The Greatest Show On Earth."

In the previous weeks, newspapers and broadcast stations had been cooperative in publicizing the circus' Raleigh engagement. Nevertheless, Irvin Feld, the manager of the circus expected "a lot of ink" right up until the show's arrival.

Our firm had been one of the first agencies retained by Feld in 1970 when he took over the giant traveling extravaganza. As a former advance man for the show, he knew all the tricks of the publicity and promotion trade, and expected results.

Feld had purchased the Ringling Brothers Circus, and after reorganizing its marketing and performance schedule sold it to the giant Mattel Toy Company. After the sale, Feld continued to manage the show.

The Feld organizational marketing plan had been innovative and effective. Moving the show from the "big top" to indoor facilities had been a positive move. Feld hired a team of advance men, and each was assigned approximately six markets in which the circus would appear. Their job was to work with individual public relations and advertising agencies in each of their respective territories in purchasing advertising, obtaining publicity and making sure that everything was in order for the show to set up and begin performances with a minimum of problems.

The role of the agencies was to make things easy for the advance man. Agency duties were numerous, sometimes quite odd and could vary from year to year. The advance man usually arrived in a market three to four months prior to the actual show date. He expected office space to be available from which he would work during his regular visits. The months prior to the arrival of the show were busy, and the frenetic pace and numerous demands dominated the schedules of many small agencies that signed on with the show.

Among other chores, the agency was required to assist the advance man in gaining the cooperation of local authorities, organize special promotional deals with television and other media, recommend vendors for special needs such as food for performing animals, make arrangements with medical and dental personnel available to treat the performers, if needed, work with an advance clown who would put on shows at schools, and other public venues and meet with media representatives and promote the coming performances.

A key agency responsibility was to identify underprivileged groups of young people who would be eligible for free tickets to a special circus performance and to consider their requests for free tickets. My wife, Marie, was given this assignment for two reasons: 1. She actually wanted the chore, and 2. She was far better than anyone in the agency at dealing with the various groups that came with hands outstretched, seeking free passes.

Each year, Marie managed the distribution of some 5,000 free tickets to a performance staged specifically for underprivileged children. Early on, Marie discovered to her puzzlement that virtually everyone considered himself or herself an underprivileged child when there were free circus tickets to be had. Law enforcement officers, politicians, even members of the Governor's Office claimed entitlement to the free tickets.

A number of employees of non-profit agencies demanded tickets, even though they served adults and others who were not necessarily underprivileged. Over time, Marie, to her credit, developed a rigorous process for determining eligibility for the tickets. However, she remained a soft touch for a sad story.

Of all the tasks assigned to the agency, however, obtaining publicity for the big show in all available media was most important. It was this task that occupied Mobbs and me on that quiet Saturday afternoon a week prior to the scheduled performance in Raleigh.

The circus was currently playing a date in Columbia, South Carolina. It was scheduled to complete that date and travel to Raleigh for its next show. As Mobbs and I considered ways to focus attention on the upcoming performance, he casually mentioned that what we did "might not matter if the railroad strike occurs."

That was the first I had heard about a possible railroad strike. "How would a strike affect the circus?" I asked.

"Train couldn't run," said Mobbs. "Our trainmen are union. They wouldn't work. Even if they did, the switchers along the way would not be working. The train couldn't move. We would be stuck in Columbia."

"Could you use trucks?" I asked.

"We couldn't bring the elephants," said Mobbs. "They are not accustomed to traveling by truck. They would probably panic and cause trucks to wreck. The only safe way would be for the elephants to walk. We may have to consider that."

Mobbs' comment got the old neurons working and a news release immediately formed in my mind.

I turned to my typewriter and wrote the following:

Ringling Brothers and Barnum and Bailey Brothers Circus said Saturday it is considering walking the show's elephants from Columbia, South Carolina to Raleigh, North Carolina if a threatened strike by railway workers prevents the circus train from using the rails.

The release explained why the elephants could not be trucked into Raleigh and noted that "The Greatest Show on Earth" valued its longtime reputation for never having missed a performance.

Mobbs looked at the release; then looked at me. We both grinned, recognizing that the story would probably get good play in the local paper. "I'm going to hand deliver this for the Sunday paper," I said, "if you will stand behind it."

"Take it to the paper," said Mobbs. "We'll see what happens."

Neither of us expected what actually did happen. By the time I returned to my office the phones were going crazy. Newspapers from throughout the nation were calling for more details.

The city editor at *The News and Observer* apparently gave a copy of the news release to the Associated Press, which put a provocative new lead on it, and sent it out on its nationwide system.

The AP lead stated, "In the longest elephant walk since Hannibal crossed the Alps, Ringling Brothers and Barnum and Bailey Circus is making plans to march more than a dozen elephants from Columbia, S.C., to Raleigh, N.C., to avoid missing a show date. In New York, the AP writer thought the story was cute and sent it out worldwide. The AP story contained more details, but it was the lead that caught the attention of much of the world's press.

Throughout Saturday afternoon, Mobbs and I answered the phones, seeking to minimize the certainty of an animal walk. After all, we had no idea of the status of the railroad strike. The news media, however, called railway union officials who agreed that a strike was possible, and that fueled the flames of the story.

Late on Saturday we cut off the phones and left the office. The story was played on Saturday evening on most of the television stations in the state, and captured big headlines in the Sunday papers.

On Monday, when we arrived at the office and turned on the phones, they immediately began to ring. Many of the calls were from television stations and the major television networks. They wanted to know the best locations to set up cameras. Even the BBC called and wanted to film the walk.

In the midst of the bedlam, my secretary pointed at me with a concerned look.

"It's Mr. Feld, from Washington," she said quietly.

The conversation with Irvin Feld was brief and one-sided. "Jefferys," he said, "Tell Mobbs that if we walk those elephants from Columbia to Raleigh, he will have to lead them....and you will have to follow with a shovel." As I was hanging up the phone, I heard a chuckle in his voice as he said, "these damn phones are going crazy."

Feld knew a good publicity story when it fell in his lap, and he apparently was enjoying it.

By the next day, however, the railway union settled without a strike, but the story was already being published throughout the nation and in numerous foreign countries.

Feld and the circus management team apparently were pleased with the publicity stunt. Our firm continued to handle the circus promotion in the area for several more years, and each one had its odd and often memorable moments.

The Clown Show at
The Governor's Mansion

In mid-March, 1973, Republican James Holshouser had been Governor of North Carolina for only a few weeks, and was still basking in his recent historic victory over Democrat Hargrove Bowles.

The Holshouser family had settled into the Governor's Mansion just in time to celebrate their daughter Ginny's birthday with a gala party in the elegant old building with members of her Girl Scout troop attending. The Holshouser daughter's birthday coincided with the visit to the Triangle area of the Ringling Brothers and Barnum and Bailey advance clown whose responsibilities were to appear wherever an opportunity for media publicity might exist.

In the past, we had scheduled clown visits with former Governor Bob Scott in his office in the Capitol Building. Scott enjoyed the visits and loved to say that he couldn't tell the difference between the Ringling Brothers clown "and the clowns from the legislature who came to his office." The media generally gave the visit a good play.

With the Governor's young daughter having a birthday party, it seemed a perfect fit for the clown to visit the Mansion and entertain the children. I turned the task over to my wife Marie, who coordinated everything with Mrs. Betty Barber, the social secretary for the Mansion. The media welcomed the opportunity to visit the mansion for what was the first social event of the new administration. Among the media was a reporter from *The News and Observer*.

The party was a success. The clown was funny, and the children appreciated the opportunity of having a 'real circus clown' present. Ms. Barber and Marie established good rapport, and there were even brief discussions regarding Marie's joining Mrs. Holshouser's personal staff.

At some point during the festivities, Ginny Holshouser invited the *N&O* reporter for a short tour of the mansion, including the bedroom of Governor and Mrs. Holshouser. The unscheduled, unmonitored tour was discovered only after the fact, and Mrs. Barber and Mrs. Holshouser were aghast. They worried that the reporter had snooped into the drawers of the bedroom bureau, and would report on the kind of bras and other personal items worn by Mrs. Holshouser.

Mrs. Barber was especially upset, inasmuch as it was she who had coordinated the media, the clown and the birthday events. When she called our office, it was hard to determine whether she was fuming or weeping.

I gave her call to Marie, whose official duties at the firm, were to do anything that I did not want to do. In retrospect, I have to acknowledge that hers was often a difficult job, but never a thankless one.

Mrs. Barber was adamant: "I know how *The News and Observer* loves to embarrass Republicans," said Mrs. Barber. "Its story will be awful. You must kill that story," she said.

Mrs. Barber had no way of knowing it, but if Marie or I could have caused *The News and Observer* to "kill" a story it was planning to publish, our fees would be so enormous, we would only have to work a few days a year.

Frankly, having worked at the "old reliable" for several years and understanding reaction to such a request, I lacked the courage to even suggest what Mrs. Barber was demanding. Marie consulted with me a moment and then told Mrs. Barber she would do whatever she could.

I suggested that I call Editor Claude Sitton, with whom I had a cordial relationship, gradually work into the conversation information about the new administration, and then let Marie explain how upset Mrs. Barber and Mrs. Holshouser had become.

Sitton chuckled when he heard the details. He almost laughed out loud, when Marie told him that the Governor's people had demanded that we "kill the story."

"We are not going to run a story about Mrs. Holshouser's underwear," said Sitton. Then he added, "If you need to make some points with the Governor's Office, you can tell them that you have talked with the editor of the paper and you "killed that story."

Marie called Mrs. Barber, assured her that she had "killed the story" and that she would probably be pleased with the article in the morning paper.

A couple of days later Marie received the following from Mrs. Holshouser:

"Dear Marie:

"Thank you for all of your assistance in obtaining the tickets for Ginny, her Girl Scout Troop, Mrs. Barber and myself. We thoroughly enjoyed ourselves and had a wonderful 'fun' evening.

"Thank you also for the kindness you have shown us and for your understanding concerning the reporters.

Sincerely,"

Pat Holshouser.

Mrs. Holshouser's letter was followed the next day by a letter from Betty Barber who wrote:

"Dear Marie:

"How sweet of you to be so thoughtful. It is no wonder that your business is a success. Tell your husband he had better hold on tight to you, because you are the kind of person that makes any business a success.

"Also, thank you for being so understanding concerning the newspaper reporter. I admire the way you handled the situation.

"Looking forward to working with you in the future."

Sincerely,

Betty

Shortly after the two letters, communication between the new Republican Governor and our office fell silent. The Holshouser folks had discovered that we were Democrats who had been involved in numerous Democratic campaigns.

The next communication we had with a representative from the Holshouser administration was from Boyd Miller, who had recently been appointed Coordinator of the Governor's Highway Safety Program.

Miller visited our office as a preamble to canceling a media research program we were conducting for the Governor's Highway Safety Program and halting distribution of a new film recently produced to combat driving under the influence. The meeting was cordial, but tense.

In an interview with Ned Cline of the Greensboro News and Record, Miller said there was "nothing political about the cancellation of the research grant." However, he gave no reason for the cancellation. He did not seem the least bit concerned when he was told that aborting the project at the mid-point, rendered all of the work useless. No one else in the Republican administration sought to continue the project and it became dormant.

A Tuxedo, A Top Hat,
And The Ride of A Lifetime

In his daily N&O column, *Byways of The News* Charles Craven turned an unfortunate alcoholic into a popular figure known as "Little Man." Readers never knew his real name. He made a living by distributing posters of upcoming entertainment and political events throughout the city, and when work was slack he had a regular route of panhandling.

His panhandling route brought him by our office on a regular basis, and my wife Marie could never refuse his request for a dollar or two "to buy a sandwich." She and everyone else who knew him were aware that the money was going for strong fortified wine, his beverage of choice.

When he had handbills or posters to distribute, Little Man was reliable. He would stop drinking long enough to discharge his duties in a responsible manner. Therefore, when there were circus posters to be distributed, Little Man was THE MAN.

We had employed Little Man on a number of occasions to distribute political flyers and handbills as well as other materials, and he had performed that work for the Ringling Brothers and Barnum and Bailey Circus for many years.

Among our many duties for the circus was to arrange for prominent citizens to ride on the elephants during the annual "animal walk" from the rail siding to the Dorton Arena where the circus performed for many years prior to construction of the RBC Center. We generally managed to persuade radio and television reporters and anchors to ride the elephants, and because many of them did not enjoy the experience, we had to recruit new riders every year.

My regular request to *Raleigh Times* editor and now *News and Observer* columnist A.C. Snow became a kind of standing joke; we both knew Snow would never mount one of the huge animals, most of which stood nearly 10 feet tall.

I am not sure, but it was probably Marie's idea to honor Little Man for his years of bill posting for the circus by dressing him in a tuxedo and top hat and having him ride the lead elephant in the pending animal walk.

We were certain that Little Man's participation would yield numerous headlines, and we were pleased when he was thrilled to participate. The VIP Formal Wear store located not far from our offices in downtown Raleigh agreed to provide the clothes, including a starched white shirt.

Marie took Little Man to the barbershop for a fancy haircut and shave. Because no one knew where he lived, a shower was apparently out of the question.

The buildup to the Little Man ride gained much attention. Craven devoted a number of columns to it, and was present on the big day, as were other news media people. Little Man, in keeping with his work ethic, remained sober for the engagement.

Little Man's participation encouraged others to ride and the animal walk was a rousing success. The VIP Formal Wear owners were not so pleased, however, when we returned the tuxedo and top hat. They sniffed the garments briefly and decided that the proper place for them was in a furnace.

Some months later, Little Man fell ill, probably from years of alcoholism. His condition worsened, and he died, with no relatives and no means of obtaining a decent funeral or burial.

Marie, who on numerous occasions had befriended him, was distressed over the idea of a burial in potter's field and the lack of flowers. She called Ringling Brothers, Barnum and Bailey Circus, and the circus agreed to pay for a nice wreath for the casket.

Attendance at Little Man's funeral was sparse. It consisted of Charles Craven, Marie, and Verna Helms, an employee of our firm, and the workmen who dug the grave. Craven's column the next day provided a brief tribute to the sad little man who for one day was a "Big Man" with *The Greatest Show on Earth.*

Disasters Averted – Almost

Beginning in the 1920s and continuing through the decades, there probably is no other organization that improved the health, nutrition, hygiene and overall quality of life for rural Tar Heel families more than the Home Demonstration Clubs of North Carolina, which now operate under a different name.

Under the leadership of Jane McKimmon, the State's first Home Demonstration Agent, the organization worked tirelessly to establish home demonstration clubs in every county in North Carolina. The agents taught club members which foods were more nutritious and how to can and preserve them. They also provided valuable advice on assuring appropriate hygiene in homes that did not have bathrooms or indoor plumbing of any kind.

Although the Home Demonstration Clubs' work was aimed primarily at rural housewives, they developed valuable educational programs for both boys and girls growing up on countless North Carolina farms.

As a member of a farm family and a long-time reader of Dr. Clarence Poe's *Progressive Farmer* magazine, I was aware of the good work done by the clubs, and I was both pleased and proud when Dr. Eloise Cofer of N.C. State University, director of the statewide program, asked me to write and produce a multimedia presentation commemorating the organization's first 50 years in North Carolina.

The multi-media presentation was to be the centerpiece of a massive 50th anniversary gathering of members of Home Demonstration Clubs from throughout North Carolina at the Memorial Auditorium in Raleigh. The program was to include Governor Bob Scott, officials from the University and representatives of the respective clubs. An attendance of about 2,500 was anticipated.

Over a period of several weeks, I researched the history of the program, interviewed a number of people who had played key roles in its evolution, gathered hundreds of archival pictures, shots dozens of slides and hundreds of feet of 16mm film.

When I completed the script, the film was edited, slides and old photos were assembled, narration, music and sound effects recorded and the whole hour-long program was organized for review by Dr. Cofer and members of her staff.

The review team was pleased with our work, and we proceeded to schedule a series of rehearsals at the Memorial Auditorium. A multi-media presentation, which can present a story in a highly dramatic fashion, is a complicated procedure. Every element must be precisely synchronized or the entire presentation can be ruined. Much of the program is automated, but key parts must be manually operated, requiring both technical ability and artistic judgment. For that part of the presentation, I enlisted a long-time and trusted colleague, Jere Snyder, with whom I had worked on many motion picture productions.

Snyder was recovering from a broken ankle, which was still in a cast, but he had been able to participate in the editing of the film footage and the overall organization of the presentation. He also had experience in similar projects.

As we rehearsed the rather elaborate and complicated presentation at Memorial Auditorium, we worked with a couple of technical people who were associated with the auditorium. One of our first concerns was the sound system. We wanted to connect our recorded narration, music and sound effects to the auditorium's sound system so that everyone attending would be able to hear the program without distortion.

"No problem," said the auditorium technician. "We'll just 'patch' your sound material into the auditorium system. We've done it many times."

On the night before the big meeting, we conducted our final rehearsal, and were again assured by the technician that connecting our sound to the auditorium's system was as simple as ABC. We set up the projectors, with everything perfectly synchronized and locked everything in place, confident that the program would be presented with no problems.

Next morning, Snyder and I arrived at the auditorium early. We inspected all of the technical gear, and finding no problems, we decided to patch in our recorded soundtrack to the auditorium system and establish a proper sound level for the presentation. For this, we needed the assistance of the auditorium sound technician.

"Uh Oh!" the technician exclaimed as he sought to plug in the sound cord from our presentation to the auditorium system. "This won't work. I've never seen a cord like this."

My heart skipped several beats. "You said there would be no problem," I said. "We went over this a half dozen times."

"I didn't look at the end of the connecting cord," said the technician

"So how do we connect our sound system into the auditorium?" I demanded. "A couple thousand people will be here in an hour."

"I don't know," whined the technician. "Do you have another kind of connecting cord?"

Snyder limped over to the connection portal on the wall, and took down some numbers. "Maybe you can go to Southeastern Electronics and get a connection cord that matches these numbers," he said. Southeastern Electronics was nearly a mile away. By now, the early arrivals were filing into the building.

I rushed out, jumped into my car and sped off to the electronics store. Dozens of cars were entering the parking lot at the auditorium. I was experiencing a full blown panic attack. I sincerely wanted to throttle the auditorium sound technician for his negligence.

The clerk at the electronics store was no help. He had never heard of the kind of connecting cord we were seeking. Trying to control my panic, I decided to go to Audiophonics, a sound studio operated by technical whiz Larry Gardner. Gardner's studio was about two blocks away from the Memorial Auditorium. If anyone could solve our problem, Larry Gardner could. By the time I neared his studio, the traffic was so heavy I could not get to the building. I decided to circle the block and park in a no-parking zone.

As I drove around the block, I saw a most bizarre sight. My colleague Jere Snyder, his ankle encased in a hard cast, was making his way up the sidewalk. In his arms, he carried an enormous appliance. From where I was, it appeared to be half the size of a refrigerator. Snyder was making pretty good time on his injured leg.

I stopped in mid traffic and yelled out my window, "What's that, Jere?"

"It's an amplifier, and I think it will work," he replied. Apparently, Snyder had the same idea as I regarding enlisting Larry Gardner's help. Gardner had recommended the huge sound amplifier, and said he had used it before at the auditorium

By the time I could find a parking space, Snyder had set up the amplifier and was testing it. It appeared to be adequate. The auditorium sound technician had disappeared, apparently fearing for his safety.

I began to breathe a bit easier. The auditorium was filling rapidly, but Snyder assured me everything would go off smoothly. My only task was to stand in front of the huge screen and cue the technicians high up in the projection booth when it was time to start the program.

Our plan was for me to hold up one finger, to signal a dimming of the lights and two fingers to start the projector. When it was time for my first signal, I raised my hand with one finger extended. The auditorium went totally dark, and a lengthy pause ensued. The technicians high in the projection booth had not gradually dimmed the lights; they had turned them off entirely.

Having given up smoking, I did not have a match or a flashlight, but thankfully, one of the ladies on the first row had a book of matches. She gave the matches to me, I lit one, held up two fingers and the presentation began.

Now, totally stressed out, I made my way to seats reserved for me by my wife, Marie. For the next 59 minutes and 45 seconds, the presentation moved along flawlessly and then....one of the three final slides appeared upside down....then another....then another. A titter of laughter filled the auditorium. As the lights came on, the applause was generous, but mixed with laughter.

I considered jumping from the second story window, but Governor Scott graciously commented on other aspects of the presentation, deflecting attention from the final seconds while I wracked my stressed out brain, trying to figure out how three slides could have appeared upside down after multiple rehearsals.

Snyder and I were baffled. It seemed impossible, but everyone saw it. We simply could not come up with an answer.

Dr. Cofer had asked me to provide all of the materials along with the script after the presentation. I waited as long as I could to deliver the materials, trying to come up with a reasonable explanation for the error. I was not successful.

Gentlewoman that she was, Dr. Cofer did not seem upset at all by the error. "I thought it added a bit of levity that was needed," she said. Then she asked me to present my invoice for payment.

Jokingly, I said, "Dr. Cofer, if there is any problem in paying my bill, I guess I'll just have to do the presentation again."

Laughing loudly, she said. "Oh no! We'll pay. We'll pay."

For over a decade, the matter of the upside-down slides remained a mystery. Every time I recalled the incident, my face flamed with embarrassment and frustration. Then, I received a call from a former employee, J.W. Ligon, who had worked for our firm for a number of years after his discharge from the U.S. Army where he had been a writer for *The Stars and Stripes* newspaper.

After leaving our firm, Ligon had returned to school, obtained a law degree and established a thriving insurance business in San Francisco. He also had become involved in a fellowship program that required him to make amends for various injuries he had inflicted on others.

In the long-distance phone call, Ligon confessed that it was he who caused the slides to be upside down, those many years earlier. He reminded me that he had photographed some of the slides in the presentation, and he wanted to know which of those he had made were being used. He arrived at Memorial auditorium as we were leaving and went to the projectors to take a look. When he replaced the last three, he put them into the projector upside down.

"I know how embarrassed you were," said Ligon. "It has taken me a long time to be able to tell you what I did."

The pain in Ligon's voice was far greater than the offense, and I quickly told him that all was forgiven. Then I added, "You're damn lucky you are a continent away. If you were here, I just might kick your butt." We both laughed, and remained friends.

The Unintended Consequences of Good Intentions

In 1983, many cities and towns of North Carolina were experiencing what former President Lyndon Johnson described in his address setting forth his vision for "a great society," as "two giant and dangerous forces – the forces of growth and decay."

While some municipalities accommodated unprecedented growth by expanding on the edges, their inner city areas languished with empty storefronts and dying downtowns. Governor Jim Hunt sought to address the problem by initiating a pilot program among three typical municipalities of varying sizes: Tarboro in eastern North Carolina, Salisbury, in the Piedmont, and Asheville, in the western part of the State.

The goal of the program was to aggressively promote the opportunities for the establishment of small and mid-size businesses in downtown areas where building were available, and if the program achieved success, share the strategies and tactics that worked with other similarly situated cities and towns.

The pilot program was administered through the State Department of Commerce's Office of Business Development, headed by Oppie Jordan, a highly motivated executrix with considerable experience in working with the Main Street Re-Development Program. The program was funded for 18 months by a number of North Carolina corporations – NCNB National Bank, Carolina Power and Light (now Progress Energy) United Carolina Bank, Carolina Telephone and Telegraph Company (now Sprint), Virginia Power and Light Company (VEPCO) and the Z. Smith Reynolds Foundation. Our firm was retained to handle the promotion.

The participating municipalities agreed to appoint a marketing team, consisting of members of the community with skills and experience in economic development and a project director to coordinate the efforts. They also agreed to assist in identifying buildings that were eligible for the tax incentives when rehabilitated as well as other buildings and building sites available for purchase or lease, to prepare market studies indicating the need for and potential profitability of business and to assist potential investors in obtaining financing.

The promotional needs and opportunities were two-fold. Businesses in the targeted municipalities needed to be educated regarding ways they could assist and benefit from the program, and potential regional and national entrepreneurs needed to be made aware of the opportunities in the targeted municipalities.

Our promotional efforts consisted of several components: The preparation and production of a comprehensive description of the targeted municipalities and the opportunities they presented in printed materials and in a documentary style video. The video was produced for broadcast on a national cable channel, and the printed materials were for those who responded to the video. Additional printed materials were produced for each of the respective municipalities that could be used for multiple promotional purposes.

News releases and feature articles for national, regional and local publications were prepared and disseminated, and sample speeches were prepared for local use to explain the dimensions of the program to local business groups. A list of some 3,500 prospective businesses was developed, and each prospect was targeted with direct mail material following the broadcast of the video.

Within a few days following the broadcast of the video, Ms. Jordan began receiving inquiries from interested parties. Among them was a Lancaster, Pennsylvania architect and developer named Owen

Kugel. Kugel had specialized in creating new uses for old buildings in Lancaster, and he presented an impressive portfolio of his work.

Kugel was interested in pursuing opportunities in the municipalities targeted for North Carolina's pilot program, or so he said. Moreover, he was anxious to visit North Carolina and help bring new businesses to downtowns.

In person, Kugel was as impressive as his portfolio. He proposed that municipalities facing the same type of problems as those in the pilot program sign consulting contracts with his firm, OK Developers, and he would take the lead in developing available buildings and bringing new businesses and residents to downtowns.

The promotional effort in behalf of the pilot communities attracted the interest of other small cities and towns, some of which were eager to conduct similar programs.

Like a pied piper playing a catchy tune, Kugel quickly attracted a parade of small towns ready and willing to sign contracts with him. In a matter of a few weeks, Kugel had signed contracts with municipalities from Asheville to Kinston. Soon, however, business people became aware of the staggering fees he was charging and began to watch Kugel with a wary eye, wondering how an individual operator, would be able to simultaneously attract businesses to an increasing number of towns, each of which was, in reality, competing with other cities and towns.

Simple arithmetic quickly showed that Kugel, charging an average of $5,000 per month for each municipality was on target to make a sizeable financial haul. Moreover, his agreements with the municipalities did not actually promise any concrete return. It merely promised effort and implied results.

Almost as quickly as they had signed contracts, Kugel's clients began to complain. City councilmen began to question the fees and the lack of results, and soon, lawsuits were being filed.

Like a row of dominoes, Kugel's clients began to cancel their contracts. Among those who bailed in one concerted action were Asheville, Greenville, Fayetteville, Kinston and Reidsville. Not satisfied simply to cancel its contract, Reidsville filed suit to recoup the money paid to Kugel. Others either threatened or actually filed lawsuits in the following weeks.

Faced with cancellations and lawsuits, Kugel hurriedly left North Carolina with nothing to show for his work but several thousand dollars in fees. In Asheville, Salisbury and Tarboro the pilot program continued, and the efforts to recruit new businesses in the downtown areas began to show real progress. The Pack Square area of Asheville, the main targeted area rebounded from desolation to a trendy, lively urban center of boutiques, restaurants and other shops.

Salisbury's downtown experienced a rebirth, also, and Tarboro enjoyed vigorous revitalization. When the pilot project was completed and evaluated, the results were impressive. More than 122 inquiries had been made to the Office of Business Development, 22 new businesses had been recruited, producing 120 new jobs, and some $32 million in new investments in the three municipalities was pending. The mayors of all three participating municipalities were pleased with the results and planned a continuation of the effort.

One of the goals of the pilot program was to provide a blueprint for other municipalities to follow in revitalizing downtowns and recruiting new business. The materials developed for the pilot program were to be made available to cities and towns that wanted to conduct similar programs.

By the time the program was completed and its results tabulated, however, Republican James Martin had replaced Democrat Jim Hunt who had originated the idea. Martin had installed his own team in the Department of Commerce, who were *underwhelmed* by the pilot program and its results. Although the pilot program provided a clear and practical way for local governments and the private sector to revitalize decaying downtowns, the final report was never disseminated to other municipalities that might have benefited from the information. The materials long ago were relegated to the trash heap.

Thirty years later, throughout North Carolina, the "two giant and dangerous forces of growth and decay" that decades ago began converging on cities and towns continue their relentless path.

A Challenge to The
News and Observer's Dominance

In an upstairs meeting room at a hotel near the Crabtree Valley Shopping Mall, more than a dozen of Raleigh's prominent businessmen were gathered in a secret meeting.

With rapt attention they listened as I went over the key points of a market study that had been conducted to determine the feasibility of establishing a new newspaper in the city of Raleigh. The study had been commissioned as a result of the anger many old Raleigh residents felt toward the two existing newspapers –*The News & Observer* and the *Raleigh Times.*

Being mad at *The News and Observer* and to a lesser degree *The Raleigh Times* was nothing new in Raleigh and many other places in eastern North Carolina. Former *N&O* publisher Frank Daniels, Jr., once told me, that one of his goals in life was to be able to go to lunch in downtown Raleigh "without someone calling me a son-of-a-bitch." Daniels recalled that his grandfather, the late Josephus Daniels, had told him that people would be mad at the paper every day, "but hopefully," said the senior Daniels, "it won't be the same people every day." In the late fall and early winter of 1978, many Raleigh residents, were incensed at what they perceived to be the unfair manner in which both papers had used their news and editorial columns to influence the 1978 local elections.

In the election, the first black sheriff had been elected, a candidate for county commissioner who had led in a first primary was defeated in a runoff when his Mormon religion became a major issue in the papers, and a popular former district attorney was defeated in his bid for a legislative seat when his trial on an old charge of driving under the influence received sensational coverage.

Those assembled in the room were members of the moderate/conservative faction of the Democratic Party, a rapidly declining segment of the voting population, many of whom would eventually change their political affiliation to Republican.

Discussions of starting publications to challenge the dominance of Raleigh's two daily newspapers had been held numerous times over the years, generally after hard-fought elections in which the losers were embittered by the newspapers' coverage of the candidates and the issues. This time, the discussions were more serious. Those seeking a new voice in the city had put up a substantial amount of money to determine the feasibility of starting a new publication in the city.

Among the group were the owners and executives of some of Raleigh's oldest and most successful firms -- Cliff Benson, a Democratic activist and owner of Carolina Building Company (Now Stock Building Supplies), Ralph Ingram and Richard Goodman, real estate developers and co-owners of Goodman Toyota, Richard Helmold of Helmold Ford and Jim Edwards, owner of Inland Construction Company. In the days to follow, the group in the room would increase to a total of more than 20 business and professional people including Wake County Commissioner Elizabeth Cofield, I. Beverly Lake, Jr., who would become Chief Justice of the North Carolina Supreme Court and Zack Bacon, a successful realtor and investor.

The group initially indicated a preference for a daily newspaper to challenge the two established papers, but when they learned the cost of launching a daily newspaper and sustaining it long enough for it to have a reasonable chance of achieving profitability, they agreed that the best chance for achieving their goal was through a weekly publication.

In the mid and late 1970s, alternative weekly publications were being launched in many cities and towns, principally for the same reason the Raleigh group wanted a new voice – dissatisfaction with the existing papers' editorial and news policies.

Many of the new publications quickly failed, but several found traction and became successful. Among the successful alternative weeklies was *The Real Paper* published in Boston. The publication was the subject of a *Time* magazine article, and the publisher of the paper granted me a full day to study the operation of the paper and provided details on its fiancés and expenses.

When I laid out the cost of launching and operating a first class weekly newspaper and the potential profitability that would most likely not begin for three years, I fully expected the group to give up its plan. Many others had abandoned their dreams after confronting the reality of the cost of publishing and the difficulty of competing with long established daily newspapers.

Publishing is an enchanting temptress that has led many otherwise hardnosed business people down the garden path. In the mid-1970s, Jim Goodmon, chairman of Capitol Broadcasting Company, was considering purchasing a publication called *The Leader,* founded by Margaret Knox in The Research Triangle Park. He asked me to evaluate the publication and give him an opinion as to whether he would be wise to purchase it.

My evaluation quickly confirmed my suspicions: *The Leader* had never made a profit. It had barely provided enough money to keep itself afloat despite Ms. Knox's relentless quest for advertising. Goodmon rejected my advice and purchased the publication. A few months later, he told me he regretted the purchase because *The Leader* "did nothing but hemorrhage money."

However, the rather large numbers displayed by the slide projector did not send the potential investors scurrying from the room. The study I had conducted indicated that an investment of $3 million would be required to launch a credible newsweekly publication and sustain it for three years.

That investment along with a revenue stream from the sale of advertising would enable the publication to employ competent professionals, assure circulation sufficient to be of value to advertisers and become an effective alternative voice in the area. If the projections that I had made for advertising revenue were reached, the proposed publication could achieve profitability in three years and in five years become a valuable asset. It would not be easy, however, and I was careful to warn the potential investors of the uncertainty of my projections and the assumptions on which they were based.

The group was quick to grasp a key factor that eliminated some of the risk of a publication startup. Collectively they controlled enough advertising to immediately establish income that would offset some of the initial expenses. Before the evening ended, the businessmen in the room reached a decision to move forward with the publication of a weekly news magazine that would be called the *Raleigh Newsweekly*.

They retained me to put the plan into effect and to serve as editor and publisher of the publication on a three-year contract. They authorized the preparation of an offering statement for investors and set the launch for mid-1979. Their assurance that the $3 million initial investment would pose no problems gave me consid-erable confidence and I moved quickly to establish an editorial, advertising, distribution and production organization.

One of the dirty little secrets of the publishing business is that subscription fees do not contribute significantly to a publication's bottom line. For a new publication, the cost of acquiring paid subscribers is greater than the value of the subscription. Moreover, if the publication should fail or be required to suspend publication, the obligation to subscribers becomes a serious liability. Those who have paid in advance must be refunded portions of their subscription fees or provided with an alternative publication of comparable value.

The profitability of a publication depends primarily on its advertising revenue. The subscriptions are used as bargaining chips to demonstrate to potential advertisers the size and composition of the publication's readership. The newly established board of directors agreed that the new publication would be distributed free to 35,000 homes in selected zip codes in Raleigh and its suburbs. Coincidentally, *The News & Observer* was close to reaching a decision to terminate its agreement with B-D Distribution Company that had distributed its successful Adpak shopping publication. We were able to retain the experienced firm headed by Marshall Lambert to distribute the new publication to the same homes that had been receiving the Adpak.

As we were putting all of the pieces in place, I received a phone call from Bernie Reeves who seemed both distraught and angry. He had learned of the plans for the *Raleigh Newsweekly* just weeks before he planned to launch his own publication, *The Spectator.* I was as distraught as Reeves to learn that two alternative publications were to be launched within days of each other. In his frustration, Reeves demanded that *The Raleigh Newsweekly* abandon its plans.

When Reeves told me that his new publication would be principally concerned with the entertainment scene in Raleigh, I was relieved. I did not feel that the two publications would be competitive with each other editorially. However, they would compete for advertising, and that was what seemed to trouble Reeves more than anything.

I tried to assure Reeves that there was room for both, but he continued to express anger and frustration. We ended our conversation when Reeves declared that "I'm willing to die to make my publication successful."

I assured Reeves that his commitment was stronger than mine. Although I was willing to do my best to make the *Raleigh Newsweekly* successful, I had no intention or thought of giving my life for the new publication.

When the *Raleigh Newsweekly* was launched in mid-June, 1979, many Raleigh readers were surprised at its content. Instead of engaging in a political or ideological battle with *The News and Observer,* we sought to produce an interesting and informative publication that pretty much avoided politics. There was never an intention for the publication to be a strong conservative voice, but a voice that sought to offset some of the more liberal positions espoused by the N&O with more moderate opinion.

Soon after the paper was launched, I was startled to learn that the investors had not raised the $3 million that the feasibility study indicated would be needed. Instead, they had raised slightly less than $1 million.

I confronted the board with my concern. Without the $3 million, I felt that the project was seriously under-capitalized and that it faced an uncertain future. I was so concerned that I drafted a letter that I asked every member of the board of directors to sign, indicating that I had advised them that the startup required at least $3 million and that if it failed because of under capitalization, its failure would not be blamed on me.

The directors signed the letter and agreed to make up the difference by increasing their advertising budgets to produce a larger income stream that the advertising department did not have to solicit each week. Moreover, they agreed to borrow additional funds if and when they might become necessary to assure the stability of the publishing project.

Over the course of the next eight months, the staff of the *Raleigh Newsweekly* consistently produced editions that were engaging, interesting, informative and useful. Readers were enthusiastic. Alas, advertisers did not share the enthusiasm of the readers.

Persuading advertisers to allocate part of their advertising budgets to the new publication was a hard sell that attracted only a few of the major advertisers. Even the investors who had promised to support the paper with a major share of their budgets reneged on their promises and continued to place the lion's share of their advertising dollars with *The News and Observer* and local broadcast stations. The advertising department was demoralized by the reluctance of the investors to support their own publication.

By the fall of 1979, the initial investment was running low, and the investors went to the bank to sign personal notes for money to keep the publication afloat. By then interest as well as inflation rates were reaching alarming heights. By early 1980, they were approaching 20 percent, making borrowing money to prop up a new publication that showed no promise of achieving a 20-percent profitability very dicey.

Ralph Ingram, who had been elected president of the Raleigh Newsweekly Publishing Company and a few other investors, asked me to join them to discuss the crises. With the interest rates continuing to escalate, I could see no clear path to profitability. Continuing the money-losing operation seemed to me to be unwise, but necessary in order to sustain continuity until a solution could be found.

I suggested that we seek a partnership with an established daily newspaper that would like to enter the Raleigh market. The Durham Herald Sun seemed like a logical choice, but it was not interested. Neither was the Greensboro News and Record. However, the owners of the Winston Salem Journal were interested, and we met with the publishers and editors, but after due consideration they determined the time was not right because of the high inflation and interest rates.

We also met with Jim Goodmon of Capitol Broadcasting, who after a bad experience in publishing was not interested. Conservative legislator and businessman John Carrington had expressed interest, but was unwilling to take on the expense in the uncertain economy.

Reluctantly, with great sadness, publication of *The Raleigh Newsweekly* was suspended in mid-February, 1980, an editorial success, but a business failure.

The Spectator, under Bernie Reeves' guidance, continued for a number of years, able to pay its bills, but as disclosed when it was finally sold never a consistently profitable enterprise.

In the decades that were to follow, production and distribution of new publications became far easier and much less costly, and today, as many major daily newspapers struggle to survive, alternative publications that focus on local issues are thriving. As the late Johnny Carson was fond of saying, "Timing is everything."

A Book From Hell

In my office on a small, secluded farm east of Raleigh, Charles Heatherly and I awaited the arrival of the State Bureau of Investigation (SBI) agents with more than a bit of nervousness. We felt certain that we had done nothing wrong, but an SBI investigation is cause for concern.

In a matter of days, a book we had published on North Carolina Lt. Governor Jim Gardner, a Republican candidate for governor in 1992, had ignited a statewide controversy, resulting in the SBI investigation and our pending interview with two agents. The accuracy of the book had not been challenged. Indeed, the chairman of the State Republican Party, Jack Hawke, had declared the book accurate following a reading immediately after a pre-arranged media launch of the book. He had unkind words to say about the book, but nothing that challenged the accuracy of its content.

Instead of challenging its accuracy, the Republican Party alleged that the book was subsidized by unknown parties, and, therefore, its publication constituted an unlawful political action committee and an illegal contribution to Democratic candidate Jim Hunt.

Heatherly and I were caught off guard by the Republican allegation. We were prepared to defend the accuracy of the book, but were disconcerted by the charge actually lodged by the Republicans.

The book, *Jim Gardner, A Question of Character*, was a tough, unblinking examination of a politician who had sought to craft a new media image of himself after decades of failed business endeavors, bankruptcies, failure to pay debts and a political record devoid of any accomplishments of consequence.

292

Gardner had a remarkable ability to gloss over his failures, blaming others, taking credit where credit was not due, and appeal to voters who looked only superficially at candidates. The objective of the book was to cast a bright light of reality on Gardner, his record and his promises. From a source close to Republican Party Chairman Hawke, we heard that Hawke had, among other descriptions, described the publication as "a book from hell." Heatherly and I were pleased with Hawke's description and used it in our marketing efforts.

As a book-length assessment of the record of a candidate for governor from one of the two major parties, the publication of the *Jim Gardner, A Question of Character,* represented a political first in North Carolina. Historically, newspapers reported on the records of the candidates. Their reporting was usually done in piecemeal fashion, with a comprehensive report a rarity. Television generally aired brief "sound bites" and truncated reports on candidates that barely scratched the surface. Gardner's extensive record of failure and his persistent effort to avoid responsibility for his past actions made him an ideal candidate for the kind of journalistic effort that Heatherly and I conducted.

Heatherly and I had formed a small publishing company to handle publication of the book, the printing, marketing and promotion. In addition, we had entered into a distribution deal with the Downhome Press, an established book publishing company headed by Jerry Bledsoe, a highly regarded journalist and author of best-selling books.

The Republican allegation was triggered by an offhand comment I had made to a newspaper reporter prior to the press conference at which the book was introduced to the media and the public. The reporter asked if there were other investors in the company. At the time, my brother-in-law, a Wilson resident, was interested in participating in the publishing company as a silent investor. A decision regarding his participation had not been made, and I told the reporter that we might have other investors. At the press conference, the question was again asked, and my reply, quite accurately, was that there were no investors other than Heatherly and me.

Republicans, unable to find inaccuracies to challenge, seized on what they believed was a contradiction. Their initial complaint was to the State Board of Elections that, lacking investigative ability, asked the SBI to conduct the investigation and turn its findings over to Wake County District Attorney Colon Willoughby.

Though we were nervous about the SBI investigation, Heatherly and I were very much aware that the Republican allegation and the subsequent SBI investigation had been like a shot of steroids on book sales. Nearly 200 news stories were published in State media. Orders poured in. At B. Dalton's bookstores in malls around the state, *Jim Gardner, A Question of Character* was displayed on the bestseller stands at the front of the stores.

In addition to individual sales, we received a number of bulk sales from groups that wanted to either give away or sell copies at special political events.

For his traditional fall fish fry at Atlantic Beach, held to mobilize Democrats for the upcoming election, Marvin Speight invited us to set up a table to sell and sign books. Between each speaker, the master of ceremonies would remind people of the availability of the books. By the time the fish were being served, hundreds of people were ignoring the food as they stood in the bright beach sunlight reading *Jim Gardner, A Question of Character* and chuckling over some of its passages. One of the guests noted as he purchased a copy that "when a bunch of Democrats had rather read than eat, it must be a damn interesting book."

During the event, an Eastern North Carolina Superior Court Judge came to the table to purchase a book. He looked at the cover and remarked, "I always knew Jim Gardner was a jackass. I just wanted to see it in black and white."

Despite our denials, many people tended to agree with the Republicans that our publishing venture was a clandestine effort in behalf of Jim Hunt, conceived and orchestrated by the Hunt gubernatorial campaign. Hawke, calling the book a "bunch of hogwash," said it was written and published by a couple of "Democratic operatives whose snouts had been in the Democratic trough for years." Other Republicans denounced the book even before it was written.

Some Democrats genuinely believed that Heatherly and I had written the book to curry favor with Hunt and obtain positions in his administration, should he win the election.

All of them had it wrong. We agreed with Samuel Johnson, who said, "Only a blockhead writes for anything other than money." Our plan to write and publish the book was merely a response to business conditions as the economy sought to transition from the 1991 recession that had begun during the last years of George H.W. Bush's presidency. The project began much as other projects, as an idea that might or might not be productive.

Like most businesses, the public relations, advertising and political consulting business is cyclical, subject to the ups and downs of the general economy and the timing of political campaigns, and in early 1992, with the economy still in the late stages of recession, business at Grady Jefferys and Associates was decidedly slow.

Heatherly, a long-time colleague and friend and I were discussing ways that we might improve our incomes for the coming year. Although we frequently worked together on joint projects, each of us operated separately.

"Got any great ideas for making money this year?" asked Charles.

"I think I'll write another book," I said. In the previous year, Wayne Pennington, another public relations professional, and I had published *The PowerHouse,* a comprehensive explanation of the way the North Carolina General Assembly impacts the lives of citizens. The book had done well, selling more than 15,000 copies prior to publication, and it was continuing to sell.

"What's the subject?" asked Heatherly.

"I'm thinking of writing a book about Jim Gardner," I said. "He'll be running for governor against Jim Hunt, and there will be a lot of interest in him. I can probably sell a lot of copies to both Democrats and Republicans."

Heatherly was immediately interested. "If you need any help," he said, "I'm available."

A few days later, business picked up. I became involved in several projects, and gave little thought to a book about Gardner. A couple of weeks passed, and I received a phone call from Heatherly. "Have you started on the Gardner book?" he asked.

"Not yet," I replied. "I've been busy."

"If you are not going to do it, I am," said Heatherly.

I was not ready to abandon the idea, so we agreed to write the book together. From numerous published sources and court records, the repository of Gardner's congressional papers at the UNC-Chapel Hill library, research at the U.S. Department of Justice in Atlanta, an exhaustive review of newspaper coverage from past years on microfilm at the Wake County Public library, interviews with a number of Republicans, including party Chairman Hawke and numerous other men and women who had known Gardner over the years, including many who had suffered economic hardship in dealings with him, we developed a portrait of the politician and the person that had not been previously published. Initially, Gardner agreed to be interviewed, but for unknown reasons, reneged on his agreement.

Only three people whom we contacted would not provide comment or answer questions about Gardner –

then Governor Jim Martin, David Wilson, a former associate who had sued Gardner, and Gardner, himself. Contrary to what some people believed, neither Jim Hunt nor anyone in his campaign was involved in the plan to publish the book.

In an unusual arrangement with Wilber Hardee, we obtained an exclusive first-hand account of what the founder of the popular national restaurant chain believed was an unethical deal in which J. Leonard Rawls and Gardner plied him with whiskey and gained control over the newly emerging competitor to McDonalds Hamburger chain. To obtain the exclusive account, Heatherly and I agreed to assist Hardee in writing and publishing his memoirs. Several months after the 1992 election, we completed the draft of his book from interviews with Hardee and notes provided to us, and Hardee was able to get it published prior to his death.

The first draft of the Gardner manuscript was submitted for review to a number of former journalists, lawyers, and people with political experience. The extensive review had given us confidence in the accuracy of our reporting and writing. We also were confident that our publishing project did not constitute an unlawful political action committee.

Nevertheless, we did not welcome the visit from the two female SBI agents. We had no idea what to expect. The two agents were interested primarily in whether the corporation we had formed was engaged in donating books to the Jim Hunt campaign. They asked for a review of our sales invoices to assure that the books were being sold.

I felt that having to provide the names of people who had purchased books would be an unfair invasion of privacy and I expressed my concern to one of the agents. She informed me that all information would be held in confidence.

"I don't care who you've sold books to," she said. "You can sell 'em to Adolph Hitler if you want to – just so long as you sell them."

Heatherly, who kept the financial records of the publishing company, provided the requested invoices, and the two SBI agents appeared to be satisfied with the information we had provided.

On the following Monday, District Attorney Willoughby announced that the SBI investigation had disclosed no wrong doing on our part. No charges would be brought.

Heatherly and I were relieved. We continued to sell books at a rapid pace, sometimes, several hundred per day. Based on the success of the book, we fully expected other similar books to be published in the years that were to come. Over two decades, however, *Jim Gardner, A Question of Character* remains the only publication of its kind in North Carolina, and after two decades, the book which originally sold for $6.95 is available from some collectors for as much as $40 a copy.

After Words:

After decades of toil in the strange fields of television, publishing, advertising and politics, I look back with many regrets, and forward with only small hope.

Those of us who were pioneers in television as the medium spread across the country have little in which to take pride. Except for obvious technical improvements, excellence is missing from a medium that cried out for excellence. In the second decade of the 21st century, television, taken in its entirety, is a national disgrace. Television that is slightly better than awful is excessively celebrated, while the awful continues to be patiently tolerated.

In advertising, the short-lived "creative revolution," an effort to make the content of ads less boring, more interesting and, thus, more effective, died as quickly as it was born, the victim of number crunchers who did not understand or appreciate the goals of those who sincerely wanted to change or at least challenge the status quo.

In the field of politics, the tools of modern communication are used to impugn the character of honorable men and women and often to promote the ascendancy of scoundrels. During every election cycle, our most far-reaching communications medium becomes a cesspool of half-truths, dissembling, obfuscation and outright lies.

No one seems to be unduly bothered that our treasured democracy has become a system of government by bribery. Politicians who accept enormous sums of money from interest groups and then do the bidding of their contributors can put no other label on it.

No one present at the beginning planned it this way. For television, there never seemed to be an overarching purpose much less a *plan* for the medium other than to attract the largest number of viewers possible for every program. Content quality and certainly excellence never were a part of the equation for television – and are not today.

Will things get better? The media world is in a state of chaos, where the only certainty is *uncertainty.* There is no crystal ball in which the outcome of today's chaos is revealed. However, chaos does have a record of giving birth to better things and better times. Will politics improve? Or will the abuses continue to grow worse until we embrace Jefferson's belief that "the roots of the tree of liberty must periodically be nourished by the blood of tyrants."

What can those of us who were there at the beginning and through the decades and set no worthwhile standards or left no suitable models for the future say in our defense? Not much. As we toiled in those strange fields, we adopted the culture of our surroundings and allowed ourselves to be subsumed by unworthy systems.

Some of us wish we had done better.

####

Other Works by the Author
Books & Publications

Fighting Annexation
How To Protect Your Property
Rights Against Municipal Tyranny

Buyout or Handout
What You Need To Know
About the Tobacco Buyout
Controversy

Jim Gardner:
A Question of Character
With Charles Heatherly

The PowerHouse
How North Carolina's
General Assembly
Serves Citizens

Sheltering A Heritage
North Carolina's Historic Buildings

Genuine Hyde
The Wit and Wisdom of North Carolina
Senator Herbert Hyde

North Carolina
The Goodliest Land under The Cope of Heaven

As The Twig Is Bent
The Report of The North Carolina Bar Association's
Penal System Study Commission's
Investigation of the Juvenile Correction System

The Tree of Life
Condensed History of The North Carolina Railroad
With John Gilbert

Crossties Through Carolina
The First Hundred Years of Railway
Steam Power in North Carolina –
With John Gilbert

Crossties Over Saluda
A Portrait of Railway Power on The
Nation's Steepest Standard Gauge
Mainline Railway Grade
With John Gilbert

Other Works
Documentary Films, TV Programs and Videos

North Carolina
A Special Kind of Splendor
*(Recipient of the International
Council on Non-Theatrical Events'
Cine Golden Eagle Award for
Motion Picture)*

North Carolina
The Goodliest Land
*(Recipient of Bronze Medal at the
New York Film Festival)*

Voice of the People
*How The North Carolina
Legislature is organized and
enacts laws*

**Roanoke: Genesis of
Nationhood**
*The story of the first English
attempt to settle America at
Roanoke Island, North Carolina*

Behind Bars
*The Investigation of North
Carolina's Penal System by the
North Carolina Bar Association*

Quest for Justice
How North Carolina's Courts Work

Confronting the Challenge
*The rigors of basic training for U.S.
Army recruits at Fort McClellan,
Alabama and Fort Dix, New Jersey*

The Democrats
*Leadership for Our Times
Progress and problems in North
Carolina under Democratic
governors and legislatures*

Mountain Doctor
*The story of Dr. Gaine Cannon's
efforts to bring medical care to a
remote mountain region.
(A WSOC-TV primetime special)*

Pick Up the Pieces
*The story of a young boy's struggle
to overcome emotional disability.
(A WSOC-TV primetime special)*

Segregation: How It Was
*A candid discussion of segregation
by the first black mayor of the City
of Raleigh, North Carolina State
Capitol and a Shaw University
Professor of Sociology*

Continued from previous page

Levels of Danger
Famous North Carolina race drivers demonstrate the effects of various levels of intoxication on driving performance

Police Pursuit Driving
Film adaptation of landmark book by a North Carolina trooper

Auto Insurance: Why It Costs So Much for Young Drivers
An examination of the rate of accidents by young drivers and their effect on insurance costs: (Winner of First Place Award by National Association of Independent Insurance Agents)

The Way We Were:
The Way We Are:
A history of the first 200 years of Raleigh, North Carolina's Capital City

Practicing School Bus Safety
Famous performing orangutan Poppi demonstrates safe school bus riding for youngsters

Tide of Victory
How a little known mountain lawyer defeated the political establishment and became Governor of North Carolina